Beginning Git and GitHub

Version Control, Project Management and Teamwork for the New Developer

Second Edition

Mariot Tsitoara

Apress®

Beginning Git and GitHub: Version Control, Project Management and Teamwork for the New Developer, Second Edition

Mariot Tsitoara
Antananarivo, Madagascar

ISBN-13 (pbk): 979-8-8688-0214-0　　　　ISBN-13 (electronic): 979-8-8688-0215-7
https://doi.org/10.1007/979-8-8688-0215-7

Managing Director, Apress Media LLC: Welmoed Spahr
Acquisitions Editor: James Robinson-Prior
Development Editor: James Markham
Coordinating Editor: Gryffin Winkler
Copyeditor: Kim Burton

Cover designed by eStudioCalamar

Cover image by WangXiNa@Freepik.com

Distributed to the book trade worldwide by Apress Media, LLC, 1 New York Plaza, New York, NY 10004, U.S.A. Phone 1-800-SPRINGER, fax (201) 348-4505, e-mail orders-ny@springer-sbm.com, or visit www. springeronline.com. Apress Media, LLC is a California LLC and the sole member (owner) is Springer Science + Business Media Finance Inc (SSBM Finance Inc). SSBM Finance Inc is a **Delaware** corporation.

For information on translations, please e-mail booktranslations@springernature.com; for reprint, paperback, or audio rights, please e-mail bookpermissions@springernature.com.

Apress titles may be purchased in bulk for academic, corporate, or promotional use. eBook versions and licenses are also available for most titles. For more information, reference our Print and eBook Bulk Sales web page at http://www.apress.com/bulk-sales.

Any source code or other supplementary material referenced by the author in this book is available to readers on GitHub (https://github.com/Apress). For more detailed information, please visit https://www.apress.com/gp/services/source-code.

Paper in this product is recyclable

This book is dedicated to the generous individuals who have made the Git community an incredible environment to work in. Your contributions have resulted in one of the most valuable tools in the tech world. Thank you!

Table of Contents

About the Author

Mariot Tsitoara is a software engineer with a passion for the open web. He has been involved with Mozilla as a rep and a tech speaker since 2015 and has spoken extensively about open source and new technology, including Rust, WebVR, and online privacy. You can reach him at mariot@tsitoara.fr.

About the Technical Reviewer

Mihajatiana Maminiaina Rakotomalala was initially inspired by movies highlighting futuristic technology and hacking to ignite his passion for IT.

His journey began as an IT support engineer, demonstrating a keen understanding of network monitoring and management and server maintenance.

Venturing into web application development, he contributed significantly to creating dynamic websites using JavaScript frameworks like ReactJS.

Simultaneously, he broadened my technical knowledge by installing and troubleshooting different operating systems and applications providing essential problem resolution services to users.

Currently serving as an IT engineer in the government sector, he oversees setting up and improving the IT infrastructure.

Acknowledgments

I would like to express my gratitude to my parents, Jeanne and Tsitoara, for the incredible opportunities they have provided me. Without their support and sacrifices, I wouldn't be where I am today.

I give special thanks to my wonderful wife, Miora, and my amazing daughter, Maeva.

I am also grateful to my siblings, Alice, Elson, Thierry, Eliane, Annick, and Mamitiana, for being exceptional role models and offering unwavering support. To my lifelong friends, Christino, Johanesa, Laza, Lova, Miandry, Mihaja, and Rindra, who have taught me so much, I dedicate this book to you.

I must acknowledge my coworkers for imparting their knowledge of Git and being helpful and enjoyable to work with.

Introduction

This book has a clear objective: to serve as the resource I wish I had when I started my tech career. Each chapter is designed to teach you only what you need to know as a beginner. It's not an exhaustive reference book, but it will equip you with the necessary knowledge to significantly impact your career.

By the end of this book, you will understand the essential tools for version control and project management.

Who This Book Is For

This book is aimed at absolute beginners with Git and GitHub, as well as those who have some experience but want to deepen their understanding. If you're seeking the most effective way to quick-start your journey in the right direction, this book is for you.

How to Use This Book

Git is a straightforward tool to learn, but practical experience is crucial for grasping its concepts. The best way to learn is by applying it directly to one of your real projects. Reading the book without engaging in the exercises will prolong your learning curve.

PART I

Version Control with Git

CHAPTER 1

Version Control Systems

This chapter introduces you to version control systems. By the end of this chapter, you will understand Git version control and its historical background. The primary goal is to recognize the scenarios that necessitate version control and to comprehend why Git is a reliable and secure choice.

What Is Version Control?

As the name implies, *version control* involves managing multiple versions of a project. It tracks every change made to project files (additions, edits, or deletions). Each change is recorded, allowing for easy undoing or rolling back.

To effectively implement version control, you need to utilize version control systems. These systems facilitate navigation through changes and provide a swift way to revert to previous versions when needed.

Teamwork is a significant advantage of version control. When multiple individuals contribute to a project, tracking changes can become chaotic, increasing the risk of overwriting each other's work. With version control, team members can work on separate copies of the project (referred to as branches) and merge their changes into the main project only when they, or other team members, are satisfied with the work.

Note This book was written from a developer's perspective; however, the concepts and principles discussed apply to any type of text file, not just code. Version control systems can track changes not only in text files but also in various non-text files such as images or Gimp files.

3

© Mariot Tsitoara 2024
M. Tsitoara, *Beginning Git and GitHub*, https://doi.org/10.1007/979-8-8688-0215-7_1

Why Do I Need One?

Have you ever worked on a text project or code that required you to recall the specific changes made to each file? If yes, how did you manage and control each version? Perhaps you attempted to duplicate and rename files using suffixes like Reviewed, Fixed, or Final? Figure 1-1 illustrates that kind of version control.

Figure 1-1. *Compressed files with suffixes to track versions*

The figure illustrates the approach that many people adopt to handle file changes. However, this method can quickly become unmanageable. It is easy to lose track of file identities and the specific changes made between them.

To effectively track versions, one suggestion is to compress the files and append timestamps to their names. This arrangement organizes the versions based on their creation dates. Figure 1-2 demonstrates this type of version tracking.

Figure 1-2. *Compressed files with prefixes sorted by date*

The solution depicted in Figure 1-2 may seem ideal, but it becomes evident that there is no way to determine the contents or descriptions of each version.

To address this issue, some developers employ a solution similar to the one shown in Figure 1-3. They include a separate file containing a summary of the changes made. This helps provide clarity and context to each version.

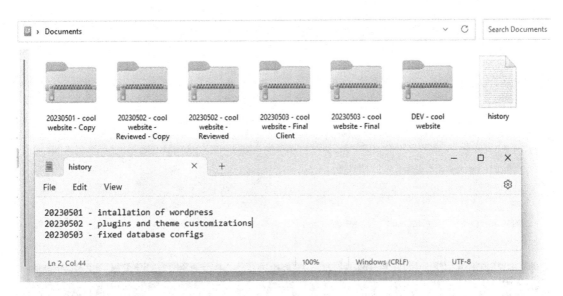

Figure 1-3. *A separate file to track changes in the project*

Figure 1-3 portrays the inclusion of a separate file within the project folder containing concise descriptions of the changes made. Additionally, note the presence of compressed files that store previous versions of the project.

However, this system falls short in comparing each version and tracking file changes. Memorization becomes necessary, especially as the project grows and the folder expands with each version.

Consider the challenges that arise when new team members join your project. Would you resort to emailing files or versions back and forth? Or would you opt to work on the same remote folder? In the latter case, how would you determine who is working on which file and what changes have been made?

Furthermore, have you ever desired to undo a change made years ago without disrupting the entire project? The need for an unlimited and powerful Ctrl+Z arises.

All these issues can be resolved using a version control system (VCS). A VCS tracks every change made to each file in your project and provides a straightforward method for comparing and reverting those changes. Each project version is accompanied by a description of the modifications and a list of new or edited files. When additional individuals join the project, a VCS can precisely identify the author of a specific file edit at a given time. This saves you valuable time, as you can focus on writing instead of meticulously tracking each change. Figure 1-4 depicts a versioned project managed by Git, showcasing the combination of all the solutions discussed in this chapter: change descriptions, teamwork, and edit dates.

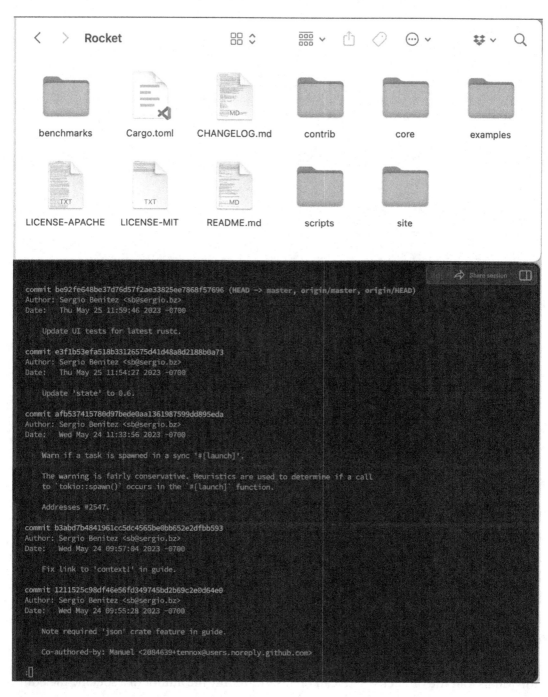

Figure 1-4. *A project versioned by Git*

Let's find out more about version control systems.

What Are the Choices?

There are many flavors of version control systems, each with its own advantages and shortcomings. A VCS can be local, centralized, or distributed.

Local Version Control Systems

These were the first VCSs created to manage source code. They worked by tracking the changes made to files in a single database that was stored locally. This meant that all the changes were kept on a single computer, and if there were any problems, all the work would be lost. It also meant that working with a team was out of the question.

One of the most popular local VCSs was a *source code control system* (SCCS), which was free but closed source. Developed by AT&T, it was widely used in the 1970s until the introduction of a *revision control system* (RCS). RCS became more popular than SCCS because it was open source, cross-platform, and much more effective. Released in 1982, RCS is currently maintained by the GNU Project. One of the drawbacks of these two local VCSs was that they only worked on one file at a time; there was no way to track an entire project with them.

To help you visualize how it works, Figure 1-5 illustrates a simple local VCS.

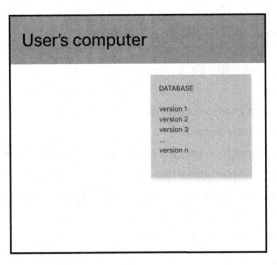

Figure 1-5. *How a local VCS works*

As you can see in Figure 1-5, everything is on the user's computer, and only one file is tracked. The versioning is stored in a database managed by the local VCS.

Centralized Version Control Systems

Centralized VCS (CVCS) stores the change history on a single server to which the clients (authors) can connect. This offers a way to work with a team and allows monitoring a project's pace. They are still popular because the concept is simple and easy to set up.

The main problem with CVCS, like local VCS, is that a server error can result in losing all of the team's work. A network connection is also required since the main project is stored on a remote server.

Figure 1-6 shows how it works.

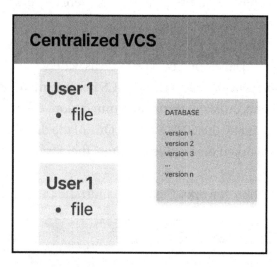

Figure 1-6. *How a centralized VCS works*

Figure 1-6 shows that a centralized VCS works similarly to a local VCS, but the database is stored on a remote server.

The main problem teams face using a centralized VCS is that once someone uses a file, it is locked, and other team members cannot work on it. As a result, they have to coordinate among themselves to modify a single file. This creates significant delays in development and leads to frustration for contributors. Moreover, the more members there are on the team, the more problems arise.

To address the issues of local VCS, the *concurrent version system* (CVS) was developed. It was open source and could track multiple sets of files instead of just one. Many users could also work on the same file simultaneously, hence the word *concurrent* in the name. All the history was stored in a remote repository, and users would keep up with the changes by checking out the server, which involved copying the contents of the remote database to their local computers.

Apache Subversion (SVN) was developed in 2000 and offered everything that CVS could, with an additional benefit: it could track non-text files. One of the main advantages of SVN was that, instead of tracking a group of files like the previous VCS, it tracked the entire project. Thus, it essentially tracked the directory instead of individual files. This meant that renaming, adding, and removing files were also tracked. These features, combined with its open source nature, made SVN a very popular VCS, which is still widely used today.

Distributed Version Control Systems

Distributed VCS works similarly to centralized VCS but with a significant difference: no main server holds all the history. Instead, each client has a copy of the repository (including the change history) rather than checking out a single server.

This greatly reduces the risk of losing everything since each client has a clone of the project. With a distributed VCS, the concept of a "main server" becomes blurred because each client has all the power within their own repository. This greatly encourages *forking* within the open source community. Forking refers to cloning a repository to make your own changes and have a different perspective on the project. The main benefit of forking is that you can pull changes from other repositories if you see fit, and others can do the same with your changes.

A distributed version control system is generally faster than other types of VCS because it doesn't require network access to a remote server. Nearly everything is done locally. There is also a slight difference in how it works: instead of tracking the changes between versions, it tracks all changes as *patches*, which can be freely exchanged between repositories, so there is no main repository to keep up with.

Figure 1-7 illustrates how a distributed VCS works.

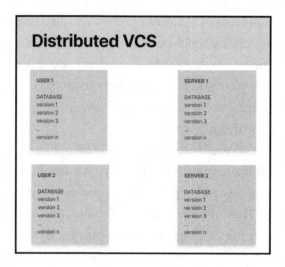

Figure 1-7. *How a distributed VCS works*

Note   When looking at Figure 1-7, it may be tempting to conclude that there is a main server that the users are keeping up with. However, in the case of a distributed VCS, it is important to note that it is only a convention many developers follow to have a better workflow. In reality, there is no requirement for a centralized main server in a distributed VCS setup. Each client has its own repository, and changes can be exchanged directly between repositories without needing a central server.

BitKeeper SCM was a proprietary distributed VCS that was released in 2000. Similar to SCCS in the 1970s, BitKeeper SCM was closed source. It offered a free Community version that lacked many of the advanced features of the full BitKeeper SCM. Despite this limitation, being one of the first distributed VCSs, it gained popularity even within the open source community.

The popularity of BitKeeper played a significant role in the creation of Git. In 2016, the source code of BitKeeper was released under the Apache License, making it an open source software. The current BitKeeper project is at `www.bitkeeper.org`. While the development has slowed, the BitKeeper community is still actively contributing.

What Is Git?

Remember the proprietary distributed version control system BitKeeper SCM from the last section? Well, the Linux kernel developers used it for their development. The decision to use it was wildly regarded as a bad move and made many people unhappy. In 2005, BitKeeper SCM ceased to be free, leading to the need for a new VCS for the Linux kernel development. Since no suitable alternative was available, the decision was made to develop a new VCS from scratch, creating Git.

Git shares similarities with BitKeeper SCM, a distributed VCS, but it offers several improvements. It is known for its speed and efficiency, particularly when handling large projects. The Git community is highly active, with numerous contributors involved in its development and maintenance. To learn more about Git, visit the official website at `https://git-scm.com`.

The features and workings of Git will be explained in more detail later in this section.

What Can Git Do?

Remember all those problems at the beginning of this chapter? Well, Git can solve them all. It can even solve problems you may not have been aware of. The following are some of the key capabilities of Git.

- Track changes

  - Navigate back and forth between versions.

  - Review the differences between different versions.

  - Check the change history of specific files.

  - Tag specific versions for easy referencing.

- Collaboration and teamwork

  - Exchange "changesets" between repositories.

  - Review the changes made by other team members.

11

- Branching and merging

  – Git's branching system allows you to create copies of the project, called *branches*, where you can work independently without affecting the main repository.

  – Merging enables you to incorporate changes in a branch back into the main source.

- Stashing

  – Git provides a stashing feature that allows you to safely set aside your current edits, creating a clean working environment to focus on a different task.

  – Stashing is useful when temporarily storing changes while working on a different feature or priority task. You can later retrieve and apply those changes to your current working environment.

Git's versatility and robust feature set make it a valuable tool for version control, enabling efficient collaboration, flexible branching, merging capabilities, and the ability to track changes effectively.

As a little appetizer, here are some of the Git commands you will learn in this book.

```
$ git init # Initialize a new git database
$ git clone # Copy an existing database
$ git status # Check the status of the local project
$ git diff # Review the changes done to the project
$ git add # Tell Git to track a changed file
$ git commit # Save the current state of the project to database
$ git push # Copy the local database to a remote server
$ git pull # Copy a remote database to a local machine
$ git log # Check the history of the project
$ git branch # List, create or delete branches
$ git merge # Merge the history of two branches together
$ git stash # Keep the current changes stashed away to be used later
```

As you can see, the commands are self-explanatory. Don't worry about knowing all of them by heart; you will learn them one by one. And, you won't need to always use all the commands. You will mostly use git add and git commit. This chapter focuses on the commands commonly used in a professional setting. But before diving into that, let's explore the inner workings of Git.

How Does Git Work?

Unlike many version control systems, Git works with snapshots rather than differences. This means that instead of tracking the difference between two versions of a file, Git captures a complete snapshot of the project's current state.

This approach contributes to Git's exceptional speed compared to other distributed VCSs. It allows for swift and effortless switching between versions and branches.

In contrast to centralized version control systems, Git operates differently. You don't need to communicate with a central server to perform work. As a distributed VCS, each user has their own independent repository with a complete history and changesets. Consequently, most actions in Git are performed locally, except for sharing patches or changesets. While a central server is not necessary, many developers still use one as a convention for easier collaboration.

Let's discuss how Git identifies and associates changesets with respective users. When Git captures a snapshot, it computes a checksum for it. This checksum allows Git to determine which files have changed by comparing their checksums. This mechanism enables Git to track changes between files and directories while checking for file corruption.

The main feature of Git is its "three states" system, which consists of the working directory, the staging area, and the git directory.

- The working directory represents the current snapshot of the project that you are actively working on.

- The staging area is where modified files are marked in their current version, indicating they are ready to be stored in the database.

- The git directory serves as the database where the project's complete history is stored.

In essence, Git operates in the following manner: you modify the files in the working directory, then add each file you want to include in the next snapshot to the staging area using the `git add` command. Once the files are added to the staging area, you can create a snapshot of the project by committing the changes using the `git commit` command. In Git terminology, a modified file added to the staging area is known as *staged*, and a file that has been committed and added to the database is *committed*. Therefore, the life cycle of a file in Git progresses from modified to staged to committed.

What Is the Typical Git Workflow?

To help you visualize the concepts discussed in this section, I will briefly demonstrate a typical workflow using Git. Don't worry if you don't fully understand everything; subsequent chapters guide you through the setup process.

On your first day at work, you must add your name to an existing project description file. Since it's your first day, a senior developer will review your code.

To begin, you need to obtain the project's source code. You can ask your manager for the server where the code is stored. In this demo, the code is stored on GitHub, which means that the Git database is hosted on a remote server provided by GitHub. You can access it through a URL or directly on the GitHub website. In this case, the clone command is used to retrieve the database, but you could also download the project as a zip file from the GitHub website. By cloning the repository, you receive a complete copy of the project files along with its entire history.

So, to obtain the source code, you can use the clone command followed by the repository's URL. Figure 1-8 is an example.

```
$ git clone https://github.com/mariot/thebestwebsite.git
```

```
mariot@macbook-pro GitHub % git clone https://github.com/mariot/thebestwebsite.git
Cloning into 'thebestwebsite'...
remote: Enumerating objects: 494, done.
remote: Counting objects: 100% (494/494), done.
remote: Compressing objects: 100% (296/296), done.
remote: Total 494 (delta 213), reused 424 (delta 167), pack-reused 0
Receiving objects: 100% (494/494), 408.65 KiB | 2.16 MiB/s, done.
Resolving deltas: 100% (213/213), done.
mariot@macbook-pro GitHub % 
```

Figure 1-8. *The result of the* git clone *command*

Git then downloads a copy of the repository into the current directory you are working from. Once the cloning process is complete, you can navigate the newly created directory and inspect its contents, as demonstrated in Figure 1-9.

```
mariot@macbook-pro GitHub % cd thebestwebsite
mariot@macbook-pro thebestwebsite % ls
LICENSE                    package.json          webpack.config.js
README.md                  src                   webpack.config.prod.js
nginx                      tsconfig.json         yarn.lock
mariot@macbook-pro thebestwebsite % ▊
```

Figure 1-9. *The contents of the repository are shown*

If you want to examine the recent changes made to the project, you can utilize the log command to display the commit history. Here is an example of how it looks, similar to Figure 1-10.

```
$ git log
```

```
commit 065070a03528fc4ae90fe08be6919692312992f5 (HEAD -> master, origin/master, origin/HEAD
)
Author: Mariot Tsitoara <mariot.tsitoara@gmail.com>
Date:   Fri May 15 09:05:55 2020 +0200

    Prepare README for production

commit e20078848e641e09f8c9a762981837b802094354
Merge: 5149769 6074d74
Author: Denys Vitali <denys@denv.it>
Date:   Sun Apr 19 08:38:43 2020 +0000

    Merge pull request #41 from Brawlence/master

    Changed Contrast & Inverted controls behaviour

commit 6074d74daf11b921c162aaae2eae7a636f565c46
Author: Brawlence <42910943+Brawlence@users.noreply.github.com>
Date:   Sun Apr 19 10:33:55 2020 +0300

    Changed Contrast & Inverted controls behaviour

    They are fixed in the top right corner of the screen (and thus easily accessible no mat
ter how far one had scrolled down), if the space is available (max-width>1080) and revert t
:▊
```

Figure 1-10. *A typical Git history log*

Running this command presents a chronological list of commits, including the commit hash, author, date, and commit message. It provides an overview of the project's history and the changes made.

Nice! Now, you should create a new branch to work on to avoid messing up with the project. You can create a new branch by using the branch command and checking it out with the checkout command.

```
$ git branch add-new-dev-name-to-readme
$ git checkout add-new-dev-name-to-readme
```

Now that the new branch is created, you can modify the files. You can use whatever editor you want; Git tracks all the changes via checksums. Now that you have made the necessary changes, it is time to put them in the staging area. As a reminder, you put modified codes ready to be snapshotted in the staging area. If you modified the README.md file, you could add it to the staging area using the add command.

```
$ git add README.md
```

You don't have to add every file you modified to the staging area, only those you want to be accounted for in the snapshot. Now that the file is staged, it is time to commit it or put its change in the database. You do this by using the command commit and attaching a brief description.

```
$ git commit -m "Add Mariot to the list of developers"
```

And that's it! The changes you made are now in the database and safely stored. But only on your computer! The others can't see your work because you worked on your own repository and a different branch. You must push your commits to the remote server to show your work to others. But you must show the code to the senior dev before making a push. If they are okay with it, you can merge your branch with the main snapshot of the project (called the *main branch*). So first, you must navigate back to the main branch using the checkout command.

```
$ git checkout main
```

You are now on the main branch, where all the team's work is stored. But by the time you worked on your fix, the project may have changed, meaning that a team member may have changed some files. You should retrieve those changes before committing your own changes to the main. This limits the risk of conflicts, which can happen when two or more contributors change the same file. You must pull the project from the remote server (also called *origin*) to get the changes.

```
$ git pull origin main
```

Even if another coworker changed the same file as you, the risk of conflicts is low because you only modified a line. Conflicts only arise when multiple people have modified the same line. Everything would be okay if you and your coworkers each changed different parts of the file.

Now, it's time to commit your version to main. You can merge your branch with the merge command.

```
$ git merge add-new-dev-name-to-readme
```

Now that the commit has been merged into the main, it is time to push the changes to the main server. You do that by using the push command.

```
$ git push
```

Figure 1-11 shows the commands used and the results.

```
mariot@macbook-pro thebestwebsite % git branch add-new-dev-name-to-readme
mariot@macbook-pro thebestwebsite % git checkout add-new-dev-name-to-readme
Switched to branch 'add-new-dev-name-to-readme'
mariot@macbook-pro thebestwebsite % vim README.md
mariot@macbook-pro thebestwebsite % git add README.md
mariot@macbook-pro thebestwebsite % git commit -m "Add Mariot to the list of developers"
[add-new-dev-name-to-readme a843219] Add Mariot to the list of developers
 1 file changed, 1 insertion(+), 1 deletion(-)
mariot@macbook-pro thebestwebsite % git checkout master
Switched to branch 'master'
Your branch is up to date with 'origin/master'.
mariot@macbook-pro thebestwebsite % git pull origin master
From https://github.com/mariot/thebestwebsite
 * branch            master      -> FETCH_HEAD
Already up to date.
mariot@macbook-pro thebestwebsite % git merge add-new-dev-name-to-readme
Updating 065070a..a843219
Fast-forward
 README.md | 2 +-
 1 file changed, 1 insertion(+), 1 deletion(-)
mariot@macbook-pro thebestwebsite % git push origin master
```

Figure 1-11. *A simple Git workflow*

It's that simple! And again, don't worry if you don't understand everything yet. This is just a little demo of how Git is usually used. It is also unrealistic: no manager would give a new recruit an all-access pass to their main repository like that.

Summary

This chapter offered a sneak peek at Git, which has many more powerful features to learn about. Before moving to the next step, ask yourself: How will Git help me in my projects? Which features are the most important? Will Git improve my workflow?

The main takeaway from this chapter is the difference between distributed and centralized VCSs. Team workflows using CVCS is less organized and leaves too many developers unfulfilled. Therefore, you must learn more about distributed VCS to keep up with the times.

You've seen the typical workflow of a team using Git in this chapter. It's the workflow most teams use in professional environments and the open source community. This workflow will increase your productivity even if you plan to work alone.

Don't worry about understanding all of Git right now; focus on what it can do for you. You will become familiar with it after a couple of chapters. Next, let's focus on installing Git on your system.

CHAPTER 2

Installation and Setup

Now that you know what version control is and how Git works, you are ready to learn how to install and set it up, which is quite easy.

Installation

The files required to install Git are available at `https://git-scm.com/downloads` for all systems. Follow the link and choose your operating system.

Figure 2-1 shows that GUI clients are available for Git. However, I recommend not venturing into that area until you complete Part III of this book. It is important to familiarize yourself with Git commands before using GUI clients; otherwise, you may waste a lot of time trying to resolve a simple issue that could be easily resolved using basic Git commands in seconds.

© Mariot Tsitoara 2024
M. Tsitoara, *Beginning Git and GitHub*, https://doi.org/10.1007/979-8-8688-0215-7_2

Figure 2-1. *The download section of git-scm.com as of June 2023*

Once familiar with Git commands, you can explore GUI clients and see for yourself. There is a chapter about GUI clients in Part IV of this book. However, please refrain from using any GUI client beforehand because it may significantly prolong your learning process.

Note   Git is bundled with two GUI tools: gitk, which is used for reviewing history, and git-gui, which is used for basic commands. These tools are explained in Chapter 15. Therefore, the previous advice still applies, and it is recommended to follow it before delving into the GUI tools.

Windows

Installing Git on Windows systems is a straightforward process. After opening the link (`https://git-scm.com/download/win`), the download should start automatically, and you are directed to the confirmation page, as shown in Figure 2-2. If the download doesn't start automatically, you can manually download the build corresponding to your Windows version.

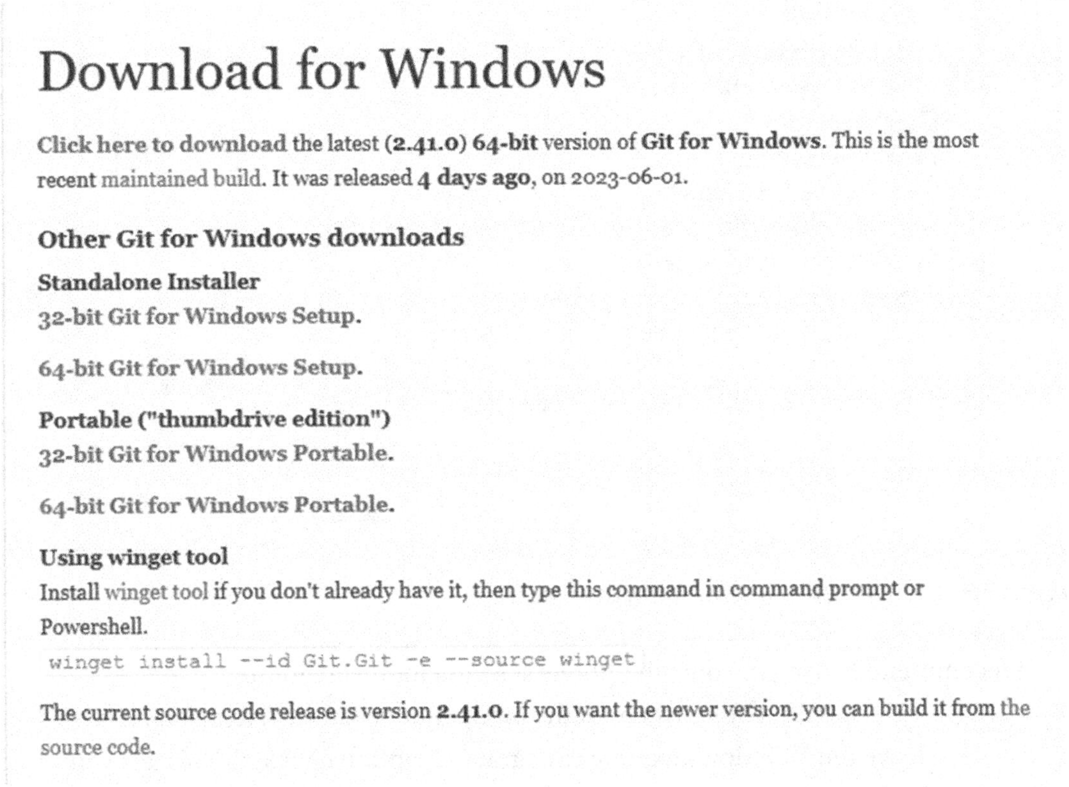

Download for Windows

Click here to download the latest (**2.41.0**) **64-bit** version of **Git for Windows**. This is the most recent maintained build. It was released **4 days ago**, on 2023-06-01.

Other Git for Windows downloads

Standalone Installer
32-bit Git for Windows Setup.

64-bit Git for Windows Setup.

Portable ("thumbdrive edition")
32-bit Git for Windows Portable.

64-bit Git for Windows Portable.

Using winget tool
Install winget tool if you don't already have it, then type this command in command prompt or Powershell.

```
winget install --id Git.Git -e --source winget
```

The current source code release is version **2.41.0**. If you want the newer version, you can build it from the source code.

Figure 2-2. *The Git download screen for Windows*

To begin the installation, execute the downloaded exe file. The first screen is the license declaration, which outlines the terms and conditions. Reading the license agreement thoroughly (although it's often skipped) is recommended. Once done, click Next to proceed to the component selection screen, like the one shown in Figure 2-3. On this screen, you are prompted to select which components to install.

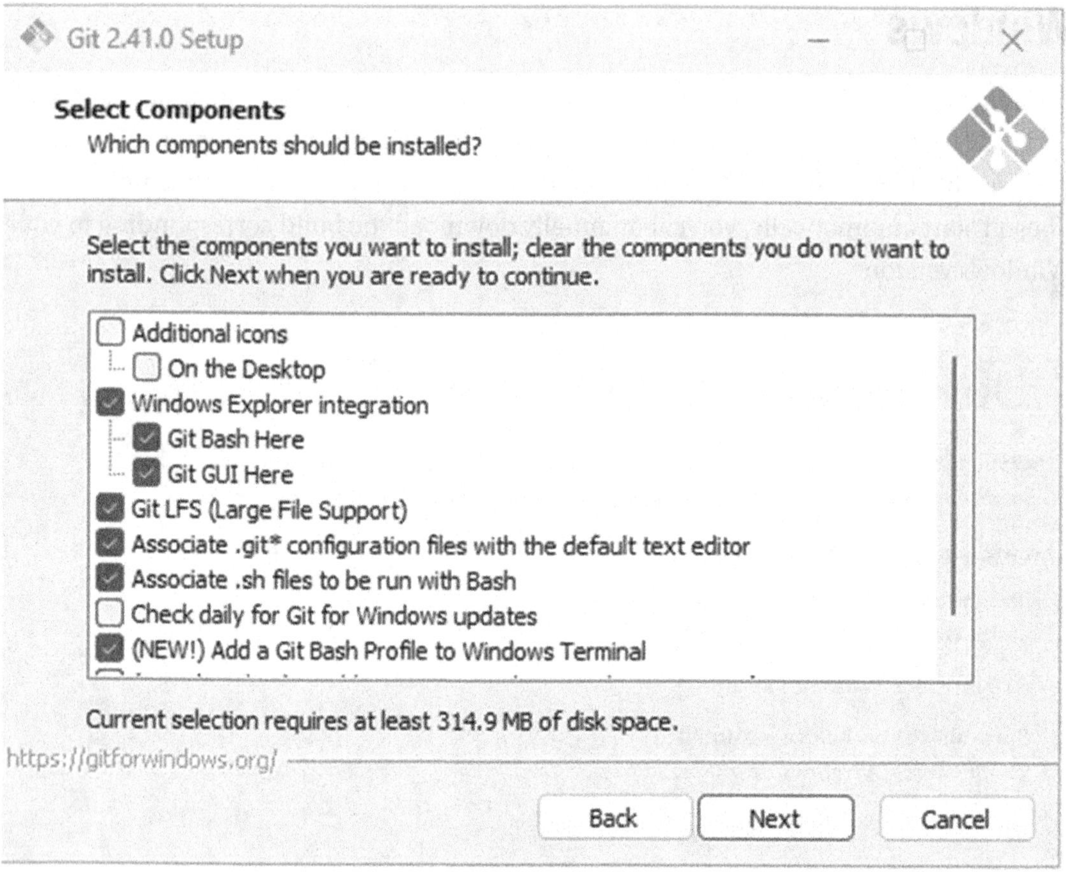

Figure 2-3. *Select the components to install*

I recommend leaving the default options selected for installation.

As Figure 2-3 depicts, you must check the components you wish to install. It is advisable to leave the "Windows Explorer integration" option checked. This lets you conveniently access Git by right-clicking a folder and finding the options to launch Git in the default GUI or the Bash (command window) context menu. The other components are self-explanatory, so deciding whether to install them is at your discretion.

Note   If you didn't install the Windows Explorer integration and want to open the command window in a folder, you must open the extended context menu. To do this, you can use the Shift+right-click keyboard shortcut. This provides additional options, including opening a command window in the selected folder.

After making your choices, click Next, and you are presented with the default editor selection screen, as shown in Figure 2-4. Git requires you to define a default editor since you need an editor to write commit descriptions and comments.

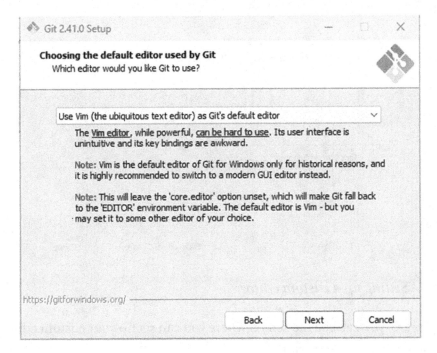

Figure 2-4. *Default editor selection*

As shown in Figure 2-4, Vim is the default editor for Git. You can select your preferred text editor from the drop-down list. The first two options, Nano and Vim, work within the console or command window, eliminating the need to open another program. The list includes popular editors like Sublime Text, Atom, and Visual Studio Code. If your preferred editor is not listed, you can choose the last option, and a new input field appears (as shown in Figure 2-5), allowing you to provide a link to the editor's main executable file.

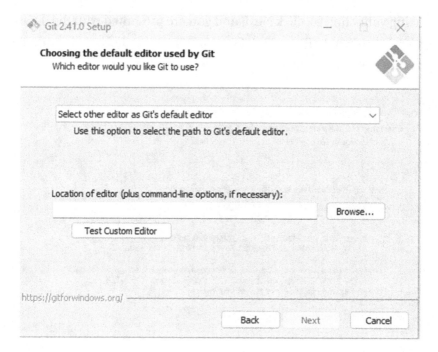

Figure 2-5. *Setting up a custom editor*

In Figure 2-5, you can see the screen where you can set up your custom editor if it is not listed in the drop-down options.

I have decided to stick with the default option and use Vim for this book. However, it does not make a difference in this book if you use any other editor. If you are interested in learning Vim (which takes some time), you can explore the Vim Tutor program that comes with Vim or try out a fun video game at https://vim-adventures.com/. Additionally, you can refer to the comprehensive guide at www.vi-improved.org/vimusermanual.pdf, which spans more than 300 pages.

Do not worry, though, as this choice is not permanent. You can change your preferred editor at any time. You learn how to do this in the last section of the chapter.

Caution   Never start or participate in an editor war while online. Just choose your preferred text editor and refrain from discussing it with anyone. I still bear scars from my previous experiences during the Emacs vs. Vim war.

The next step is to choose the name of the initial branch, as shown in Figure 2-6. This is the name of the first branch created when initializing a new repository. Traditionally, the default name has been "master". However, many teams prefer "main" as the default branch name.

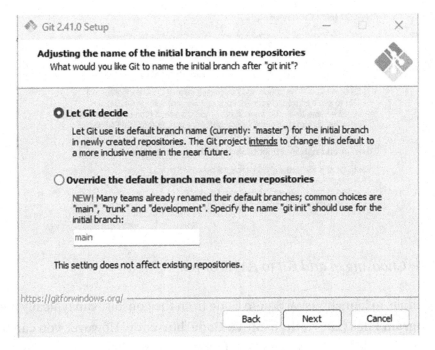

Figure 2-6. *Choosing git init default name*

The choice of branch name does not have any impact on your Git journey, so you can select the name that you are most comfortable with. Additionally, it's worth noting that you can always change the branch name when initializing a repository or at a later stage. I use "main" for new projects, while my team at work uses "devel".

Once you have chosen your favorite editor, you can proceed to the next screen, which is the PATH environment adjustment screen as shown in Figure 2-7. The PATH environment variable holds a list of directories where executable programs are located. It is necessary so that you don't have to enter the full path to an executable when you want to run it in the console; you only need to type its name.

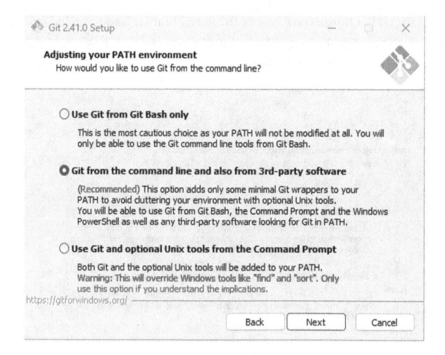

Figure 2-7. *Choosing to add Git to PATH or not*

For example, to launch Visual Studio Code from the console, you typically need to type **C:\Program Files (x86)\Microsoft VS Code\bin\code**. However, you can type the code to launch by adding C:\Program Files (x86)\Microsoft VS Code\bin to the PATH.

The same principle can be applied to Git if desired. If you prefer to use Git with its own isolated console called Git Bash, select the first option. In this case, you would need to launch Git from the Apps list or the context menu of a folder (if you installed the Windows Explorer integration).

However, if you want to be able to use Git globally, it is recommended to leave the default option checked to add Git to your PATH environment. By doing so, other tools can also utilize Git, and you can work with Git from any command window. I highly recommend choosing this option for greater convenience and flexibility.

The last option is invasive because it adds numerous Git commands to your PATH and potentially overwrites some of Windows' default tools. It is recommended to choose this option only if you have a valid reason. In most cases, there is no need for such a modification.

Please select an option shown in Figure 2-7 and proceed to the next step accordingly. Next, you reach the SSH executable adjustment screen, shown in Figure 2-8. You can choose between using the bundled OpenSSH or an external SSH executable. Unless you have a specific reason to use a different SSH executable, it is recommended to use the bundled one.

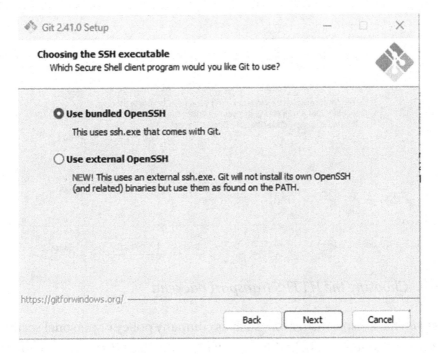

Figure 2-8. *Choosing an SSH executable*

Afterward, you encounter a screen regarding HTTPS connections, as depicted in Figure 2-9. You must select the library for sending data over HTTPS on this screen. As you progress through this book, you learn about connecting to remote servers since Git is a distributed VCS. To share your commits with others, it is crucial to establish secure and encrypted connections to protect your data from potential theft or unauthorized access.

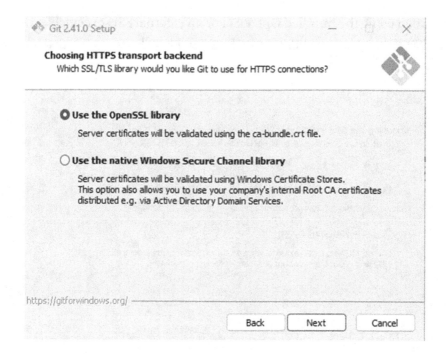

Figure 2-9. *Choosing the HTTPS transport backend*

Unless you have a specific reason, such as company policy or personal security setup, it is recommended to stick with the default option for HTTPS connections.

The next step involves line endings. This step presents you with a selection screen, which should resemble the one shown in Figure 2-10. Different operating systems handle text files differently, particularly when it comes to line endings. Considering the likelihood of collaborating with a team that uses various operating systems, Git needs to convert line endings to and from each style before sharing commits.

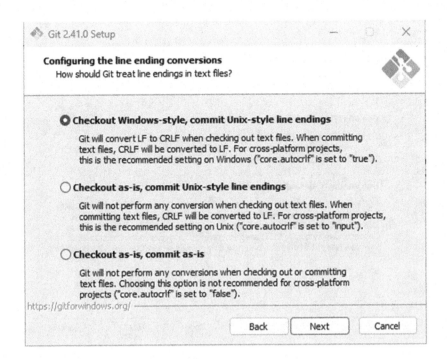

Figure 2-10. *Line ending conversions*

Selecting the default option for line endings is advisable if you are using Windows. The other two options can potentially cause issues with your commits if you are not careful with line endings. You can proceed to the next step once you have chosen the default option.

Caution   This step is crucial because Windows and macOS use "\r\n" to end lines, whereas Linux uses "\n". If you do not convert line endings appropriately, your files can become difficult to read, and Git may detect numerous changes even if you made minimal modifications. It is important to ensure proper line-ending conversion to maintain consistency and avoid unnecessary complications in your Git workflow.

In the next step, you choose a default terminal emulator or console. This is a straightforward selection screen like the previous ones, as shown in Figure 2-11. Git Bash requires a console emulator to function properly, so you must make a choice. The default emulator is MinTTY, while the alternative option is Windows' default console.

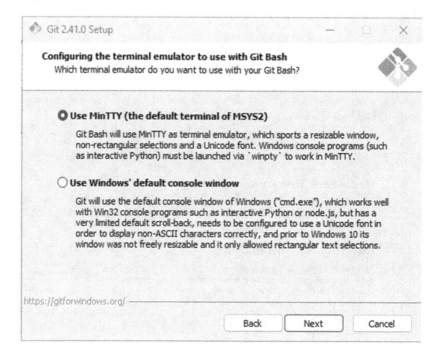

Figure 2-11. *Choosing a terminal emulator*

I recommend sticking with the default option for the terminal emulator, as MinTTY offers improved functionality compared to the Windows console window. Click Next to proceed to the final steps.

Next, you select the default behavior for the `git pull` command. Choose the default behavior as shown in Figure 2-12.

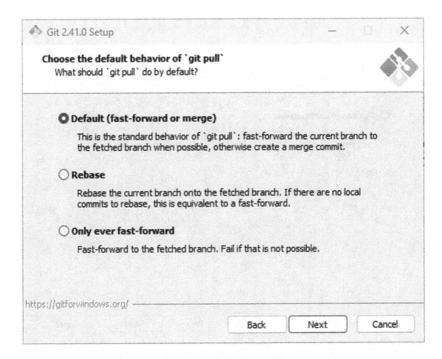

Figure 2-12. *Configuring default git pull behavior*

You have reached the end of the installation process. There are just a few adjustments to make on the extra options screen, as depicted in Figure 2-13 and Figure 2-14. This screen allows you to enable additional features that complement your Git installation. For instance, the Git Credential Manager enhances secure connections to remote servers and integrates well with other Git tools.

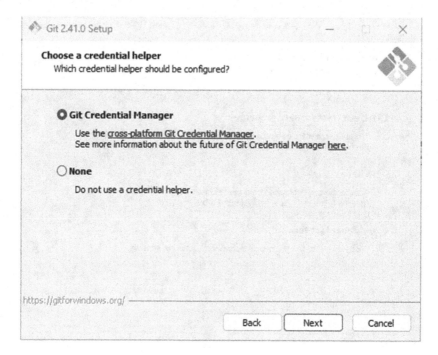

Figure 2-13. *Configuring credential helper*

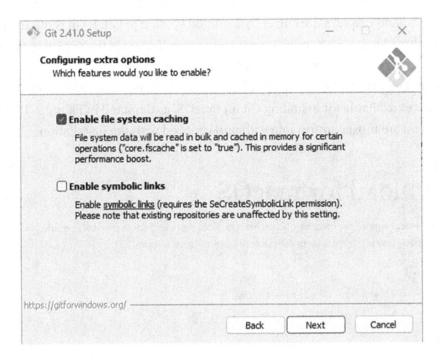

Figure 2-14. *Configuring extra options*

Unless you have a specific reason not to, it is recommended to leave the default options as they are. Once you have made your selections, launch the installation and allow it to complete. Congratulations! Git is now installed on your Windows system. The next section explains how to set it up properly.

macOS

If you have previously done software development on macOS X, it's likely that Git is already installed on your system, because it comes bundled with Xcode (https:// developer.apple.com/xcode/). You can check if Git is installed by running the following command in your console.

```
$ git --version
```

This command displays the currently installed version of Git. If Git is not installed, you are prompted to install Xcode's command-line tools. Select the option in the prompt to install Git, and you can skip the remaining steps in this section.

To install Git on macOS, visit `https://git-scm.com/download/mac`. There are several choices available for installing Git on macOS, as depicted in Figure 2-15. Choose the option you are most comfortable with and proceed with the installation.

Download for macOS

There are several options for installing Git on macOS. Note that any non-source distributions are provided by third parties, and may not be up to date with the latest source release.

Homebrew

Install homebrew if you don't already have it, then:

```
$ brew install git
```

MacPorts

Install MacPorts if you don't already have it, then:

```
$ sudo port install git
```

Xcode

Apple ships a binary package of Git with Xcode.

Binary installer

Tim Harper provides an installer for Git. The latest version is 2.33.0, which was released almost 2 years ago, on 2021-08-30.

Building from Source

If you prefer to build from source, you can find tarballs on kernel.org. The latest version is 2.41.0.

Installing git-gui

If you would like to install git-gui and gitk, git's commit GUI and interactive history browser, you can do so using homebrew

```
$ brew install git-gui
```

Figure 2-15. *Downloads for macOS*

I recommend using Homebrew (`https://brew.sh/`) to install Git and its tools on macOS. Run the `brew install git git-gui` command in your terminal. This command installs Git along with its dependencies. The installation process may take some time as it installs the necessary components.

Installing Git on macOS is relatively easier, especially if Homebrew is installed.

Linux

If you are using a Linux distribution, the installation of Git can vary depending on your distribution. However, most popular distributions have Git available in their package manager. Let's discuss the commands for some common Linux distributions.

The following are for Ubuntu and Debian.

```
$ sudo apt-get install git
```

or

```
$ sudo apt install git
```

The following is for Fedora.

```
$ sudo yum install git
```

or

```
$ sudo dnf install git
```

If you use a different distribution, you can visit the Git website's Linux download page (`https://git-scm.com/download/linux`) to find the appropriate installation commands for your specific distribution. The commands provided should be like the ones shown in Figure 2-16, with instructions for various Linux flavors.

Download for Linux and Unix

It is easiest to install Git on Linux using the preferred package manager of your Linux distribution. If you prefer to build from source, you can find tarballs on kernel.org. The latest version is 2.41.0.

Debian/Ubuntu

For the latest stable version for your release of Debian/Ubuntu

```
# apt-get install git
```
For Ubuntu, this PPA provides the latest stable upstream Git version

```
# add-apt-repository ppa:git-core/ppa  # apt update; apt install git
```
Fedora

```
# yum install git  (up to Fedora 21)
# dnf install git  (Fedora 22 and later)
```
Gentoo

```
# emerge --ask --verbose dev-vcs/git
```
Arch Linux

```
# pacman -S git
```
openSUSE

```
# zypper install git
```
Mageia

```
# urpmi git
```
Nix/NixOS

```
# nix-env -i git
```
FreeBSD

```
# pkg install git
```
Solaris 9/10/11 (OpenCSW)

```
# pkgutil -i git
```
Solaris 11 Express

```
# pkg install developer/versioning/git
```
OpenBSD

```
# pkg_add git
```
Alpine

```
$ apk add git
```
Red Hat Enterprise Linux, Oracle Linux, CentOS, Scientific Linux, et al.

RHEL and derivatives typically ship older versions of git. You can download a tarball and build from source, or use a 3rd-party repository such as the IUS Community Project to obtain a more recent version of git.

Slitaz

```
$ tazpkg get-install git
```

Figure 2-16. *Downloads for Linux and Unix*

Since you are already familiar with your Linux distribution, you may have a preferred method of package management or specific steps to install software. Feel free to use the method you are most comfortable with to install Git on your Linux system.

After you use the command corresponding to your distribution listed in Figure 2-16, Git is installed!

Caution   Like the editor war, the distribution war is a big no-no online.

Setting up Git

Before using Git, you must do a little setup. This setup is typically done only once because all the configuration is stored in an external global file, which means that all your projects share the same settings. However, there is also a way to configure projects individually, which is covered later.

Since Git is a distributed version control system, there will come a time when you need to connect to remote repositories. To ensure no identity mistakes, you must provide Git with some information about yourself. Don't worry. It won't ask for any fun facts!

To set up Git, open Git Bash (for Windows systems) or the default console window (for Linux/ macOS or Windows systems that modified their PATH environment). In the command prompt, specify your name and email address to Git using the following commands.

```
$ git config --global user.name "Mariot Tsitoara"
$ git config --global user.email "mariot.tsitoara@gmail.com"
```

Note the `global` argument, which indicates that the configuration is applied to all future Git repositories. This means you won't have to set up your name and email again in the future.

Using the `config` command, you can also change your default editor. If you ever want to switch your editor because you found a new one or uninstalled your previous one, the `config` command is there to assist you. For example, you would use the following command to change the default editor to Nano.

```
$ git config --global core.editor="nano"
```

The Git configuration file, which stores your setup, can be found in your home folder. For Windows, it is located at C:\Users\YourName\.gitconfig. It is at /home/yourname/.gitconfig for Linux and macOS.

You can manually edit this file if you prefer to make changes directly.

Summary

Let's review what we've learned so far! First, you should have Git installed on your system by now. The installation process is very easy on Windows and even easier on macOS and Linux. I suggest keeping all the default options (even if they aren't shown in the preceding screenshots) if you are unsure what you need.

Next, there is the setup. You only need to do this once in every system where you install Git. Git uses your name and email to sign every action you make, so setting this up first is necessary.

And that's it! You are now ready to use Git with all its glory. Head to the next chapter to jump-start with Git.

CHAPTER 3

Getting Started

You're finally ready to dive into Git! This chapter introduces you to some key Git
terminologies and concepts that are essential for any project. After that, you learn how
to set up a project, make changes, review those changes, and navigate between different
versions. So, let's get started!

Repositories

A repository serves as a storage for your project and keeps track of all its changes. You
can think of it as a "change database." However, it's important to note that a repository is
simply a regular folder on your system, making it easy to work with.

To manage a project with Git, you must set up a repository specifically for that
project. The process of setting up a repository is straightforward. Just navigate to the
desired folder where you want to track your project and instruct Git to initialize a
repository there.

To start a project and set up a repository, follow these steps.

1. Create a directory for your project.

2. Navigate into the directory using the command prompt or
   terminal.

3. Initialize a Git repository by executing the appropriate command.

See? It's very easy. Let's convert those statements into commands. But first, let's open
a console to enter the commands.

Follow these instructions to open a console or terminal on different operating
systems.

- Linux: Launch your favorite terminal using the shortcut Ctrl+Alt+T
  for Debian-like distributions.

© Mariot Tsitoara 2024
M. Tsitoara, *Beginning Git and GitHub*, https://doi.org/10.1007/979-8-8688-0215-7_3

- macOS: Press Cmd+space to bring up Spotlight and search for the Terminal app. Open it.

- Windows: There are two options available: cmd and PowerShell.

  - cmd: Press Windows+R to open the Run dialog, then type **cmd** and press Enter.

  - PowerShell: Press Windows+R to open the Run dialog, then type **powershell** and press Enter.

Note   If you had them open before installing Git for the first time, restart these consoles. Additionally, Git for Windows offers the Git Bash console emulator, which provides a similar environment to Linux and macOS consoles. If you're using Windows, I highly recommend using Git Bash to have a consistent experience with users on different operating systems.

To open Git Bash and execute the commands, please follow these steps.

1. Open Git Bash from the Apps list or the contextual menu.

2. In the Git Bash terminal, type the following commands.

```
$ mkdir mynewproject
$ cd mynewproject/
$ git init
```

The `mkdir` command creates a directory (folder) named "mynewproject." The `cd` command navigates to the "mynewproject" directory. Finally, the `git init` command initializes a Git repository in the current directory.

After executing the `git init` command, Git provides you with the location of the repository, like shown in Figure 3-1.

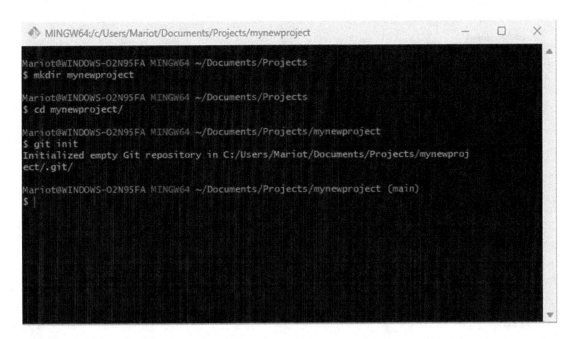

Figure 3-1. *Initialization of a new repository*

Note   mkdir and cd are system commands the operating system manages, whereas init is a Git command. Every Git command begins with git.

Git creates a directory called .git that contains all your changesets and snapshots. To check it out, show hidden files from your File Explorer settings. The repository looks like the directory shown in Figure 3-2.

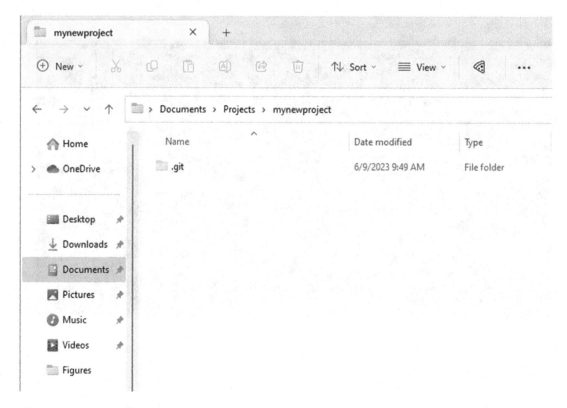

Figure 3-2. *An empty repository*

And if you open the `.git` directory, you find many more items in the Git database. Figure 3-3 shows an example.

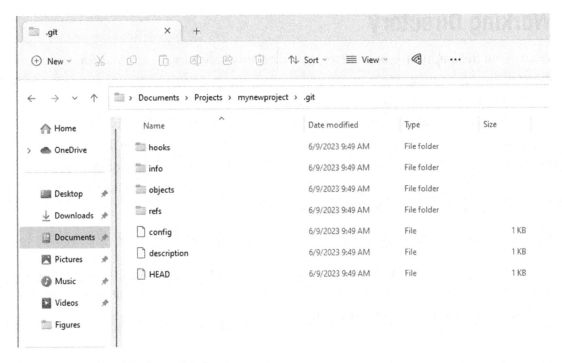

Figure 3-3. *Inside the* `.git` *directory*

Chapter 1 mentioned that instead of tracking changes between versions, Git takes snapshots? Well, all those snapshots are stored in the `.git` directory. Each snapshot is called a *commit*, which is covered shortly.

The HEAD file in the `.git` directory points to the current "branch" or subversion of the project you are working on. The default branch is called "main," but it is just like any other branch; the name is simply an old convention.

You should also know that initializing is the only way to create a repository. You can copy an entire repository with all its history and snapshots. This process is called *cloning*, which is explored in another chapter.

EXERCISE: CREATE AN EMPTY REPOSITORY

Our first exercise is quite simple. Just create an empty repository anywhere on your system. You can use either the default console or Git Bash.

Working Directory

What about the empty area outside the .git directory? That area is called the *working directory*, which contains the files you will be working on. Typically, the most recent version of your project resides in the working directory.

Each file you work with is in the working directory. There is nothing particularly special about this area except that it's where you directly manipulate the files. It's important to note that you should never modify the files inside the .git directory.

Git detects any new files you add to the working directory. You can check the status of the directory by using the status command.

```
$ git status
```

For example, if you create a new file called README.md in the working directory, Git recognizes that the project has changed. Place your new file alongside the .git directory, as shown in Figure 3-4, and not inside it.

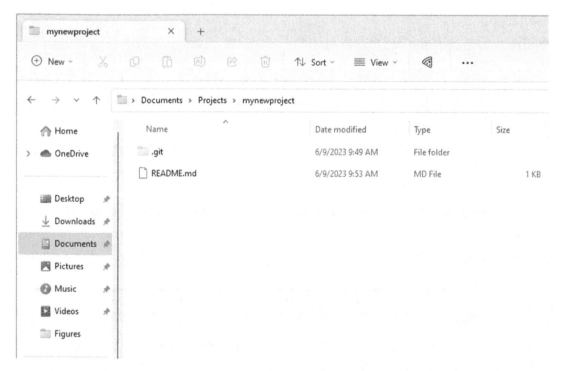

Figure 3-4. *Creation of a new file in the working directory*

If you check the status of the working directory, you receive a result like the one shown in Figure 3-5. Observe that you don't have any commits yet because you are still in the working directory and haven't taken any snapshots. The status also indicates that you are on the "main" branch, which is the default name for the initial branch created during repository initialization. There is also a list of untracked files. These are the files that have been modified or created in this instance.

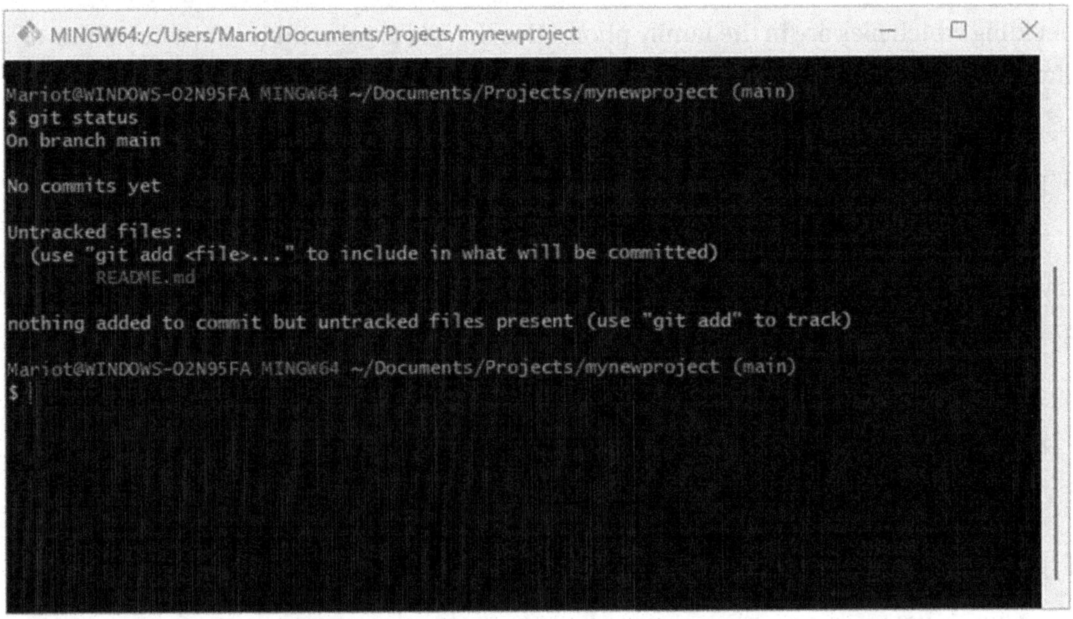

Figure 3-5. *The status of the working directory*

Essentially, the working directory is where you directly interact with your project files. It is the space where you make changes, create new files, and modify existing ones before committing them to the Git repository.

EXERCISE: CREATE SOME FILES FOR THE PROJECT

This exercise is also very easy. Create files within your project directory (repository) and check the working directory status.

Staging Area

The *staging area* is where your files go before snapshots are taken. Not every file you modify in the working directory should be included in the snapshot of the current state of the project. Only the files placed in the staging area are captured in the snapshot.

So, before taking a snapshot of the project, you must select which changed files to include. Changes in a file can involve creating, deleting, or editing it. Think of it as deciding which files are in the family photo. Use the add command to add a file to the staging area.

The following is an example.

```
$ git add nameofthefile
```

It's that simple. To stage the README.md file created earlier, use git add README.md. If you have created multiple files, you can add them individually or together, like git add file1 file2 file3.

Let's stage a new file by using the following command.

```
$ git add README.md
```

Then, let's check the status using the git status command.

```
$ git status
```

Adding a file to the staging area won't produce any visible result, but checking the status gives you a result like what is shown in Figure 3-6.

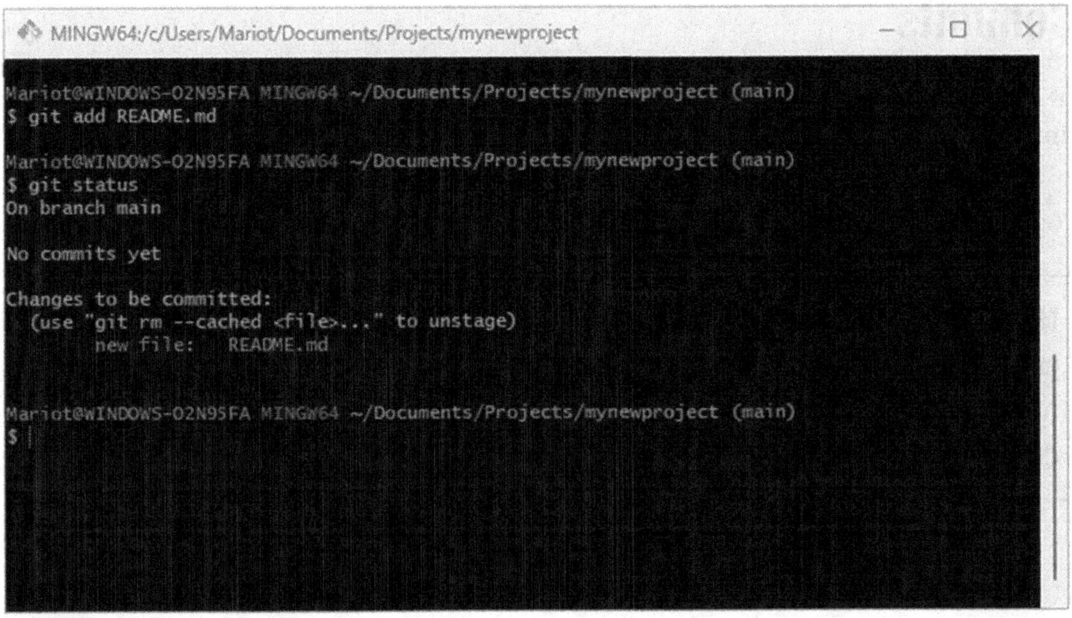

```
MINGW64:/c/Users/Mariot/Documents/Projects/mynewproject                    —    □    ✕

Mariot@WINDOWS-O2N95FA MINGW64 ~/Documents/Projects/mynewproject (main)
$ git add README.md

Mariot@WINDOWS-O2N95FA MINGW64 ~/Documents/Projects/mynewproject (main)
$ git status
On branch main

No commits yet

Changes to be committed:
  (use "git rm --cached <file>..." to unstage)
        new file:   README.md

Mariot@WINDOWS-O2N95FA MINGW64 ~/Documents/Projects/mynewproject (main)
$
```

Figure 3-6. *Staging a file*

Figure 3-6 shows that the working directory is cleaned after staging the file. That's because the git status command only tracks unstaged files, which are edited files that have not been marked for a snapshot.

Additionally, as shown in Figure 3-6, you can unstage a file using the git rm command with the --cached option.

```
$ git rm --cached README.md
```

Caution   Don't forget the --cached option when unstaging a file. If you forget it, you could lose your file!

After you have staged all the files that you want the changes to be considered, you are now ready to take your first snapshot!

EXERCISE: STAGE AND UNSTAGE YOUR FILES

Take the files you created in the previous exercise and stage them. Unstage one file and then restage it. Check the working directory status after each stage/unstage.

Commits

As discussed, a commit represents a snapshot of the entire project at a specific point in time. Git does not record individual changes to the files; it captures the project.

In addition to the snapshot, a commit includes information about the *author* of the content and the *committer* who added the changeset to the repository.

Note   The author and the committer are typically the same person unless the committer applied the changeset from another team member. It's important to remember that Git commits are interchangeable since it is a distributed version control system (VCS).

A commit represents a snapshot of the project's state, and each commit has a previous state known as its *parent commit*. The initial commit in a repository, created by Git upon repository creation, is the only commit without any parents. Subsequent commits are linked to each other through parentage. The collection of commits that are connected through parent-child relationships is called a *branch*.

Note   If a commit has two parents, it indicates that the commit was created by merging two branches.

A commit is identified by its name, which is a 40-character string obtained by hashing the commit. It is a simple SHA1 hash, so multiple commits with the same information have the same name.

A reference to a specific commit is called a *head*, and it has a name. The head you are currently working on is called HEAD.

Now, you can commit the files you staged earlier. Before each commit, it's recommended to check the status of the working directory and the staging area. You can proceed with the commit if all the files you want to commit are in the staging area (under the phrase "Changes to be committed"). Otherwise, you must stage them using the `git add` command.

To commit all the changes, use the `git commit` command.

```
$ git commit
```

Executing this command opens the default editor (refer to Chapter 2 if you want to modify yours) and prompts you for a commit message. A commit message is a short description of what has changed in the commit compared to the previous one.

For example, if my default editor is Notepad, executing the commit command displays a screen like the one shown in Figure 3-7.

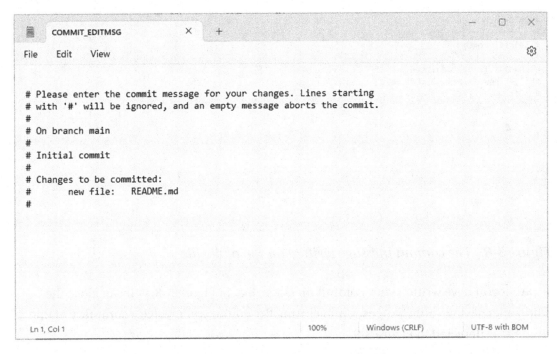

Figure 3-7. *Git opens the default editor so you can edit the commit message*

Figure 3-7 shows that the first line of the file is empty, and that's where you should write the commit message. The commit message should ideally be written on a single line, but you can also add additional lines for comments. Comments in the commit message start with the # symbol, and Git ignores them. They only provide additional information and make the commit message more descriptive. It's important to note that Git automatically includes the list of changed files in the commit comments (the same files you saw with `git status`).

In the later chapters, you will learn how to write commit messages properly. But for now, you can enter a simple message like "Add README.md to the project" on the first blank line, as shown in Figure 3-8.

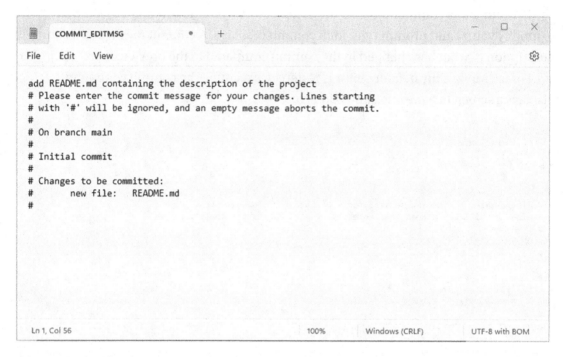

Figure 3-8. *The commit message written on top of the file*

After you have written your commit message, like in Figure 3-8, you can close the editor after saving your changes. Upon closing the editor, you receive a summary of the commit, as depicted in Figure 3-9.

```
MINGW64:/c/Users/Mariot/Documents/Projects/mynewproject                    —    □    ×
No commits yet

Changes to be committed:
  (use "git rm --cached <file>..." to unstage)
        new file:   README.md


Mariot@WINDOWS-02N95FA MINGW64 ~/Documents/Projects/mynewproject (main)
$ git commit
hint: Waiting for your editor to close the file... unix2dos: converting file C:/Users/Mariot/
Documents/Projects/mynewproject/.git/COMMIT_EDITMSG to DOS format...
dos2unix: converting file C:/Users/Mariot/Documents/Projects/mynewproject/.git/COMMIT_EDITMSG
 to Unix format...
[main (root-commit) ff9f109] add README.md containing the description of the project
 1 file changed, 1 insertion(+)
 create mode 100644 README.md

Mariot@WINDOWS-02N95FA MINGW64 ~/Documents/Projects/mynewproject (main)
$ git status
On branch main
nothing to commit, working tree clean

Mariot@WINDOWS-02N95FA MINGW64 ~/Documents/Projects/mynewproject (main)
$
```

Figure 3-9. *Summary of the commit*

The summary of the commit contains several pieces of information.

- The current branch: main

- The name of the previous commit: root-commit (since this is your first commit)

- The name of the commit: the first seven characters of the commit hash

- The commit message

- The number of files changed: one file

- The operation performed on each file: creation

Congratulations! You have taken your first snapshot. If you check the status of the repository, you see that it is clean again unless you have left some files unstaged.

EXERCISE: COMMIT YOUR CHANGES

Take your staged files from the previous exercise and commit them. Then, modify one of your tracked files, stage it again, and make a new commit. Compare the summary of each commit. What is different? In what way are those commits linked?

Quick Start with Git

Now that you are familiar with the basic concepts of Git, you can apply them in a real project. Let's imagine you want to create a folder to hold your to-do list and make it versioned so you can track when each item was completed.

To help you become more familiar with Git, complete the following exercise without assistance. If you encounter any difficulties, refer to the previous sections for guidance.

Remember the basic principles of Git.

- Modify files in the working directory.

- Add the files you want to include in the current state to the staging area.

- Create a snapshot of the project by committing the changes.

Ensure that you add the modified files to the staging area before committing, or they are not included in the snapshot. Any modified files not added to the staging area remain in the working directory until you decide to discard them or include them in a future commit.

Let's get started with the exercise! Please complete it thoroughly before moving on to the next chapter. It is essential to have a clear understanding of how Git works.

EXERCISE: A VERSIONED TODO APP

---

1. Create a new repository.

2. Create a file named TODO.txt in the directory and add some text.

3. Stage TODO.txt.

4. Commit the project with a short commit message.

5. Create two new files named DONE.txt and WORKING.txt.

6. Stage and commit those files.

7. Rename WORKING.txt to IN PROGRESS.txt.

8. Add some text to DONE.txt.

9. Check the directory status.

10. Stage WORKING.txt and DONE.txt.

11. Unstage DONE.txt.

12. Commit the project.

13. Check the directory status.

After completing this exercise, close the book and try to explain the following concepts to yourself in your own words.

- Working directory

- Staging area

- Commit

If you understand these concepts well without encountering many problems, you are ready to learn more Git commands and concepts.

Summary

This chapter is of great importance for your understanding of Git. The following are the three states that a file can be in.

- Modified: You have made changes to a file in the working directory.

- Staged: You have added the file to the staging area to prepare it for snapshotting.

- Committed: You have captured a snapshot of the entire project, including all unmodified and staged files.

If a file was part of the previous commit and you haven't made any modifications, it is automatically included in the next commit. A modified but unstaged file is considered unmodified. You need to explicitly stage those files to make Git track their changes.

You have also touched upon committing and commit messages. Opening an external editor to write commit messages may initially feel unfamiliar, but you will become more comfortable with it in time.

The next chapter delves into checking the project history, navigating between versions, ignoring specific files, and reviewing the current changes made to the project since the last commit.

CHAPTER 4

Diving into Git

Now that you are familiar with the basic commands of Git, it's time to dive deeper into its other features.

Ignoring Files

Not everything in the working directory should be tracked by Git. Certain files (configs, passwords, bad code) are generally left untracked by authors or developers. The files (or directories) to be ignored should be listed in a simple file named `.gitignore`. Note that the proceeding period in the name is important.

Let's return to the previous chapter's repository, the to-do list. Let's imagine that you want to include a private, untracked file named `PRIVATE.txt`. First, you must create the .gitignore file using your favorite text editor and write `PRIVATE.txt` in it, as shown in Figure 4-1.

© Mariot Tsitoara 2024
M. Tsitoara, *Beginning Git and GitHub*, https://doi.org/10.1007/979-8-8688-0215-7_4

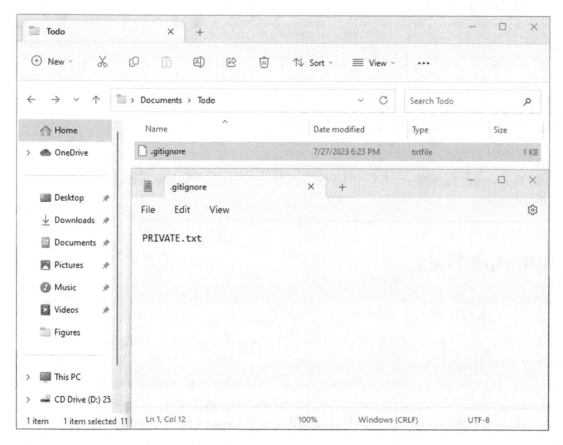

Figure 4-1. *The* `.gitignore` *file with* `PRIVATE.txt` *in it*

If you create and modify the PRIVATE.txt file (like in Figure 4-2), it won't be considered by Git when you check the status.

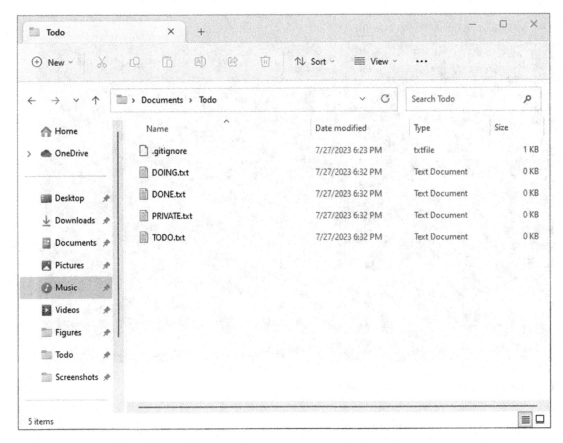

Figure 4-2. *Adding PRIVATE.txt*

Let's try to check the status.

```
$ git status
```

You get a similar result as shown in Figure 4-3.

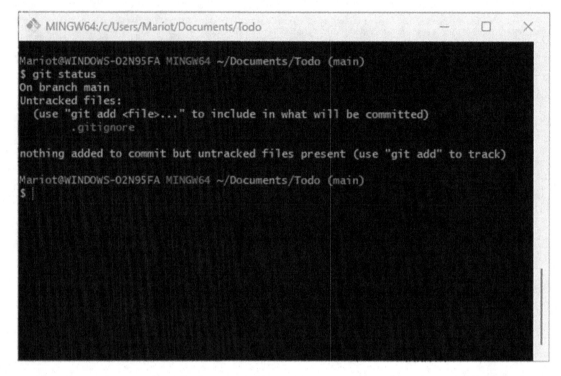

Figure 4-3. *Status of the working directory*

As you can see from the status shown in Figure 4-3, PRIVATE.txt is not tracked. However, you can also observe that the .gitignore file IS tracked. Therefore, after modifying the .gitignore file, you must add and commit it to include the changes in the Git repository.

```
$ git add .gitignore
$ git commit
```

Staging a file and committing the project result in a confirmation message summarizing the changes made (see Figure 4-4).

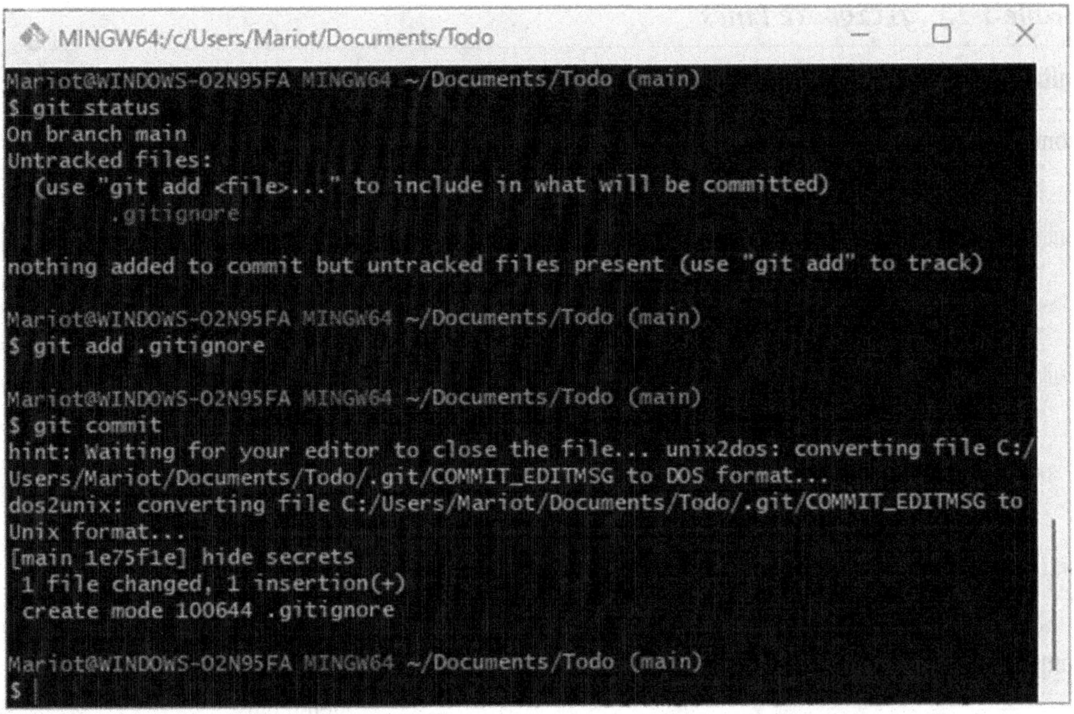

Figure 4-4. *Committing .gitignore*

Remember that the `.gitignore` global file should be placed at the root of your repository. Placing it in a directory only ignores matching files in that specific directory. It is generally considered bad practice to have multiple .gitignore files scattered across various directories unless your project is enormous. Listing all the rules in a single .gitignore file located at the root of your repository is preferable.

You might wonder what kind of files should be ignored when using Git. The general rule of thumb is to ignore all files generated by the project. For instance, in a software source code project, you should ignore the compiled outputs (such as executable or translated files). Additionally, it's recommended to exclude temporary files, logs, and large libraries (e.g., node_modules). Also, remember to exclude any personal configuration files and temporary files created by your text editor.

The .gitignore file is not limited to ignoring files by their exact names; you can also ignore directories and files that match certain descriptions. Table 4-1 is a handy reminder of all the templates you can use.

Table 4-1. *.gitignore Lines*

.gitignore Line	What Is Ignored	Example
config.txt	config.txt in any directory	config.txt local/config.txt
build/	any build directory and all files in it. But not a file named build	build/target.bin build/output.exe not output/build
build	any build directory, all files in it, and any file named build	build/target.bin output/build
*.exe	all files with the extension .exe	target.exe output/res.exe
bin/*.exe	all files with the extension .exe in the bin/ directory	bin/output.exe
temp*	all files with name beginning by temp	temp temp.bin temp_output.exe
**/configs	any directory named configs	configs/prod.py local/configs/preprod.py
**/configs/local.py	any file named local.py in any directory named configs	configs/local.py server/configs/local.py not configs/fr/local.py
output/**/result.exe	any file named result.exe in any directory inside output	output/result.exe output/latest/result.exe output/1991/12/16/result.exe

Those are the most common lines used with .gitignore. There are others, but they are only used in specific situations and almost never used in common projects. If you are using a computer language or framework, go to `https://github.com/github/gitignore` for a template of the `.gitignore` file you should use.

But what if you want to ignore all files matching a description except one? Well, you can tell Git to ignore all the files and then immediately make an exception. To exclude a file from the ignored list, you use "!". For example, if you want to ignore all .exe files except output.exe, write .gitignore like in Figure 4-5.

Figure 4-5. *How to make an exception*

Note the order of the lines. The exception comes *after* the rule!

This exception marking only works for lines describing file names, though. You can't use it with lines ignoring directories.

And that's how you ignore files! It's almost as easy as ignoring your responsibilities! The `.gitignore` file is tracked and versioned, so don't forget to stage it before committing!

Checking Logs and History

If you followed the exercises (as you should) or began to use Git for your projects, you now have a problem I promised would solve easily with Git: how to consult the history log.

This is one of the most used features of Git and one of the easiest Git commands: `git log`.

```
$ git log
```

Try it! Open your repository and run the command. You should see a view similar to the one shown in Figure 4-6.

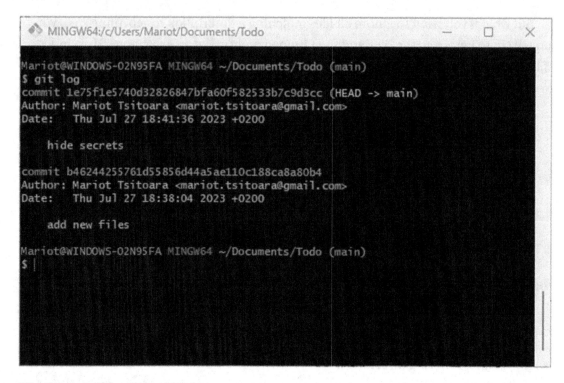

Figure 4-6. The commit log

The commit log lists (from the most recent to the oldest) all the snapshots you or others committed. It also includes the following for each commit.

- The name (unique, obtained by hash)

- The author

- The date

- The description

Since the commit names are often lengthy, let's only use the first five letters as the name. This is important for the next section.

If your commit history is very long, you can use the keyboard to do the following.

- Go forward or backward one line: key up and down OR press j and k

- Go forward or backward one window: press f and b

- Go to the end of the log: press G

- Go to the beginning of the log: press g

- Get help: press h

- Quit the log: press q

You can use many parameters with git log, as presented in Table 4-2.

Table 4-2. *The Most Common Git Log Parameters*

Command	Use	Example
git log --reverse	reverse the order of commits	
git log -n <number>	Limit the number of commits shown	git log -n 10
git log --since=<date> git log –after=<date>	only show commits after a certain date	git log --since=2023/11/11
git log --until=<date> git log --before=<date>	only show commits before a certain date	
git log --author=<name>	Show all commits from a specific author	git log --author=Mariot
git log --stat	Show change statistics	
git log --graph	Show commits in a simple graph	

Viewing Previous Versions

Now that you know how to check the history and commit logs, it is time to inspect the files to see what changes were made.

Remember those long names that are created with each commit? You are going to use those to navigate between commits or snapshots. To check your files in a specific snapshot, you must know its name. The best way to find the name of each commit is to check the history log.

To view and learn what changes have been made to your project, you can use the git show command followed by the name of the commit. You don't need to write the full name; the first seven letters suffice.

```
$ git show <name>
```

Try it with your repository! You should get a result like the one shown in Figure 4-7.

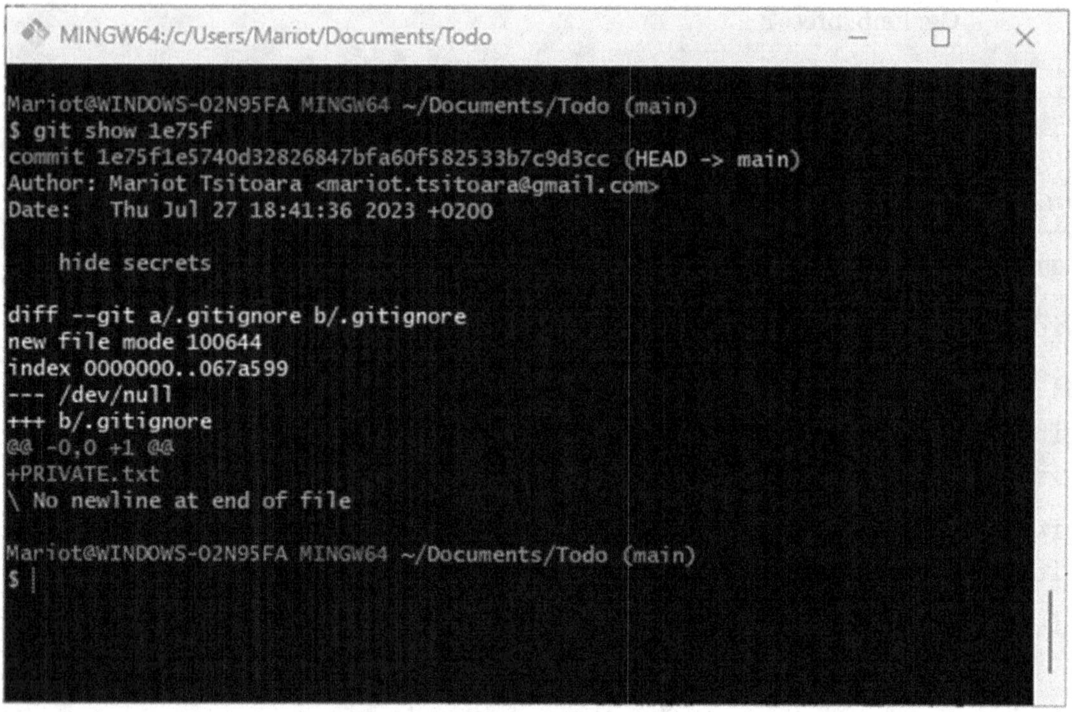

Figure 4-7. *Result of git show*

As you can see, the commit is displayed in a highly detailed manner. You can observe the differences between the selected commit and the previous one. Additions are shown in green, and deletions are displayed in red. Using the git show command, you can examine the details of any commit.

Reviewing the Current Changes

Checking previous versions is helpful, but what if you only want to review the changes you just made? Examining differences between the last commit and the current working directory is an essential feature of Git, which is very useful. The command to check these differences is simple: git diff.

```
$ git diff
```

Modify one or multiple files in your directory, and then execute the command. You get a result like the one shown in Figure 4-8, which is very similar to the result of the git show command from the previous section. They display the same view because the information shown is identical.

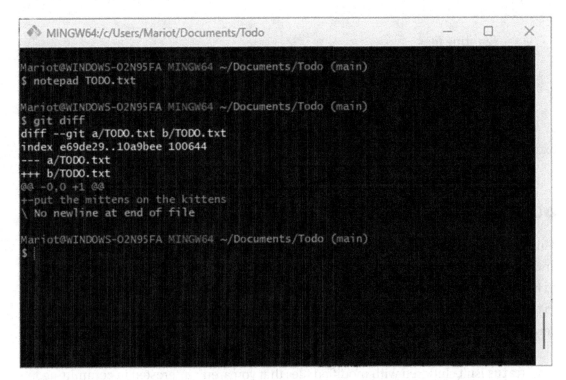

Figure 4-8. Checking all the changes done in the working directory

Most of the time, you only need to check the changes made to a single file, not the entire project. You can pass the file name as a parameter to review its differences compared to the last commit.

```
$ git diff TODO.txt
```

The main thing to remember is that git diff checks the changes made to the files in the working directory; it doesn't check staged files! You must use the --staged parameter to examine changes made to staged files.

```
$ git diff --staged
```

You should always check the diff in the staged files before committing a project so you can do a final review. You may forget to do so one day, so proceed to the next chapter to learn how to undo or modify your commits.

Before moving on to the next chapter, please make sure you are comfortable with these features.

- Ignoring files

- Checking history logs

- Reviewing local and staged changes

Congratulations if you are comfortable with these concepts and have completed the exercises! However, you aren't finished with commits yet!

Summary

This chapter was all about project history. You learned about checking logs with `git log` and `git show`. You also reviewed the current changes with `git diff`. `git log` and `git diff` will be particularly useful in the future, so make sure you understand them well. `git diff` is about comparing the current modified files to the files in the last commit. In contrast, `git log` is just a list of all previous commits.

The ability to ignore files with `.gitignore` is also a valuable skill to have, so your `git status` isn't cluttered with modified files that you aren't interested in committing. It's also a good way to ensure that a particular file (probably containing secret keys) isn't accidentally committed.

You still have a lot to learn about commits in the next chapter. Chapter 5 reviews the three states of Git files and shows how to bring back previous versions into the working directory. You also learn how to undo and modify commits. Hang tight!

Commits

The previous chapter taught you a little about the essential features of Git. By now, you should know how to check the history log and see the changes made to the current version. However, Git commits can be a complex concept, so this chapter delves deeper into them in this chapter. First, you explore (again) the inner workings of Git and its terminology. Then, you'll learn how to view and examine previous versions. Let's get started!

The Three States of Git

Before delving into the details of commits, let's revisit the basics and understand how Git works. You may already know the three states a file can be in. Regardless, don't skip this chapter; it is essential for everything you do with Git. I encourage you to read on.

As you saw in the last chapter, not all files are tracked by Git; some files are ignored (by the .gitignore file). Additionally, some files aren't ignored but are not yet tracked by Git. These are the newly created files that have never been part of a snapshot (commit).

Tracked files can be in three states.

- Modified: You changed the file.

- Staged: You changed the file and prepared it to be snapshotted.

- Committed: You took a snapshot of the entire project, and the file was part of it.

Untracked files remain as such until you decide to stage and commit them or explicitly ignore them.

Note Git doesn't track changes; it tracks snapshots. Each time you commit, the state of the entire project is saved, not just the small changes that were made.

67

Nerd fact: Git is fast because you always work on the last state of the project. When you want to see a previous commit, it just shows you the state of the project at that specific time. Many version control systems stored each change made to a file, and when you wanted to go back to a previous state, they replayed the changes in reverse. This approach caused many problems with speed and memory when the project grew large. However, Git's way of thinking avoids such issues by creating efficient databases. When you take a snapshot and a file doesn't change, it is not stored again; instead, a reference to the existing file is used.

Let's revisit the three states and explore their relationship:

- The working directory is where you work with your files. It's the directory you created before initializing the repository. Here, you can read, modify, and edit your files.

- The staging area is where you place your changed files before taking a snapshot of the entire project. You cannot create a snapshot (commit) without staging your changed files first. Only staged files (along with unchanged files) are included in the snapshot. Unstaged files (whether tracked or untracked) and ignored files remain in their current state.

- The database or .git directory stores every snapshot you've taken. These snapshots are known as *commits*.

Recall that staging concerns only the changed files you select, while committing encompasses the entire project. You stage individual files, and then commit the entire project to create a snapshot.

Navigating Between Versions

Many times, you won't only want to know what has changed in your project, but also to see the state of the project at a specific point in time, to view the snapshot you took. With Git, this is easy to achieve.

When you want to return the project to a previous state in the working directory, you can use the git checkout command followed by the commit name. However, it's important to note that this operation changes the files in the working directory. Therefore, you must ensure that you don't have any unstaged files. Untracked files are fine since Git doesn't track their states yet.

To view a project snapshot, use the `git checkout` command and pass the commit name as a parameter. It allows you to see how the project looked at that specific point in its history.

```
$ git checkout <name>
```

Let's try it! Open your current project in a text editor and take note of its contents. Then, check out a previous commit, as Figure 5-1 shows.

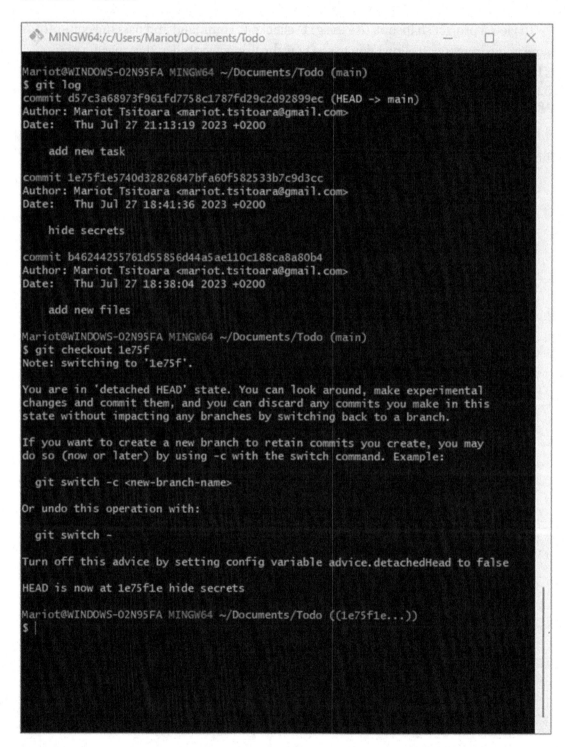

Figure 5-1. *Checking out older commits*

Warning You can't check out any other commit if your working directory isn't clean! Make sure to commit your changes before switching snapshots.

If you check your text editor, you notice that the project is now just like when you took the snapshot. That's one of the best things about Git—nothing you took a snapshot of is ever lost!

Now, let's learn some Git terminology. Instead of saying *name* when talking about commits, you use the term *head*. When switching between different commits, you need a way to know which head you are on. A head refers to a commit (there can be multiple heads in a repository), and the head pointing to the currently checked-out commit is called HEAD.

But how do you return to the normal, current working directory? Since you didn't make any significant changes to the repository, returning to the working directory is as simple as checking out the only branch you have. By convention, that branch is called main.

```
$ git checkout main
```

Try it out! Remember the two golden rules of time travel.

- Only travel back in time when the present is clean (nothing unstaged in the working directory).

- If you change the past, make sure to store the changes somewhere (in a new branch).

Don't forget to check out the current branch (main) after navigating between versions.

Undo a Commit

The time comes when you stage and commit files but later change your mind. It happens to everyone. However, with traditional methods (without versioning), it is very difficult to roll back changes, especially if they were made ages ago. With Git, it's as simple as using a single command: `git revert`.

Why not just delete the commit? That's because of the time-traveling rule from the previous section: never change the past. Whatever changes were committed must stay for the sake of history. Changing what has happened in the past is very dangerous and counterintuitive. Instead, you use git revert to create a new commit that contains the exact opposite of the commit you are trying to undo.

So, undoing a commit is just committing its exact opposite. It's that simple! To use it, you must pass the name of the commit to be undone as a parameter.

```
$ git revert <commit name>
```

You can revert any commit, but make sure to work on a clean working directory. So, don't forget to stage and commit your files before reverting a commit. Let's try it!

First, ensure that the working directory is clean, as shown in Figure 5-2.

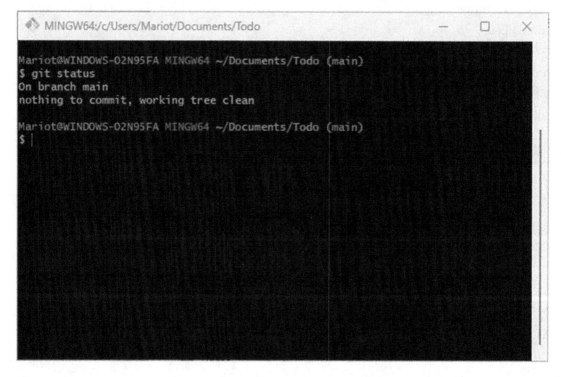

Figure 5-2. *Using git status to check the working directory*

Perfect. Now that you know the working directory is clean, it's time to check the history to determine which commit to undo. You should get a result like the one shown in Figure 5-3.

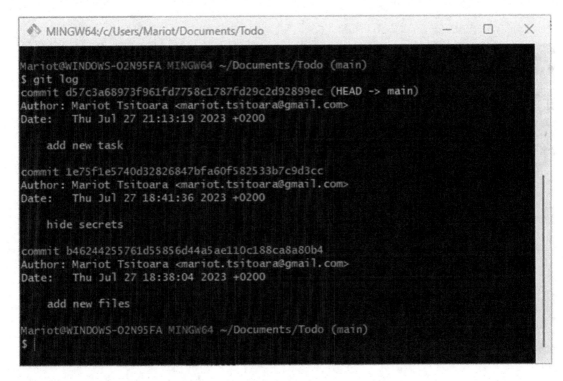

Figure 5-3. Checking commit history with git log

Note   If you don't like the way the commit history is displayed, you can pass the --oneline parameter to reduce the information shown. Figure 5-4 shows an example.

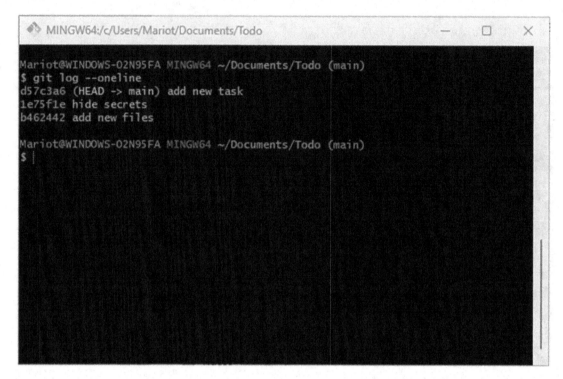

Figure 5-4. *A prettier git log output*

Let's revert the last commit! Use git revert followed by the commit name.

$ git revert d57c3a6

Since git revert only creates a new commit containing opposite changes, the rest of the procedure is the same as any new commit. Figure 5-5 shows that you are asked to describe your new commit. I suggest always keeping the default commit description, as it makes it easy to identify.

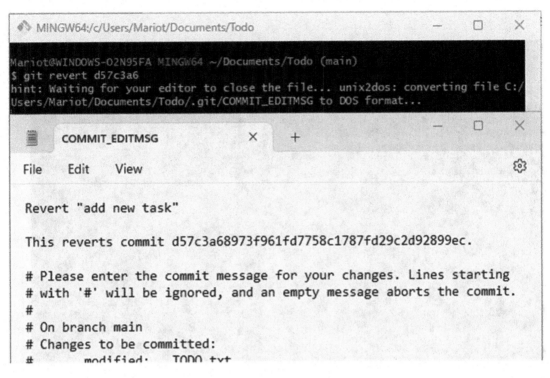

Figure 5-5. *The new commit description*

After you save the commit description (as with all commits), you are presented with a summary of the snapshot content. Figure 5-6 shows the result after running the commands and saving the commit description.

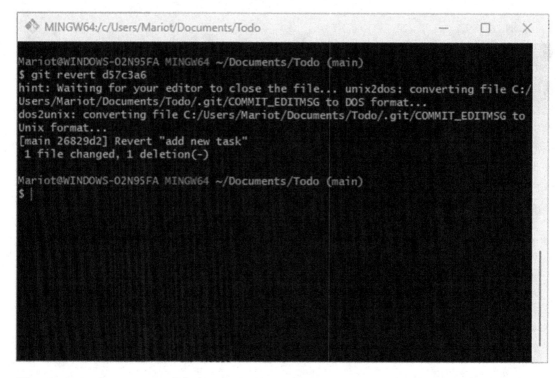

Figure 5-6. *Summary of the revert*

As you can see, undoing changes is very easy with Git. The key thing to remember is that git revert only creates a new commit containing opposite changes. This means you can revert a revert! Reverting a revert reapplies your original commit, and the two reverts cancel each other out. However, the commits remain in your history log because you can't change the past.

Note   You can change the past using various advanced Git techniques. But never do it unless you know what you're doing. It's a very bad idea, and it likely leads to more problems down the road. It's always safer to use git revert to undo changes.

Modifying a Commit

As I promised you in the last chapter, you learn how to modify a commit in this chapter. It is used when you forgot to stage a file or want to change the commit message. However, this should not be used to modify a lot of files, as doing so is counterintuitive. The next chapter discusses in detail when and where to use this feature. And I'll say it again: never try to change the past.

To modify a commit, you must use the `git commit` command, but with `--amend` as a parameter. It opens your default text editor, just like a normal commit, but with the staged files and commit message already there.

```
$ git commit --amend
```

Then, save and close the text editor, as you would for any regular commit. The term *modify* I used earlier is a bit misleading because you are not directly modifying an existing commit; you are creating a new one and replacing the current one. So, from now on, I use the term *amend* to refer to this process.

Amending a commit takes everything in the staged area and creates a new commit with those changes. If you want to add a new file to the commit or remove a file from it, you can stage and unstage them as needed. To unstage a file, you can use `git reset HEAD <file>`.

For example, let's use the TODO app again. First, edit an existing file, then create two new files named `filenottocommit.txt` and `fileforgotten.txt`, as shown in Figure 5-7.

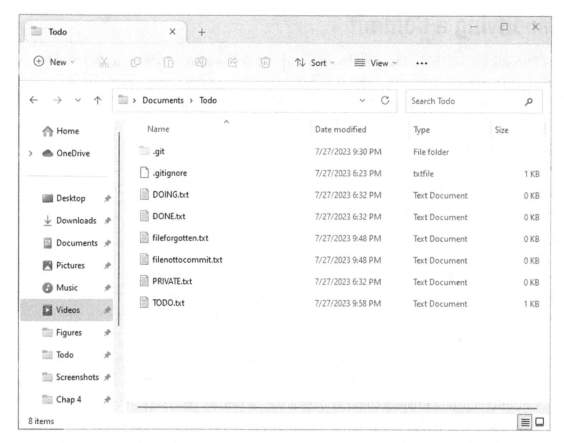

Figure 5-7. *All the files in the working directory*

You can check the project's current state by executing the git status command.

```
$ git status
```

You might have a slightly different result depending on how many files you added to the project before, but it should look like Figure 5-8.

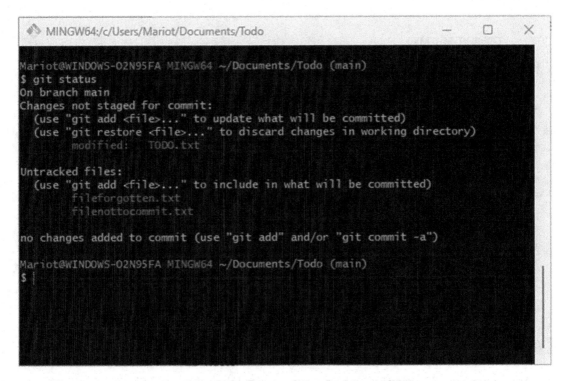

Figure 5-8. *The modified and untracked files are highlighted*

The next thing you must do is stage the files to be part of the commit. Add the changed files and `filenottocommit.txt` to the staging area to do this.

```
$ git add TODO.txt DONE.txt filenottocommit.txt
```

As you learned from the last chapter, you should always check what you've staged with `git diff --staged` before committing. However, let's pretend that you forgot to check and proceed to commit immediately.

```
$ git commit
```

Even in that case, you arrive at the commit message screen that outlines the changes to be committed, like Figure 5-9.

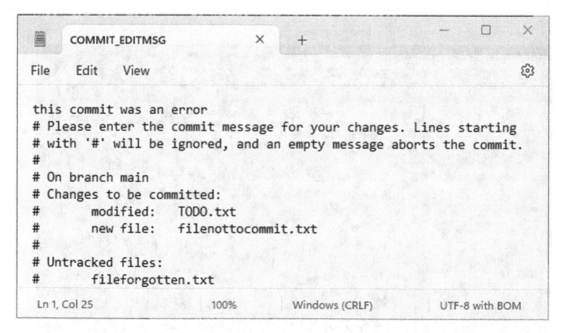

Figure 5-9. *The commit message screen is the last failsafe*

As you can see, the changes to be committed and the untracked files are outlined and highlighted. It's difficult to miss them, but let's pretend to overlook them. Write a simple commit message, save it, and close the editor. You get the usual summary shown in Figure 5-10.

```
 MINGW64:/c/Users/Mariot/Documents/Todo                                    —    □    ×

       modified:    TODO.txt

Untracked files:
  (use "git add <file>..." to include in what will be committed)
        fileforgotten.txt
        filenottocommit.txt

no changes added to commit (use "git add" and/or "git commit -a")

Mariot@WINDOWS-O2N95FA MINGW64 ~/Documents/Todo (main)
$ git add TODO.txt filenottocommit.txt

Mariot@WINDOWS-O2N95FA MINGW64 ~/Documents/Todo (main)
$ git commit
hint: Waiting for your editor to close the file... unix2dos: converting file C:/
Users/Mariot/Documents/Todo/.git/COMMIT_EDITMSG to DOS format...
dos2unix: converting file C:/Users/Mariot/Documents/Todo/.git/COMMIT_EDITMSG to
Unix format...
[main a956e63] this commit was an error
 2 files changed, 1 insertion(+)
 create mode 100644 filenottocommit.txt

Mariot@WINDOWS-O2N95FA MINGW64 ~/Documents/Todo (main)
$ |
```

Figure 5-10. *The commit summary*

Now that you've read the commit summary, you notice that you committed the wrong file and forgot to commit another. First, you should remove the last commit from your project with `git reset`. You use the `--soft` option so that the changes you made stay in the working directory. `HEAD~1` refers to the previous commit, as `HEAD` refers to the current one.

```
$ git reset --soft HEAD~1
```

After this, you can unstage the file with git reset again:

```
$ git reset HEAD filenottocommit.txt
```

Check if the commands worked as intended by reviewing the project's current status. Use the `git status` command to see if the last commit has been removed from the project and the changes are in the working directory.

```
$ git status
```

You get a result like the one shown in Figure 5-11.

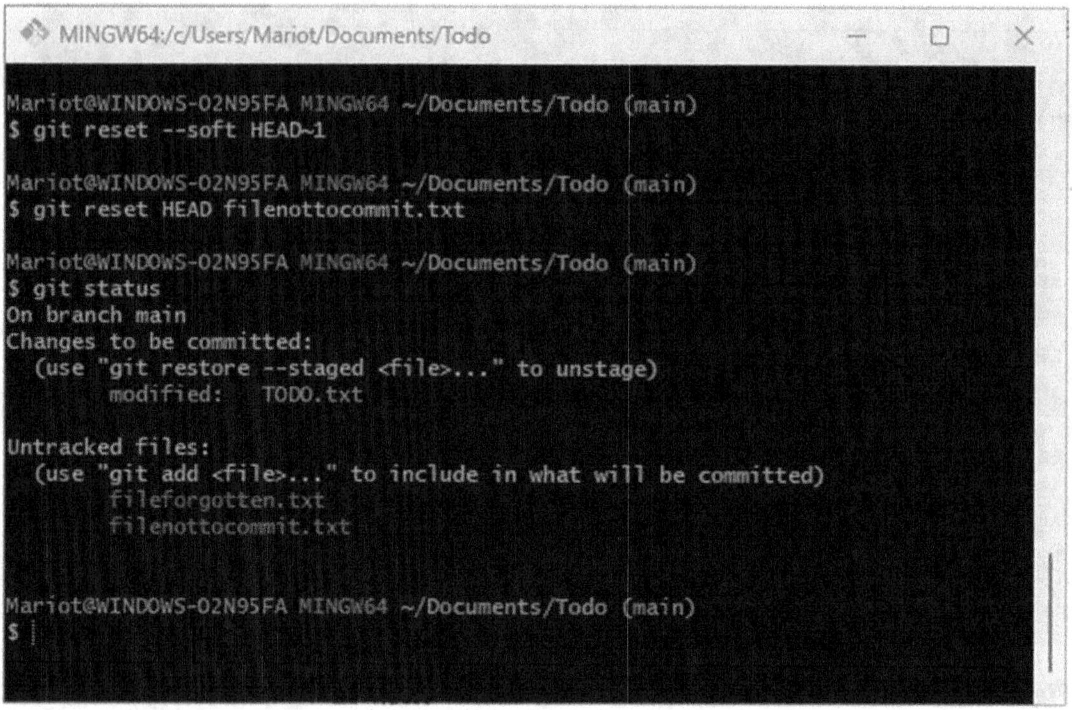

Figure 5-11. *Status of the project after resetting*

As you can see, `filenottocommit.txt` is untracked because you removed it from the staging area. Naturally, `fileforgotten.txt` is also untracked because you didn't stage it. Only `TODO.txt` remains in the staging area because you haven't made any changes after the commit.

Warning   Be very careful when you use the reset command, as it can be quite dangerous. Always make sure to double-check the command you write before executing it.

Then, stage the correct one.

```
$ git add fileforgotten.txt
```

You can commit the project now that you have staged the correct files.

```
$ git commit
```

Let's intentionally add a grammatical error to the commit message to demonstrate another feature of Git.

Amending a Commit

There is no need to modify the entire commit for simple mistakes like an error in the commit message. You need to amend it. Let's try it with our project!

```
$ git commit --amend
```

The amend process looks just like a normal commit, but instead, the commit message is already written, as you can see in Figure 5-12.

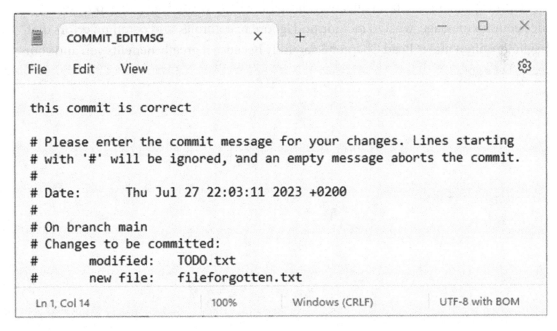

Figure 5-12. *Editing a commit message*

You can change the commit message as you wish and then save and close the editor as usual. It's that simple! Look at the new commit's name and compare it to the old one. You'll notice that they are different. That's because the commit name is a hash of the information in the snapshot—different states of the project result in different commit names.

A parting note about modifying commits: don't abuse it! Yes, making errors is not ideal when writing code, and you usually want to correct them immediately. However, errors also help you become better; keeping track of your mistakes is a great way to learn and improve.

Summary

This chapter primarily focused on navigating, undoing, and amending versions of your project. You should now be comfortable with making small corrections in your commits. Review the first section of this chapter, as it's essential for everything you do in Git. You should know the differences between the three states of Git by heart.

The next chapter is a brief one, only discussing theory. You learn how to write a nice commit message, what to include and ignore in commits, and common errors that beginners often make. Read Chapter 6 carefully because it greatly benefits you and your team. Let's go!

CHAPTER 6

Git Best Practices

Chapter 5 was one of the most important ones in this book. Make sure to return to it whenever you have doubts about commits. At this point, you should be able to create, review, and amend project snapshots without problems. Now that you know the basic features of Git, it's time to learn the best practices to make your life (and your teammates') easier. These are the things that I wish I knew when I first used Git. This chapter covers commit messages, the dos and don'ts of Git, and a list of the most common mistakes beginners make. It finishes with a reminder of how Git works.

Commit Messages

Commit messages are one of the most important aspects of version control and yet often overlooked. These messages help you understand what changes were made in the commit and, most importantly, why those changes were made. Clean and readable commit messages are essential for a better Git experience. Let's begin by identifying the problem.

The most common problem faced with Git is that commit messages are often void of sense and don't convey any meaningful information. Moreover, most of the time, the messages get less and less clear with each commit. This happens because of a misunderstanding of Git concepts: each commit must stand by itself, and if a commit requires other commits to make sense, it shouldn't exist. You should never commit a half-done project. Instead, if a task becomes too big, it's best to split it into several logical chunks, where each part makes sense independently.

A good way to gauge if you are on the right path when splitting tasks is to check the potential commit message: if you think about using a very similar commit message for multiple commits, you likely made an error when splitting the task. For example, if your task is to make many small corrections in a large website, it would make sense to divide it into smaller tasks, such as a commit for each page or a commit for each page category. So remember: your commits must be independent, atomic, and complete.

© Mariot Tsitoara 2024
M. Tsitoara, *Beginning Git and GitHub*, https://doi.org/10.1007/979-8-8688-0215-7_6

One problem many beginners also have is including too much information in the commit message, which can lead to unnecessary details clogging the commit history. A commit message should be concise and straight to the point. You don't need to list everything that has changed; instead, focus on explaining why those changes were made. The `git show` command can be used to see a complete recap of the changed files in the commit if someone is interested in the specific changes.

It's important to remember that you are not the only one who will read your code or text. Take the time to explain the context of the changes and why they were made. Thinking that you'll remember it is a mistake and should never be practiced. For every commit, ask yourself: If another person looks at my project, will they understand the timeline of changes in the project just by looking at my commit messages? Also, remember that the other person might be you in a few months; code is easily forgotten.

Your Git commit message should focus on *why* the changes were made. If someone wants to see *what* has changed, they can refer to git diff.

Git Commit Best Practices

For a better commit message and to avoid the problems listed earlier, here are some tips that you should follow from now on. These tips help your coworkers and provide you with a clear view of why a commit was made in the future. Having a good history log is imperative in a fast-paced development environment.

The following are some tips.

- Commit messages should be easy to read at a glance. When you use `git log`, long messages without newlines can be hard to read, requiring unnecessary scrolling to view everything. Keeping messages concise and well-formatted helps with easy searching and retrieval of commits.

- Keep the commit messages to a maximum of 50 characters.

- Begin the message with a capital letter for clarity and consistency.

- Avoid ending the message with a period; it's not necessary.

- Use the present tense to describe the changes made.

- Avoid using unnecessary articles or words that don't clarify the message.

- Keep commit messages consistent in style and format throughout the project.

By following these tips, you'll improve the readability and usefulness of your commit messages, making it easier for everyone, including your future self, to understand the changes made in the project's history.

Since Git commit messages are fundamental in any project, they should be consistent and not subject to abrupt changes. Using the same language and following internal logic for commit messages is essential. Changing writing styles mid-project can make it challenging to search for specific commits and understand the project's history.

Here are some best practices for writing commit messages.

- Messages must be clear and contextualized, especially in big projects with multiple developers working on different parts. Consider starting the commit message with the context or area of the project impacted by the changes, particularly in large projects.

- Avoid using vague or unclear messages such as "change CSS," "fix tests," "hotfix," "little fixes," and "updates." These messages are often misleading and require users to look at diffs to understand the changes. Always include why the changes were made and never force users to decipher the code changes to understand the commit's purpose.

- While you can expand the commit message in the body, avoid providing excessive details. The focus of the commit message should be WHY the changes were made, not a comprehensive list of WHAT changed.

- Use clear, present-time, and imperative language in your commit messages. The best commit messages are usually short, direct, and easy to understand.

To make it clearer, let's provide some examples. Table 6-1 is a handy tool to guide you in the right direction when writing commit messages.

Table 6-1. *Some Examples of the Best and Worst Commit Messages*

Best	Bad	Worst
[login] Fix typo in DB call	Fixed typo in DB call	Fix typo
refactor login function for reuse	Changing login function by moving declarations to parameters	Code refactoring
add new api for user program check	adding a new api for user program check	New user api

The examples presented in Table 6-1 should serve as guidance to help you write better commit messages. They indicate whether you are heading in the right direction when crafting a commit message.

It's important to note that these are recommended actions and not strict rules set in stone. In some exceptional cases, you may find it necessary to deviate from these guidelines to make the message clearer and more informative. The key is to balance providing sufficient context and keeping the message concise and to the point.

Ultimately, the goal of a commit message is to convey why the changes were made, making it easier for you, your team, and anyone else who reads the commit history to understand the purpose and intent behind each commit. So, while following best practices is beneficial, use your judgment to adapt the message as needed for clarity and comprehension.

What to Do

Let's enumerate the good practices you should always remember when using Git. These practices are essential to your success and will save you significant time.

- Each commit should stand on its own. Keep your commits small and independent. A commit should introduce a feature or fix a bug, not track every change you make. If a task requires multiple independent steps, separate them into multiple commits. For example, if a feature needs both an API endpoint and a frontend call, make separate commits for each, as they are not logically linked. This approach improves readability in the commit history and provides clearer commit messages.

- Write informative commit messages. Each commit message should answer a question. Why was the commit created? What problem does it solve? Since commits can be shared among many users in Git, the commit message should explain the result of applying the commit. Use the present tense in commit messages, even though the temptation to use the past tense might persist initially. Over time, you'll become more comfortable with the present tense convention.

That's it! The list of things to do in Git is concise. Just focus on writing clear messages for your small, independent commits. Now, let's look at the things you should avoid in Git.

What Not to Do

This list is a bit longer than the previous one because Git is a powerful tool that doesn't limit what you can do. However, this can also lead to more opportunities for mistakes, especially when trying to save time. Ultimately, bad practices will create more problems than they solve, so it's best to avoid them altogether.

One common mistake beginners make is trying to solve multiple problems in one commit. For example, they might fix a bug when they notice another one, then solve both problems and commit the project. This may seem fine initially, but later, it becomes difficult to identify which changes introduced the new problems. It also makes writing coherent and clear commit messages challenging. If you commit many changes from different contexts, consider splitting the commits into smaller, more focused ones.

Another related mistake is combining commits that have nothing in common. For instance, code refactoring should be in a separate commit from bug fixes or new features. Keeping them separate facilitates bug tracking and maintains a cleaner history log.

The next mistake is related to using Git as a backup system, which happens when some developers commit their changes at the end of each day, regardless of whether it makes sense. This is often driven by companies that measure productivity based on the number of lines of code produced. However, this counterintuitive approach leads to confusing commits that repeatedly try to resolve the same problem. It's essential to commit when the work is ready and not just to meet a daily quota. If you need to switch tasks, you can use concepts like branching or stashing to handle unfinished work.

Another misuse of Git is the overuse of the amend command. Amending commits should be reserved for correcting typos, adding forgotten files, or making small changes. It should not be used to introduce significant changes to a commit. If the changes are substantial enough to require a new commit message, create a new commit instead. It's essential to keep track of your mistakes and not be afraid to leave them in the codebase. Git is there to track versions and show what has changed, including errors. Trying to erase mistakes does not help anyone and may cause more problems in the long run.

Finally, the last common mistake is attempting to change history in Git. This dangerous practice can lead to confusion, frustration, and problems in the repository. Instead of trying to change the past, the correct approach is to make a new commit to introduce changes. The past should be left as it is, and developers should move forward with new commits for any updates or corrections. Let the past die. Kill it if you have to.

Note   Later in the book, you are shown how to go back in time and change history. Never do this.

How Git Works (Again)

I know, I know. You've been through this already. But I want to make sure that you are completely comfortable with it before moving on to Part II of this book.

Remember the three states of Git? They are also called the "three trees" (in fact, it is the official appellation in the docs). Let's review them once again. Figure 6-1 helps you quickly identify the trees.

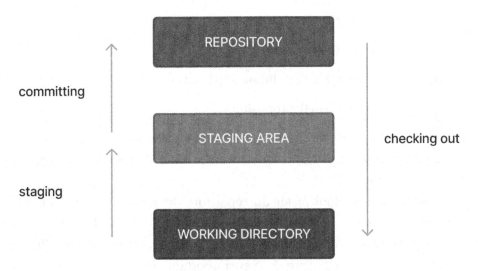

Figure 6-1. *The relationship between the three states of Git*

As shown in Figure 6-1, there's nothing new here, just a reminder. To track changes in a project, you need to take a snapshot of the entirety of it. Git doesn't track changes; it tracks versions.

You will only interact with the working directory because that's where your files can be freely edited. There is nothing to say about it; it's just the current state of your files.

The staging area is where you put your files when ready to take a snapshot of your project. Any changed files that haven't been put on the staging area (or *staging index*) are not part of the snapshot. The changes are still available in the working directory, though. So, it's necessary to check the state of the working directory before and after adding files to the staging index to ensure everything is okay.

The repository is the database of the Git architecture. You will find all your commits and history logs there. You can find it in the `.git` folder (which you should never touch unless to adjust configs). Committing takes everything in the staging area and creates a snapshot. That's why we say, "commit a project," not "commit a file" or "commit changes." Unchanged files committed in the past are already in the staging area. That's why you don't have to stage everything, just the edited files. Remember to stage new or deleted files, too!

Finally, checking out brings back the state of a project to a previous one. The working directory updates to reflect the changes, so ensure no uncommitted files are lying around.

The following are the basic steps in Git.

1. Make changes (in the working directory).

2. Stage every changed file (in the staging index).

3. Commit the project (in the repository).

It's that simple, but please be sure to understand the relationship between those states before proceeding to the next chapter. Every section after this one assumes that you are familiar with those.

But how do the commits look inside the repository? It's simple: they look like linked lists. A commit contains many pieces of information: the contents and the metadata. The contents are just the project files (changed files and references to unchanged files). The metadata contains other data that are also very important: the date of commit, committer identity, and Git messages. Another metadata present in the commit is the parent pointer or reference. It is just the name of the previous commit; if it's empty, it means the commit is the first one. So, each commit is linked to the next with a parent-child relationship.

Summary

This chapter focused on important concepts and terminologies in Git, which are essential to your success with version control. You should now understand when it's the right time to commit and how to write clear and meaningful commit messages. Remember that the commit message should answer the question: what does the commit bring? It should provide context and explain the reason behind the changes, making it easier for others, including non-developers, to follow the project's progress.

The key takeaway is that commits are the building blocks of your project, and each one should be stable and independent. Your commit messages should explain why a commit exists rather than detailing what was done.

Additionally, this chapter provided valuable tips on the dos and don'ts of Git. Remembering these practices will save you significant time and effort in the long run, especially when it comes to debugging.

This chapter concludes Part I of the book. Part II introduces a very useful tool: GitHub. You can share and track your projects in GitHub, enhancing collaboration and project management. Rest assured; the Git features promised earlier are covered in subsequent chapters after the GitHub section. Let's move forward with excitement and dive into the next part!

CHAPTER 7

Remote Git

Congratulations on completing the first part of this book! You've learned the basic features of Git, which should make you comfortable making and tracking changes. Writing meaningful commit messages might have been a bit challenging, but following the advice from the last chapter can help you improve with each commit. Additionally, you should now be able to view previous versions and access the history logs, which are crucial features for the upcoming chapters.

Now, get ready for a new challenge: working with remote repositories. In this chapter, you'll discover the importance of working with remote repositories and how it works. You'll also be introduced to typical team workflows and the correct usage of remote repositories. Since the concept of remote Git might seem complex, don't worry! You'll use an easy tool that will greatly assist you throughout the process (hint: it's in the title of this book). Let's dive into the world of online collaboration!

Why Work in Remote Git

Throughout this book, you've been working alone in your local repository. However, Git is an excellent tool for team collaboration, and it would be a shame to limit its usage to only local repositories. This section explores remote Git and explains why it's crucial for effective teamwork.

As you know, Git is a distributed version control system, meaning repositories are not centralized on a single server but spread across multiple local repositories. Each team member has their own local repository, containing their commits and history. These commits can be easily exchanged between repositories, and all files are constantly ready for editing.

For effective team collaboration, a method must be devised to ensure that all commits are readily accessible. Waiting for coworkers to arrive at work and start their computers before gaining access to their commits would be highly inconvenient.

© Mariot Tsitoara 2024
M. Tsitoara, *Beginning Git and GitHub*, https://doi.org/10.1007/979-8-8688-0215-7_7

The solution lies in having a central server host the repository, and team members can push and pull their commits to and from it. But wait, doesn't that resemble a central version control system workflow? Not entirely, though there are similarities.

Recall that distributed version control systems were developed to address the issues associated with central repositories. In Git, each client has its own repository, allowing them to work on it whenever they want. Almost all Git operations are performed locally. The remote server is just treated as a client with a repository where everyone can push their commits. This approach ensures that all changes are available to everyone at any time. Notably, this method is only used to facilitate commit exchange and is not an inherent part of Git. For Git, all repositories are considered equal; developers have agreed that some repositories are more equal than others, in the sense that they serve as designated central repositories for teamwork.

Caution   It is possible to share commits without the need for an intermediate server, but it is such a bad idea that it is not covered in this book.

Even if you work alone, having a remote repository in addition to your local one is still a good idea. That way, you have a backup of your project with all its history in a safe location. You can also access your project anytime, provided you have network access to the repository server.

Caution   Just because Git can be used as a backup system doesn't make it one. Using it for this sole purpose is not a good idea.

So, are you interested in that remote repository yet? Of course you are! It's amazing! Let's see how it all works.

How Does It Work?

Using a remote server means having a computer that holds a copy of your project and its history. You don't have to push all your commits into it; you only push the commits you want to share. Your coworkers then pull the commits that interest them and apply them to their own repositories. And that's it! Working with a remote server involves copying repositories and pushing and pulling changes. Let's see in detail how it all works.

To set up a remote repository, you first need a server capable of running the Git software. Any computer worth its salt can run Git as it is a very small software. You won't need a lot of firepower to run it properly. Even a very small computer like the Raspberry Pi is more than enough for Git.

Now that you have the server, you must find a way to communicate with it. Network access to the server is necessary so that multiple clients can push and pull from the same repository. This communication with the server should be very secure. It would be extremely disappointing if anyone with access to the server could read and edit the repository. To be able to interact with the repository, users must authenticate themselves with each Git operation. A login/password HTTPS type of authentication can be used, but it's not secure enough. Using SSH authentication is better. The principle of SSH authentication is simple: only the clients that have been predetermined can access the repository.

And that's it! Setting up a remote Git server is a straightforward task. Maintaining and securing it, on the other hand...

Note   Git doesn't distinguish between "server" and "client." They are just social constructs enforced by the developers.

Using your own server to host your Git projects is a good idea if you work alone or want to keep them private. However, it becomes a pain when you work with a team. Each team member must have access to the Git server via a network, so you need to set up a local network if your team is in the same working space. The server should also run 24/7 so that there is no delay in Git operations.

What happens if some of your coworkers are remote or in a different working space? Well, you need to hook your server up to the Internet. Thus, you also need to ramp up your security game. The more coworkers you have, the more authentication exceptions you have to manage.

Another problem with using your own Git server is that you need to deal with permissions. As seen in Chapter 1, not all developers should have writing access to the repository. Junior members, for example, need their commits reviewed by senior members before pushing to the repository. Giving them direct access to the project is a bad idea (due to their insatiable need to change history).

These are the problems that come with maintaining your own Git server. If only a tool could take care of those for us...

The Easy Way

Guess what? There is a tool that takes care of all those things for us, and its name is GitHub! GitHub is the tool of choice when dealing with remote repositories. You can think of GitHub as a code hosting server for projects using Git. It works just like your own Git server but with fewer headaches.

GitHub was created in 2008 to host Git projects and is now a subsidiary of Microsoft, which has invested a lot in open source communities. Figure 7-1 shows the GitHub home page at github.com.

Figure 7-1. *GitHub home page*

GitHub covers nearly every need of developers, whether they are open source developers wanting to share their software or professional teams seeking to work privately without the hassle of managing their own servers.

Like a social media platform, GitHub provides a space for developers to build, share, and document their projects, eliminating the need for external tools or websites. GitHub is a vital tool for open source projects as it facilitates developer collaboration and code release. Users can review and propose changes to each other's projects, follow and contribute to their favorite repositories, fostering a vibrant community of developers.

GitHub is not limited to open source projects; companies and individual developers can create private repositories accessible only to them. This allows them to benefit from the powerful features of Git while also enjoying additional tools and functionalities provided by GitHub. The platform's versatility is a key factor in its popularity, appealing to many users.

Other software companies offer services like GitHub, with GitLab and BitBucket being the most popular alternatives. GitLab is highly like GitHub in most of its features and comes in two editions: Community and Enterprise. The Community edition is open source and can be used alongside GitHub without issues. GitLab is also renowned in DevOps circles, making it an attractive option for those interested in that career.

Initially designed to host Mercurial projects, BitBucket expanded its support to include Git projects in 2011. Developed by Atlassian, BitBucket offers enterprise benefits like GitHub and has become a trusted platform in the industry.

While using a local server has advantages and disadvantages, this book chooses the easier route of utilizing GitHub for remote repositories. However, it is essential to understand how a remote repository works and why it is needed. If you still wish to use your own server, there is a guide in one of the annexes of this book to assist you. Enjoy your journey. ☺

Summary

This chapter explored the concept of remote repositories and why they are essential for team collaboration. While working locally in Git is enjoyable, sharing commits with teammates requires remote repositories. These repositories are typically hosted on servers, and developers can push and pull changes to and from them to exchange code seamlessly.

GitHub is introduced as an excellent tool for remote repositories, offering code hosting services for both open source projects and private teams. It serves as a version control system and provides a platform for developers to build, share, and document their projects, fostering a strong community of collaboration.

The chapter emphasized the importance of understanding how remote repositories work and why they are needed, even if the decision is made to use a service like GitHub to simplify the process.

The next chapter delves deeper into GitHub's vast array of features. It explores bug tracking, access control, feature requests, and many other functionalities that make GitHub a powerful platform for team development. Let's continue your journey into GitHub's capabilities!

PART II

Project Management with GitHub

## CHAPTER 8

GitHub Primer

In the last chapter, you embarked on an initial exploration of remote repositories and their significance. By now, you should understand how they function and, more importantly, the advantages they offer. Now, let's delve into the details of one of the most renowned code hosting platforms: GitHub.

The chapter begins with a brief history of GitHub to help you gain better insights into this platform. The chapter also discusses the diverse community of users who utilize GitHub and the various purposes for which they use it.

GitHub Overview

Defining GitHub is quite challenging because it encompasses numerous functionalities. Therefore, I'll use their own words: "GitHub is a development platform inspired by the way you work. From open source to business, you can host and review code, manage projects, and build software alongside 36 million developers."

GitHub isn't just a code hosting platform; it serves as a comprehensive development platform. What does that entail? It means that GitHub goes beyond storing code; it aids in planning and tracking the evolution of your projects. Its features are explored in the next section, but the key takeaway is that GitHub is designed to assist you in building and releasing your projects.

If there's one compelling reason to use GitHub, it's its development workflow. Gone are the days when project managers would write pending tasks on a whiteboard, and team members would send emails to keep track of who was working on what. There's no need for lengthy chain of back-and-forth emails to check a task's progress. GitHub efficiently manages all of these aspects.

© Mariot Tsitoara 2024
M. Tsitoara, *Beginning Git and GitHub*, https://doi.org/10.1007/979-8-8688-0215-7_8

GitHub and Open Source

GitHub has always been a close ally of open source projects; in fact, it is home to the largest open source community in the world. Since developers need a convenient place to build and share their projects, GitHub is an obvious choice. This way, all decisions and discussions concerning the projects can be accessed and joined by anyone, which is the beauty of open source.

With GitHub, the best thing you can do for an open source project is now easier than ever: contributing. When you find a project you like, you can follow it and track its progress. If you want to work on a new feature or fix a bug, you must make a clone of the project and start working on it. This process is called *forking*; it serves as the backbone of open source projects. Once you have made all the changes to your copy of the project, you can submit a pull request to the project's maintainer. This means you request that your changes be pulled and merged into the project. Other contributors review your changes and may request some additional modifications. All this communication occurs on GitHub, eliminating the need for email or instant messaging. Once all parties agree on the changes, the pull request is accepted, and your changes become part of the project!

Of course, open source projects involve more than just code; they require documentation, translators, community managers, maintainers, and more. You can contribute to projects by writing documentation, providing translations, or reviewing the changes made by other contributors. Projects also need testers and individuals to offer insights about the final products. Some projects have millions of contributors, necessitating the need for community managers responsible for the community's well-being and enforcing the internal code of conduct. Additionally, some contributors welcome and mentor beginners, which is challenging yet vital for any project.

Millions of open source projects have chosen GitHub because its workflow from idea to release is simple and accessible. Forking a project to contribute to it is the driving force behind any successful open source project. If you like a project but disagree with its direction, you can fork it and start your own version. In this case, you become the maintainer of the new project, and others can submit pull requests to you if they want to contribute. This way, everyone is happy!

Again, open source projects need documentation and tutorials for beginners. A text file (called README by convention) is sufficient for small projects. The README file should present the project and convey the problems it aims to solve.

It should also instruct users on how to install and use it, as well as how to contribute to it. Refer to Figure 8-1 for an example of a README file (also available at `https://github.com/git/git`).

README.md

Git - fast, scalable, distributed revision control system

Git is a fast, scalable, distributed revision control system with an unusually rich command set that provides both high-level operations and full access to internals.

Git is an Open Source project covered by the GNU General Public License version 2 (some parts of it are under different licenses, compatible with the GPLv2). It was originally written by Linus Torvalds with help of a group of hackers around the net.

Please read the file INSTALL for installation instructions.

Many Git online resources are accessible from https://git-scm.com/ including full documentation and Git related tools.

See Documentation/gittutorial.txt to get started, then see Documentation/giteveryday.txt for a useful minimum set of commands, and `Documentation/git-<commandname>.txt` for documentation of each command. If git has been correctly installed, then the tutorial can also be read with `man gittutorial` or `git help tutorial`, and the documentation of each command with `man git-<commandname>` or `git help <commandname>`.

CVS users may also want to read Documentation/gitcvs-migration.txt (`man gitcvs-migration` or `git help cvs-migration` if git is installed).

The user discussion and development of Git take place on the Git mailing list -- everyone is welcome to post bug reports, feature requests, comments and patches to git@vger.kernel.org (read Documentation/SubmittingPatches for instructions on patch submission and Documentation/CodingGuidelines).

Those wishing to help with error message, usage and informational message string translations (localization l10) should see po/README.md (a `po` file is a Portable Object file that holds the translations).

To subscribe to the list, send an email with just "subscribe git" in the body to majordomo@vger.kernel.org (not the Git list). The mailing list archives are available at https://lore.kernel.org/git/, http://marc.info/?l=git and other archival sites.

Issues which are security relevant should be disclosed privately to the Git Security mailing list git-security@googlegroups.com.

Figure 8-1. *Git README file*

As you can see in Figure 8-1, README files can have basic text formatting and links. They can also include images and code examples.

README files are written in the Markdown markup language. It's a straightforward language that can render simple formatting and linking. You can find a Markdown cheat sheet in the Appendix of this book!

As you can see, GitHub has a lot to offer to the open source community, and all of that is free of charge! But now, let's see what GitHub has to offer you personally.

Personal Use

Yes, open source is great, but what if it's not your jam? Or when you have a project that you want to keep to yourself? GitHub has you covered as well!

You don't have to make all your GitHub repositories public; you can also make them private. That way, only you and a few collaborators (that you choose) can access it. You can create an unlimited number of public and private repositories on GitHub; the only limit is your creativity and time. However, there is a limit on the number of contributors you can have on private repositories: 3. If you want to work with more contributors, you can sign up for GitHub Pro, a paid plan. But for almost everybody, the free plan is more than enough.

Having a personal GitHub account to showcase your work is also a good way to market yourself. That way, people can check the open source or personal projects you contribute to and even review your code. It is a portfolio demonstrating your skills and expertise to potential employers or collaborators. Additionally, many employers in the tech industry value candidates who actively participate in the open source community and have a visible presence on platforms like GitHub. So, having a well-maintained GitHub profile can benefit your career advancement and networking opportunities.

And since there are 36 million developers on GitHub, you might want to connect with some. One way to connect is to follow a particular project. When the project progresses, you receive updates and can check out the changes. Note that you automatically follow a repository you contribute to. Another way to show appreciation for a project is to star it. It's akin to liking a piece of content on social media.

Hence, the more stars a repository has, the more users are happy with it. GitHub also offers a news feed that provides news and notifications from specific projects. These projects are chosen because you contribute to or have "starred" them. The news feed is also tailored by analyzing your most-used language or tools, providing relevant updates and information. It's a great way to stay connected with projects you are interested in and to engage with the GitHub community.

Before moving on to the next section, there is a cool feature you can check out on GitHub: your contribution activity. If you enable the option, every commit you push on GitHub is registered as a contribution—even to your personal or private repositories. These activities are displayed in a nice illustration, like the one shown in Figure 8-2. They showcase your contributions throughout the year and indicate your achievements to your profile's visitors. It's a great way to visually represent your coding progress and involvement in various projects.

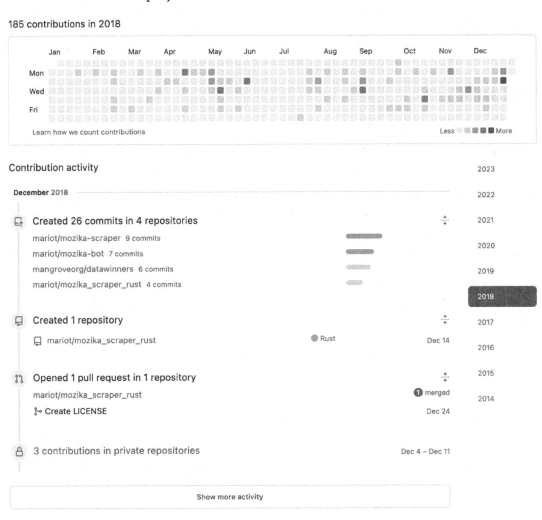

Figure 8-2. *My contribution history in 2018*

GitHub for Businesses

GitHub is not just for personal projects or open source communities; businesses also have their place there. Many businesses now invest in open source for some of their products, and what better place to find quality developers than GitHub?

GitHub offers an Enterprise plan that incorporates all the benefits of a paid plan and many additional features. These features range from the choice of hosting to security and online support. While all these features may be very attractive to businesses, a simple Free plan is enough for most people.

Summary

This chapter overviewed GitHub users and some of its small features. By now, you should have some ideas about how you want to utilize GitHub. The next chapter explores GitHub's main features and shares tips on collaborating effectively with teammates. It covers project management, code reviews, and more, and you start using GitHub with your first repositories! Get ready for action in the next chapter, and review the previous exercises to stay sharp. Let's begin!

## CHAPTER 9

Quick Start with GitHub

So far, the book has only discussed what GitHub is and who can benefit from it. Now, you will delve into its specific capabilities and main features. One of the most crucial aspects of GitHub is its project management tools, which, when used with the right development workflow, can propel a project forward with great efficiency.

This section of the book embarks on a series of exercises to familiarize ourselves with GitHub. While I could explain all the advantages of GitHub, you will gain a better understanding through hands-on exploration. Let's get started by creating a GitHub account and initiating a project.

Project Management

The ability to manage a project while adhering to a well-established path is one of GitHub's most revered features. I encourage you to follow along with me in this section because it gives you a comprehensive understanding of these features.

The first step is to create a GitHub account because you are managing your project using Git and GitHub. The process is straightforward, and you only need to provide basic information, such as your name and email, as shown in Figure 9-1.

© Mariot Tsitoara 2024
M. Tsitoara, *Beginning Git and GitHub*, https://doi.org/10.1007/979-8-8688-0215-7_9

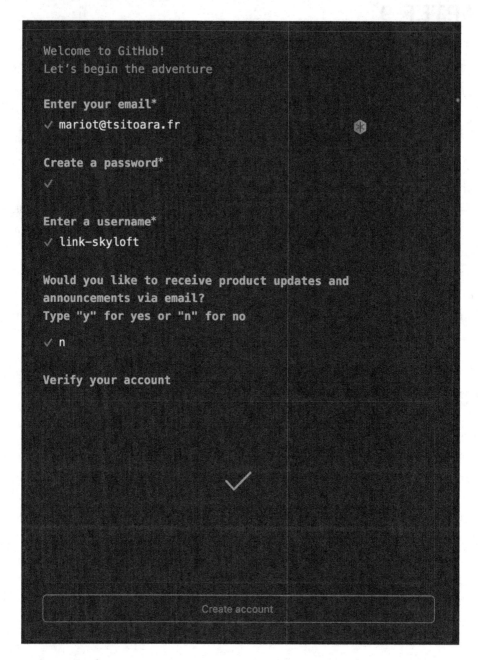

Figure 9-1. *GitHub signup page*

After signing up, you receive a confirmation link in your email. Simply follow the provided link to complete the registration process. Once done, you are directed to the GitHub dashboard, which should look like Figure 9-2.

Figure 9-2. *GitHub dashboard*

Your GitHub dashboard may appear empty now, but you'll work on filling it with some cool projects soon. You'll notice some trending repositories and news stories on the right side of the page, but you won't explore those just yet.

Now, as shown in Figure 9-2, there are three links you can follow to create a new repository: one on the left side, one in the middle, and the last one in the navigation bar. Click any of them to begin creating the repository.

The repository creation form is also straightforward, as illustrated in Figure 9-3. You only need to provide a name and a short project description. While the description is optional, try to make it concise so that users visiting your repository understand its purpose.

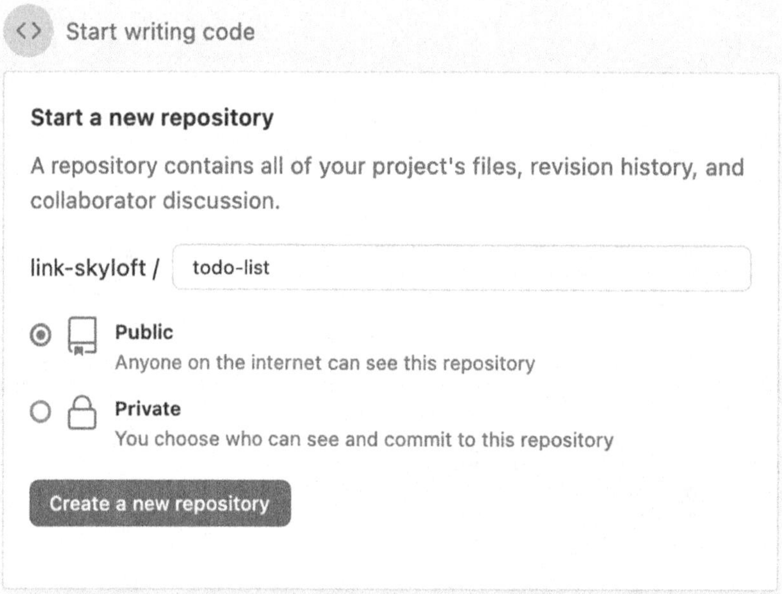

Figure 9-3. *Starting a new repository*

You can make the repository private if you prefer; in that case, only you can access it. A public repository, however, doesn't mean that anyone can freely edit it; it simply means that anyone can read it, and logged-in users can propose changes to it. However, you are still the project's maintainer and the repository's owner.

Regarding initializing the repository with a README file, you can ignore this option for now, as you aim to create a repository from scratch. You'll add the README, .gitignore, and license files later.

Once you've made your selections, click the Submit button to create your first GitHub repository! It's as simple as that! You are redirected to your project page, which has a unique link representing your repository. The link format is as follows: `https://github.com/your_username/your_repository`. For example, the new repository I created is accessible through `https://github.com/link-skyloft/todo-list`. Therefore, you cannot create two repositories with the same name. Your project page should look similar to the one shown in Figure 9-4.

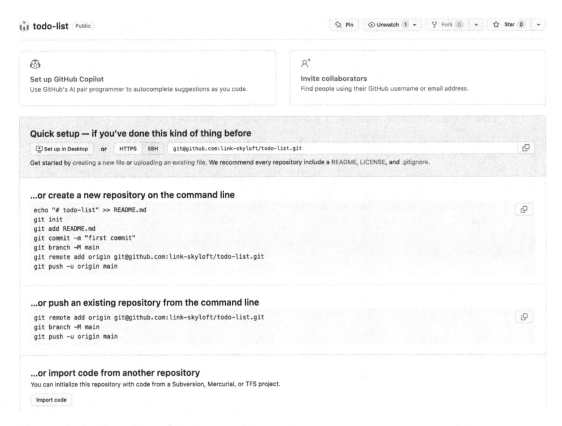

Figure 9-4. *Your brand-new repository*

As you can see in Figure 9-4, there are instructions on how to get started, whether you want to create a new repository or push an existing one. Let's proceed with pushing the to-do list! For this, you need to choose the second option.

First, you must choose an authentication method. You have two options: HTTPS and SSH. The main difference is that HTTPS uses a login/passphrase combination, while SSH uses keys. Let's opt for SSH to avoid the need to enter a passphrase with each action.

To learn more about SSH, you can check this link: `https://docs.github.com/en/authentication/connecting-to-github-with-ssh`.

To generate an SSH key, follow the instructions provided in this link: `https://docs.github.com/en/authentication/connecting-to-github-with-ssh/generating-a-new-ssh-key-and-adding-it-to-the-ssh-agent`. From the time of writing this, the website looks like the Figure 9-5.

Generating a new SSH key 🔗

You can generate a new SSH key on your local machine. After you generate the key, you can add the public key to your account on GitHub.com to enable authentication for Git operations over SSH.

> **Note:** GitHub improved security by dropping older, insecure key types on March 15, 2022.
>
> As of that date, DSA keys (ssh-dss) are no longer supported. You cannot add new DSA keys to your personal account on GitHub.com.
>
> RSA keys (ssh-rsa) with a `valid_after` before November 2, 2021 may continue to use any signature algorithm. RSA keys generated after that date must use a SHA-2 signature algorithm. Some older clients may need to be upgraded in order to use SHA-2 signatures.

1 Open Git Bash.

2 Paste the text below, substituting in your GitHub email address.

```
ssh-keygen -t ed25519 -C "your_email@example.com"
```

> **Note:** If you are using a legacy system that doesn't support the Ed25519 algorithm, use:
>
> ```
> ssh-keygen -t rsa -b 4096 -C "your_email@example.com"
> ```

This creates a new SSH key, using the provided email as a label.

```
> Generating public/private ALGORITHM key pair.
```

When you're prompted to "Enter a file in which to save the key", you can press **Enter** to accept the default file location. Please note that if you created SSH keys previously, ssh-keygen may ask you to rewrite another key, in which case we recommend creating a custom-named SSH key. To do so, type the default file location and replace id_ssh_keyname with your custom key name.

```
> Enter a file in which to save the key (/c/Users/YOU/.ssh/id_ALGORITHM):[Press enter]
```

1 At the prompt, type a secure passphrase. For more information, see "Working with SSH key passphrases."

```
> Enter passphrase (empty for no passphrase): [Type a passphrase]
> Enter same passphrase again: [Type passphrase again]
```

Figure 9-5. *Instructions on how to generate a new pair of keys*

I used the following command on Git Bash to create my SSH keys.

```
$ ssh-keygen -t ed25519 -C "mariot@tsitoara.fr"
```

Use the default file location and the email you used to sign up with GitHub. You could enter a passphrase if you want, but I don't recommend doing so because you'll need to enter it each time. If you follow the instructions, you'll get a result similar to the one shown in Figure 9-6.

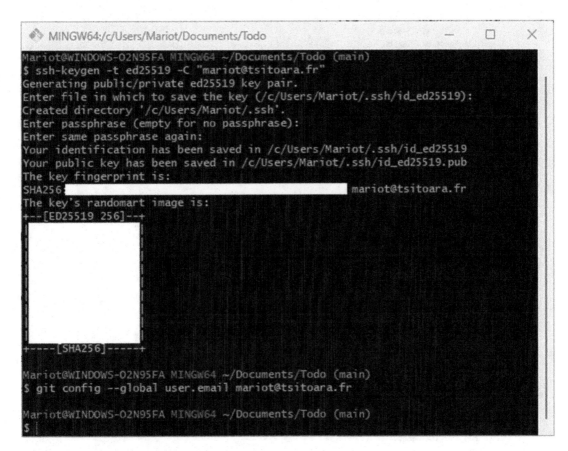

Figure 9-6. *Generating a pair of keys*

You'll also notice that I changed my email to be the same as my GitHub account.

Now that you have your keys, add them to the ssh-agent. Follow the instructions as you can see on the website shown in Figure 9-7.

Adding your SSH key to the ssh-agent 🔗

Before adding a new SSH key to the ssh-agent to manage your keys, you should have checked for existing SSH keys and generated a new SSH key.

If you have GitHub Desktop installed, you can use it to clone repositories and not deal with SSH keys.

1 Ensure the ssh-agent is running. You can use the "Auto-launching the ssh-agent" instructions in "Working with SSH key passphrases", or start it manually:

```
# start the ssh-agent in the background
$ eval "$(ssh-agent -s)"
> Agent pid 59566
```

2 Add your SSH private key to the ssh-agent. If you created your key with a different name, or if you are adding an existing key that has a different name, replace *id_ed25519* in the command with the name of your private key file.

```
ssh-add ~/.ssh/id_ed25519
```

```
1. Add the SSH public key to your account on GitHub. For more information, see
"[AUTOTITLE](/authentication/connecting-to-github-with-ssh/adding-a-new-ssh-key-to-
your-github-account)."

</div>

<div class="ghd-tool linux">

1. Start the ssh-agent in the background.

    ```shell
    $ eval "$(ssh-agent -s)"
    > Agent pid 59566
    ```

    Depending on your environment, you may need to use a different command. For
example, you may need to use root access by running `sudo -s -H` before starting
the ssh-agent, or you may need to use `exec ssh-agent bash` or `exec ssh-agent zsh`
to run the ssh-agent.

1. Add your SSH private key to the ssh-agent. If you created your key with a
different name, or if you are adding an existing key that has a different name,
replace _id_ed25519_ in the command with the name of your private key file.
    ```shell
ssh-add ~/.ssh/id_ed25519
```

1 Add the SSH public key to your account on GitHub. For more information, see "Adding a new SSH key to your GitHub account."

Figure 9-7. *How to add the keys to the ssh-agent*
```

As you can see on the website, you must first ensure that the ssh-agent is running with the following command.

```
$ eval "$(ssh-agent -s)"
```

Then, add the SSH private key to the ssh-agent with the following command.

```
$ ssh-add ~/.ssh/id_ed25519
```

You can see the result in Figure 9-8.

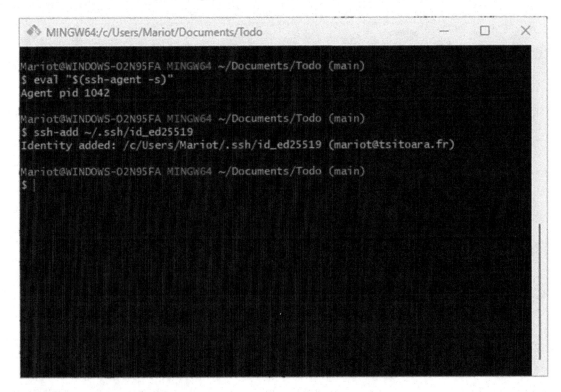

Figure 9-8. *Adding the private key to the ssh-agent*

Now it's time to add the public key to GitHub! Follow this link for the instructions: https://docs.github.com/en/authentication/connecting-to-github-with-ssh/ adding-a-new-ssh-key-to-your-github-account. The website should look like the one shown in Figure 9-9.

Adding a new SSH key to your account ⌗

After adding a new SSH authentication key to your account on GitHub.com, you can reconfigure any local repositories to use SSH. For more information, see "Managing remote repositories."

> **Note:** GitHub improved security by dropping older, insecure key types on March 15, 2022.
>
> As of that date, DSA keys (ssh-dss) are no longer supported. You cannot add new DSA keys to your personal account on GitHub.com.
>
> RSA keys (ssh-rsa) with a valid_after before November 2, 2021 may continue to use any signature algorithm. RSA keys generated after that date must use a SHA-2 signature algorithm. Some older clients may need to be upgraded in order to use SHA-2 signatures.

1 Copy the SSH public key to your clipboard.

If your SSH public key file has a different name than the example code, modify the filename to match your current setup. When copying your key, don't add any newlines or whitespace.

```
$ clip < ~/.ssh/id_ed25519.pub
# Copies the contents of the id_ed25519.pub file to your clipboard
```

> **Tip:** With Windows Subsystem for Linux (WSL), you can use clip.exe . Otherwise if clip isn't working, you can locate the hidden .ssh folder, open the file in your favorite text editor, and copy it to your clipboard.

2 In the upper-right corner of any page, click your profile photo, then click **Settings**.

3 In the "Access" section of the sidebar, click 🔑 **SSH and GPG keys**.

4 Click **New SSH key** or **Add SSH key**.

5 In the "Title" field, add a descriptive label for the new key. For example, if you're using a personal laptop, you might call this key "Personal laptop".

6 Select the type of key, either authentication or signing. For more information about commit signing, see "About commit signature verification."

7 In the "Key" field, paste your public key.

8 Click **Add SSH key**.

9 If prompted, confirm access to your account on GitHub. For more information, see "Sudo mode."

Figure 9-9. *Adding an SSH key to GitHub*

You can use a clip to copy the public key to your clipboard.

```
$ clip < ~/.ssh/id_ed25519.pub
```

You should then go to your GitHub account and access the Settings page. Under the Access section in the navigation pane on the left, click "SSH and GPG keys" and then click the "New SSH Key" button, as shown in Figure 9-10.

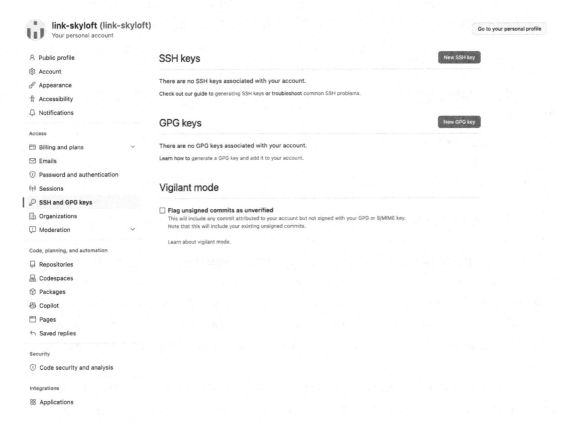

Figure 9-10. *SSH keys settings*

Choose a title for your key and paste the public key. And that's it! Now, you are using SSH to connect to GitHub. Let's push the to-do list to GitHub!

How Remote Repositories Work

In Chapter 7, you learned about remote Git and using GitHub as a remote repository store. This section is a logical extension of that chapter because you will learn how remote repositories managed with GitHub work.

When you created the repository using the GitHub website, you were provided instructions to GitHub servers and asked them to initialize an empty repository. If you recall Chapter 2, initializing a repository is simple: go to any directory and execute `git init`. That's what happened here, except not on your computer but on a server hosted by GitHub.

So, it's as if you executed the following commands on a faraway server with Git installed.

```
$ mkdir todo-list
$ cd todo-list
$ git init
```

It's the same commands used to create the local repository. So now, there is a remote repository on GitHub's servers to share your project.

Remote repositories are used, so you don't have to use your own computer to share your project. In the case of GitHub, the remote repositories are accessible by anyone, but only the owner can edit them. Teamwork is discussed in a later section.

The main takeaway is that a remote repository lets you publish your project to make it available to everyone. Anyone can clone your repository to follow your advancements to get the latest changes.

Publishing your local repository to a remote one is called *pushing*. Getting the latest commits from a remote repository to a local one is called *pulling*. Push and pull are perhaps the most used commands in Git.

But how can I inform GitHub about the remote repository I want to link with my local one? This is where the unique link to your repository comes into play. You'll use this link to push your local changes or pull any commits that you don't already have.

In conclusion, GitHub has created an empty remote repository that can only be modified by you but can be viewed by everyone. The next step is to create a local repository and connect with the remote one.

Linking Repositories

Now that GitHub has created the remote repository for us, it's time to link your own local repository to the remote one.

To list, add, or remove remotes, use the `git remote` command. For example, let's link your current remotes using the following command.

```
$ git remote
```

You shouldn't get any results because it's a brand-new repository, and you haven't linked any remote to it. Let's add one now.

Important   If you see remotes in your results, you can remove them using git remote rm [remote_name]. You shouldn't see any remote if it's a new repository.

You need the unique link to your repository to link a local repository to it, so grab yours from the previous section. Mine is `git@github.com:link-skyloft/todo-list.git`, as shown in Figure 9-4. Make sure to copy the SSH link and not the HTTPS!

You also need to create a name for your remote repository. That way, you can have multiple remotes within a single project. It may be necessary when the test and production remotes are different from each other. The default name is `origin` per convention. Although you can choose any name, it is recommended to use `origin` as the name of the remote where teammates share their work.

The command to add a link to a remote is simple.

```
git remote add [name] [link]
```

So, to add a link to the newly created repository, you'll have to execute the following command.

```
$ git remote add origin git@github.com:link-skyloft/todo-list.git
```

That's it! You can check if the remote has been added by executing git remote or git remote -v to get more information. You should get a result similar to the screen shown in Figure 9-11.

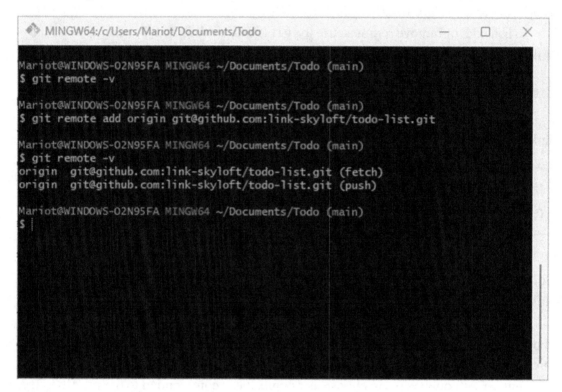

Figure 9-11. *Adding the origin remote*

And that's it! Adding a new remote is a simple, straightforward task. Now that that is cleared, let's push the project to GitHub!

Pushing to Remote Repositories

You finally got the local and remote repositories linked. It's time to push the project to GitHub so you can share your work.

The command to push changes to the remote is simple; you just need the name of the remote repository and the branch to be pushed. Since you haven't created any branches yet (branches are discussed later), the only branch is called main. The following shows the git push command.

```
git push <remote_name> <branch_name>
```

So, in this case, the command is as follows.

```
$ git push origin main
```

Git checks the authenticity of the GitHub server. Type **yes** to continue connecting; the branch will be pushed. You get a result like the one shown in Figure 9-12.

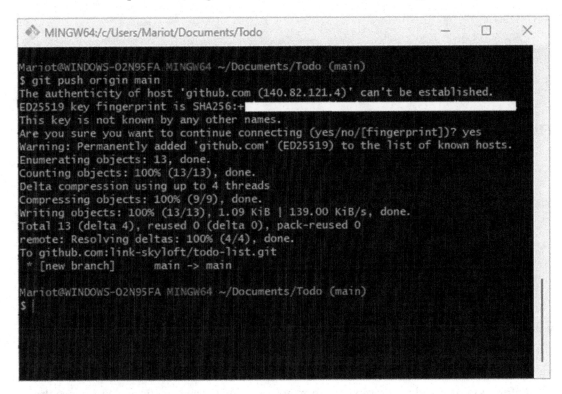

Figure 9-12.   *The first push*

Now, the project is visible on GitHub for everyone to see! Let's check it out on its project page. If you refresh the project page, you should see a page like the one shown in Figure 9-13.

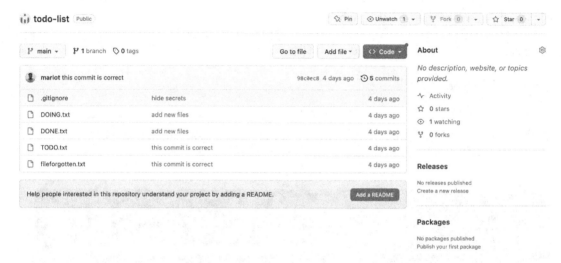

Figure 9-13. *The updated project page*

As you can see in Figure 9-13, the repository page now displays valuable information.

- The number of commits

- The last commit name and its committer

- A list of all project files

What you just did is the basis of code sharing: pushing changes. You will use this command repeatedly when working with remote repositories. It is a simple feature, but you must understand what it does. Pushing means copying all your current commits (in a specific branch) to a remote branch in a remote repository. All history logs are also copied.

Before you proceed to the next chapter, ask yourself these questions: Where are the remote repositories stored? Who has read-only access to them? Who can edit them? Also, you should understand the basics of linking remote and local repositories and why it is necessary.

Summary

In this chapter, you first interacted with remote Git repositories. They are just normal repositories stored on a remote server instead of your local machine. You saw how to create and link local and remote repositories, an often used feature. The main command you learned was git push, which copies the state of your local repository to a remote one.

The next chapter dives into project management and explores other GitHub features. You will learn how to pull changes from the remote repository and resolve push and pull issues. Let's get started!

## CHAPTER 10

Beginning Project Management: Issues

Chapter 9 offered a quick peek at using GitHub to host and share code. However, that barely scratches the surface of what GitHub can offer; it has numerous features that can assist in maturing your project. In this chapter, you start learning about managing projects with GitHub. Therefore, let's begin with the fundamental aspect of GitHub project management: issues.

Issues Overview

Planning is crucial to successfully manage any project; merely reacting to new inputs and doing things based on whims is a perfect recipe for disaster. Managing a GitHub project follows a similar principle; you must keep track of your actions before initiating them. This is why GitHub incorporates an excellent Issues feature. This section delves into discussing them and learning proper management techniques.

Throughout all the chapters in this book, you've assumed both developer and project manager roles. However, in larger projects, you might not participate in the planning phases. But for now, consider yourself temporarily promoted to project manager and lead developer (while also being the sole developer). Congratulations! One of the responsibilities of a project manager is to plan all the tasks that need completion. These plans don't need to be overly precise yet (in reality, they seldom are), but it's crucial to have a list of all the tasks that require attention. These tasks can encompass new features, bug fixes, or team discussions. In GitHub, these tasks are called *issues*.

An issue tracks the progress of new features, bug fixing, or ideas team members propose. They constitute the cornerstone of GitHub project management; ideally, no action should proceed without an associated issue. The aim of every action you undertake should be geared toward resolving an issue.

© Mariot Tsitoara 2024
M. Tsitoara, *Beginning Git and GitHub*, https://doi.org/10.1007/979-8-8688-0215-7_10

The era of organizing the next steps through tedious team meetings is long gone. Now, you clearly understand your upcoming actions and, crucially, are aware of everyone else's tasks. Proposing new ideas to your colleagues has become more straightforward than ever; open an issue to initiate a discussion with your team, eliminating the need for additional apps or email clients. The greatest benefit of utilizing issues is the everlasting preservation of history—each feature, bug, and discussion remains documented indefinitely.

Creating an Issue

To better understand issues, the most effective method is direct interaction with them. Let's return to the GitHub project page and engage with these issues.

Upon opening your GitHub project page, you'll be directed to the Code section, where your project files are showcased. Your project page should resemble mine at this stage, as depicted in Figure 10-1.

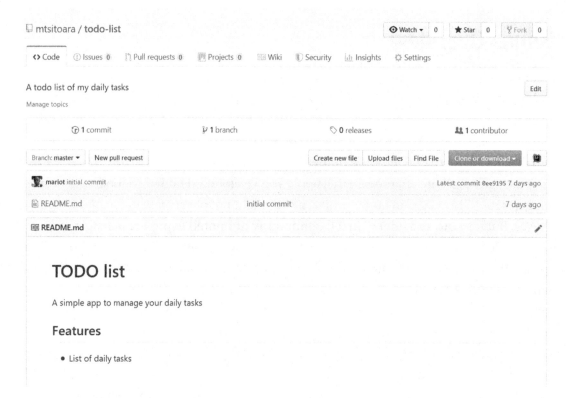

Figure 10-1. *Project page open on the "code" section*

Directly below the project name, numerous tabs showcase the various sections of your project. Your primary focus typically revolves around the Code, Issues, Pull Requests, and Projects sections. However, for the present task, let's concentrate on the Issues tab. Click it to begin. You'll land on an empty section akin to the one depicted in Figure 10-2 since your project currently lacks any issues.

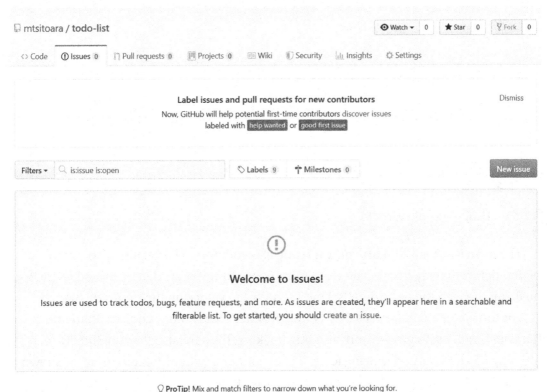

Figure 10-2. *Issues section*

Several calls to action are available to create a new issue. Click any of them, and you'll encounter a form similar to mine, as displayed in Figure 10-3.

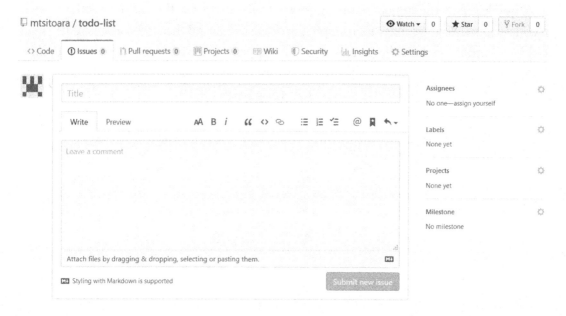

Figure 10-3. *New issue form*

The form is straightforward; only the title is mandatory. There's also a comment section below the title in case you need more space to elaborate. Let's proceed to create the first issue with the basic details. Don't modify the values on the right side just yet.

For the inaugural issue, let's discuss the product's technology choices. Remember that issues aren't solely for feature and bug tracking; they are also instrumental in initiating discussions and sharing ideas. Fill in your first issue similar to mine, as shown in Figure 10-4. My issue, "Choose the technologies to be used for the app", marks the initial step of a project.

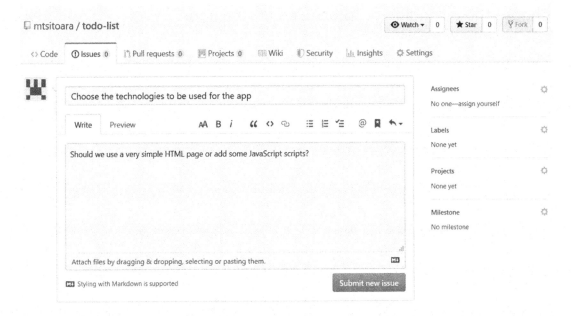

Figure 10-4. *The first issue*

Now that you've completed the basic information for the issue, submit it. You are redirected to the detailed view of your new issue. It should resemble my issue, as depicted in Figure 10-5.

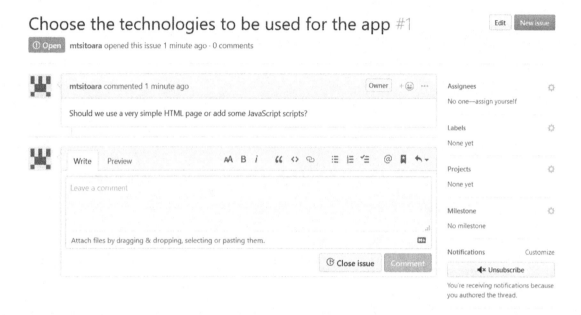

Figure 10-5. *Details of an issue*

The first noticeable aspect is that your issue has been assigned a unique number. Each issue retains its distinct number, which is never recycled. Even if an issue is deleted, its number will not be reused. This number holds significance, as you'll discover in this section.

The details page also features a comment section where team members can discuss. Additionally, a limited selection of emojis is available for use as responses. For instance, using a thumbs-up emoji to agree is more efficient than cluttering the conversation with repetitive comments like "mine too." This helps maintain smoother communication and avoids stalling the discussion.

You'll find a Subscribe button at the bottom-right corner of the page. Opting to subscribe to an issue ensures you receive notifications for any changes made to it, including new comments and updates on milestones reached.

Since you are the sole team member, there won't be much discussion. Simply add a comment or a reaction emoji and then close the issue. Closing the issue does not delete it; instead, it marks it as completed. Deleting issues is not recommended because maintaining a project history is crucial, and issues are the best way to track changes. Keep in mind that if your repository is public, anyone can read your comments. Thus, please maintain kindness and address any unpleasantness that may arise.

After commenting and closing the issue, you'll return to the issue details page, resembling mine, as shown in Figure 10-6.

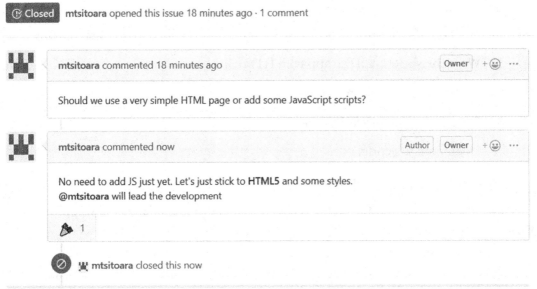

Choose the technologies to be used for the app #1

🕐 Closed   mtsitoara opened this issue 18 minutes ago · 1 comment

mtsitoara commented 18 minutes ago   Owner + 😊 ⋯

Should we use a very simple HTML page or add some JavaScript scripts?

mtsitoara commented now   Author   Owner + 😊 ⋯

No need to add JS just yet. Let's just stick to **HTML5** and some styles.
@mtsitoara will lead the development

🎉 1

⊘ mtsitoara closed this now

Figure 10-6. *A closed issue*

While it's possible to continue commenting on a closed issue, it's generally discouraged because everyone has acknowledged the issue's completion and shifted focus. Issues can also be locked, preventing further comments, a final resort to maintaining peace. We all have differing opinions, so discussing them on the Internet, especially in an open forum, can be challenging. However, maintain professionalism because everything you communicate will be visible to anyone reading.

Interacting with an Issue

You've successfully created and closed an issue, yet your involvement with them has been limited. However, what purpose does an issue serve if it doesn't impact the project? This section actively engages with issues both on GitHub and within the code.

Put on your project manager hat for the initial segment because you need to strategize the project. Until now, the TODO list app comprised multiple text files placed side by side. Let's use HTML5 to enhance its presentation. Executing this requires an action plan, and it falls upon you, as a project manager, to outline this plan.

Given that it's a simple HTML5 app, you don't need an elaborate plan—just a few essential bullet points will suffice. So, to create this app, you need to do the following.

1. Write the skeleton of the app with HTML5.

2. Add some styles to make it prettier with CSS3.

3. Describe the app in README.md.

4. Document the code.

5. Create a web page for the app.

These are the fundamental steps necessary to achieve the objective of shipping a TODO app.

Since you're familiar with creating issues, I'll leave it to you to generate an issue for each bullet point. Once completed, your Issues page should resemble mine, as Figure 10-7 depicts.

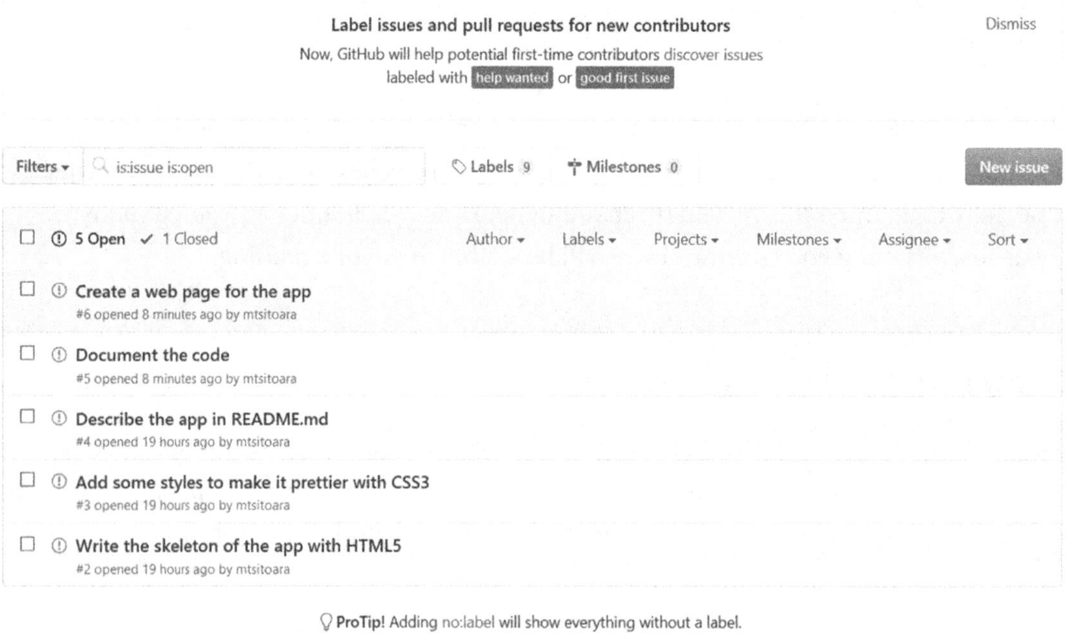

Figure 10-7. *All open tasks*

As observed, the tasks are presented in the order of their introduction, lacking distinguishing features besides their numbers. This setup can lead to confusion, particularly if there's an abundance of issues. Let's employ labels to ensure a clearer overview of all the tasks.

Labels

Labels serve precisely as you'd expect: texts that facilitate quick issue filtering. Let's directly apply them to help you become acquainted with this concept.

As depicted in Figure 10-7, the issues page contains a search bar to filter through issues. However, since you haven't assigned labels, the filtering options are limited to basic search functions. Click the Labels button next to the search bar to display all available labels. You'll then encounter a list of default labels that can be utilized, as illustrated in Figure 10-8.

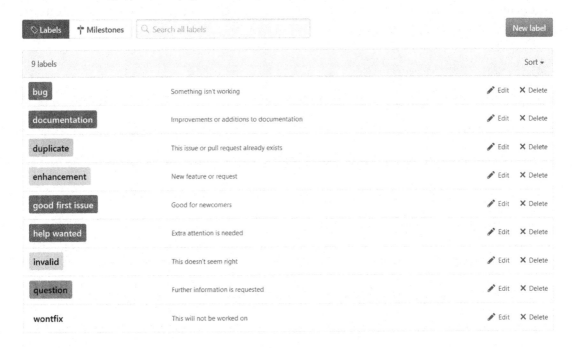

Figure 10-8. *List of the default labels*

These labels represent the most commonly used ones within the developers' community. However, they aren't mandatory or immutable; you can modify them based on your preferences and project requirements. It's generally inadvisable to alter these labels, especially when working on an open source project, as many developers are accustomed to these standard labels.

But given that this is your personal project and you serve as the project manager, you can add, edit, or remove any label as needed. For instance, the label "help wanted" might not serve a purpose if you work alone in a private setting. Labels can also signify an issue's severity; commonly used labels like "urgent" or "breaking" indicate severe issues. Additionally, labels can differentiate the origin of an issue, especially in larger projects. For instance, "frontend," "backend," or "database" labels can categorize issues into distinct groups.

Once you've made changes to the labels (although I recommend adding new ones as needed while retaining the default ones), return to your issues and access the details page. Then, assign one or more labels to each issue by clicking the Labels button. You can refer to Figure 10-9 for an example.

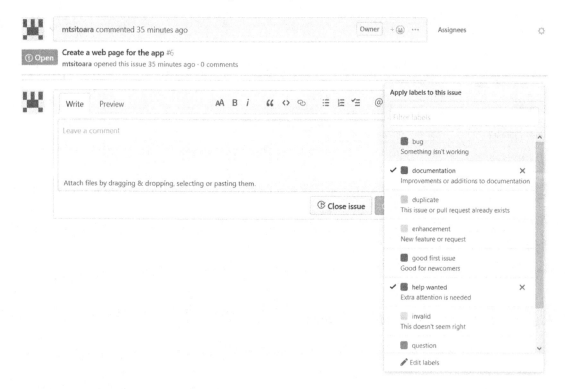

Figure 10-9. *Adding a label to an issue*

After you add the labels, a notification appears in the comment section of the issue page. Figure 10-10 shows an example.

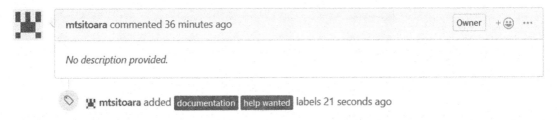

Figure 10-10. *Notification about the newly added labels*

Now, go through each of your issues and apply some labels to them. Once you've finished, return to the issues page. It should resemble mine, as depicted in Figure 10-11.

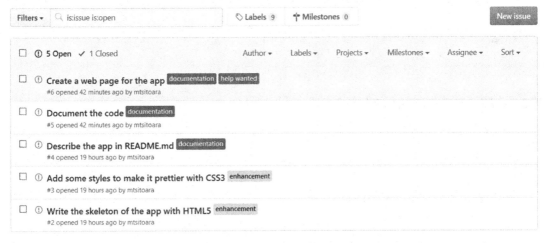

Figure 10-11. *Labeled issues*

Now that you've added labels to the issues, you can filter through them. For instance, to view all issues labeled "enhancement", click the Labels filter (as displayed in Figure 10-12), and you'll see a result similar to mine depicted in Figure 10-13.

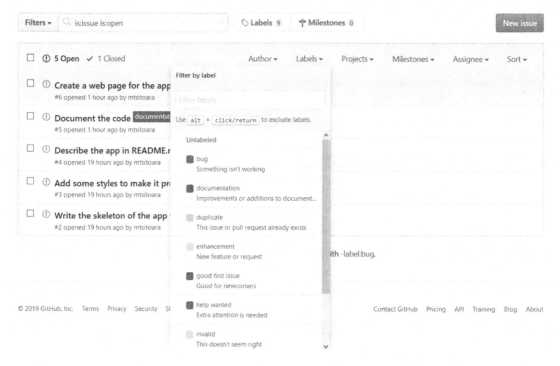

Figure 10-12. *Filtering by label*

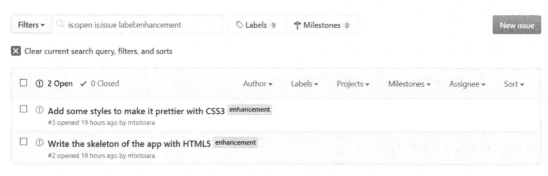

Figure 10-13. *Filtered issues*

Isn't filtering fun?! But you know what is even more fun? Assign issues to others! Let's do it.

Assignees

Now that the issues are correctly labeled, it's time to assign them to a developer. It's a relatively easy task and is not so different from labeling.

You can assign an issue to up to 10 members of your team. However, you can only assign yourself since you're the only one currently. Let's proceed! Navigate to the issues titled "Write the skeleton of the app with HTML5" and "Add some styles to make it prettier with CSS3" and assign them to yourself. Assigning an issue to a team member operates similarly to adding labels. You can refer to Figure 10-14 as an example.

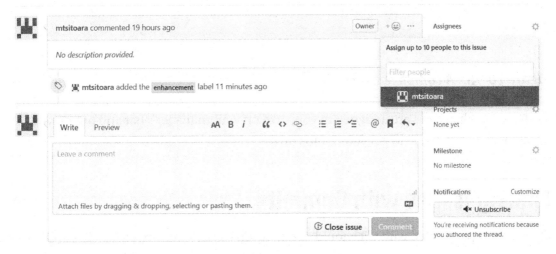

Figure 10-14. *Assigning an issue*

After you assign these two issues to yourself, you get a result like mine, as shown in Figure 10-15 on your Issues page. You can now filter through your issues by labels and assignees.

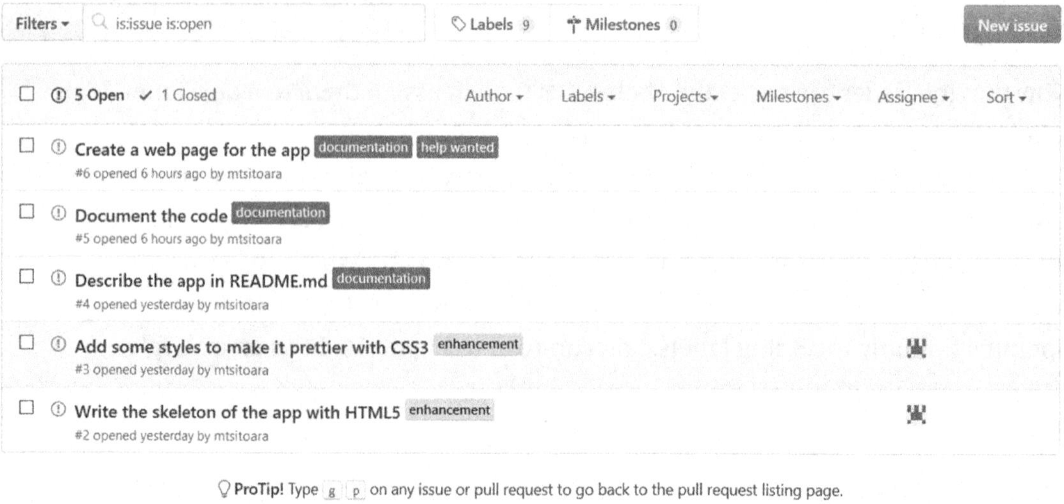

Figure 10-15. *A complete issues list*

Now that the issues are assigned to you, take off your manager's hat and put on your developer's hat. It's time to get your hands dirty!

Linking Issues with Commits

Every action performed with Git should aim to resolve an issue. When using Git, most of your work involves commits; thus, each commit should be associated with an issue. In this section, you learn how to link the commits to issues.

Firstly, let's determine which issues to address. As seen in Figure 10-15, two issues are assigned: "Write the skeleton of the app with HTML5" and "Add some styles to make it prettier with CSS3". Let's start by working on writing the app skeleton because it's a logical starting point. Therefore, access the details page of this issue and make a note of its number. As depicted in Figure 10-16, mine is issue number 2 (#2).

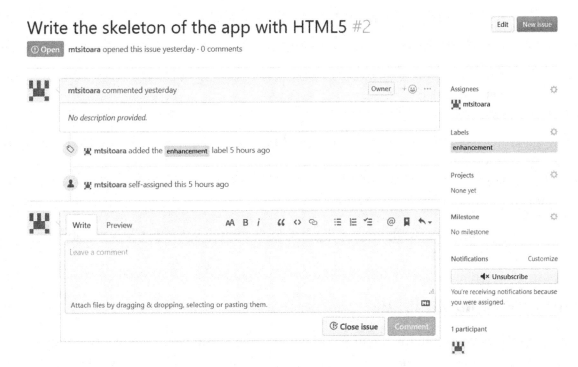

Figure 10-16. *Issue number 2 details page*

Working on the Commit

Now that you have an issue to resolve and its number, it's time to prepare the commit. Since simple HTML5 is used for this app, you only need a single file for the skeleton. So, create a file named index.html in your working directory and paste it into this code.

```
<!doctype html>
<html>
    <head>
        <meta charset="utf-8">
        <title>TODO list</title>
    </head>
    <body>
        <h1>TODO list</h1>

        <h3>Todo</h3>
        <ul>
            <li>Buy a hat for the bat</li>
```

```
            <li>Clear the fogs for the frogs</li>
            <li>Bring a box to the fox</li>
        </ul>

        <h3>Done</h3>
        <ul>
            <li>Put the mittens on the kittens</li>
        </ul>
    </body>
</html>
```

I'll let you stage the newly created file, but don't commit it yet; first, let's talk about the commit message.

Referencing an Issue

You are prepared to commit the project in its current state; however, you need to modify the commit message to link the commit to an issue. The most common method to link a commit to an issue is by referencing the issue number within the commit message.

Thus far, you've solely used very concise commit messages, aiming to keep them within a single line. However, as you now require a more detailed way to describe the commits, you'll structure the commit messages as follows: a title, a body, and a footer separated by a blank line. Refer to Figure 10-17.

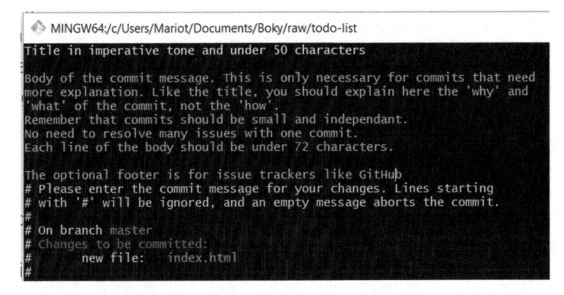

Figure 10-17. *The commit message structure*

Caution   Don't forget the blank line between each part of the commit message. It is important.

The body and footer sections within the commit structure are optional and should only be used when necessary, particularly the body. People tend to skim, often reading only the title before moving on. Therefore, ensure the title is self-explanatory even without the body.

The footer section is now the focus; it's designated for issue trackers like GitHub. Utilize the footer to reference issues by their numbers. For instance, to reference the issue you're addressing, include its number in the footer preceded by a #. Once GitHub detects this formatting, it automatically links the commit to the referenced issue.

Note   You can put the references to the issues anywhere in the commit message, even in the title. But this practice is very ugly and should be discouraged.

Combining all of that, let's make the commit with a proper commit message. Look at the example of my commit, as shown in Figure 10-18.

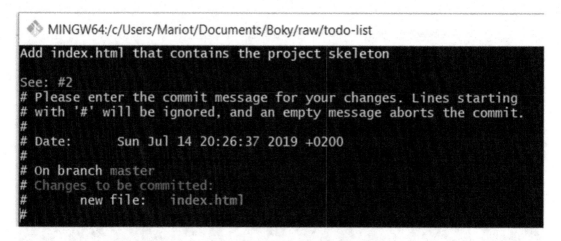

Figure 10-18.   Commit message linked to issue #2

I skipped the body part in my commit message because it was unnecessary. I only needed to link this commit to issue #2, so I put that number in the footer.

Now, push it! Look at the previous chapter if you forgot how.

Next, let's go back to the issue's details page. The first thing you notice is that a new comment has been added: the reference to the commit. It should look like mine depicted in Figure 10-19.

Figure 10-19.   A reference to the last commit

This a very useful feature of GitHub that you will certainly use; show all the commits linked to a particular issue. That's why no commit should be pushed without being tied to an issue. It's better for the management of the project.

If you tap the name of the commit shown on the reference (see Figure 10-19), you see a familiar screen. I'll let you discover which screen is depicted in Figure 10-20.

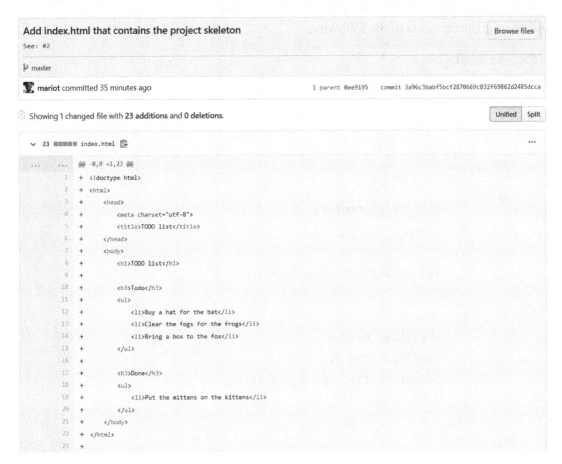

Figure 10-20. *A detailed view of a commit*

That's right! It's the `git show` view. There is no need to get lost in Git commands to see what a commit does; you can directly see it in GitHub!

Now that you have resolved the issue, go back to its details page and close it. Let's resolve the next one!

Closing an Issue Using Keywords

It was nice to work on an issue and close it, right? There is still something even more fun: closing an issue by using keywords in a commit message!

First, you must decide which issue to resolve. The next issue is "Add some styles to make it prettier with CSS3," which has the number 3. Let's resolve it! Open index.html and change the contents to the following.

```
<!doctype html>
<html>
    <head>
        <meta charset="utf-8">
        <title>TODO list</title>
        <style>
            h1 {
                text-align:center;
            }
            h3 {
                text-transform: uppercase;
            }
            li {
                overflow: hidden;
                padding: 20px 0;
                border-bottom: 1px solid #eee;
            }
        </style>
    </head>
    <body>
        <h1>TODO list</h1>

        <h3>Todo</h3>
        <ul>
            <li>Buy a hat for the bat</li>
            <li>Clear the fogs for the frogs</li>
            <li>Bring a box to the fox</li>
        </ul>
```

```
    <h3>Done</h3>
    <ul>
        <li>Put the mittens on the kittens</li>
    </ul>
  </body>
</html>
```

Stage the file, but don't commit yet. The following are keywords to close an issue.

- close

- closes

- closed

- fix

- fixes

- fixed

- resolve

- resolves

- resolved

Using one of these words followed by an issue number, mark it as resolved and close it. The commit resolves issue #3, so it puts that in the commit message footer. Your commit message should look like mine (see Figure 10-21).

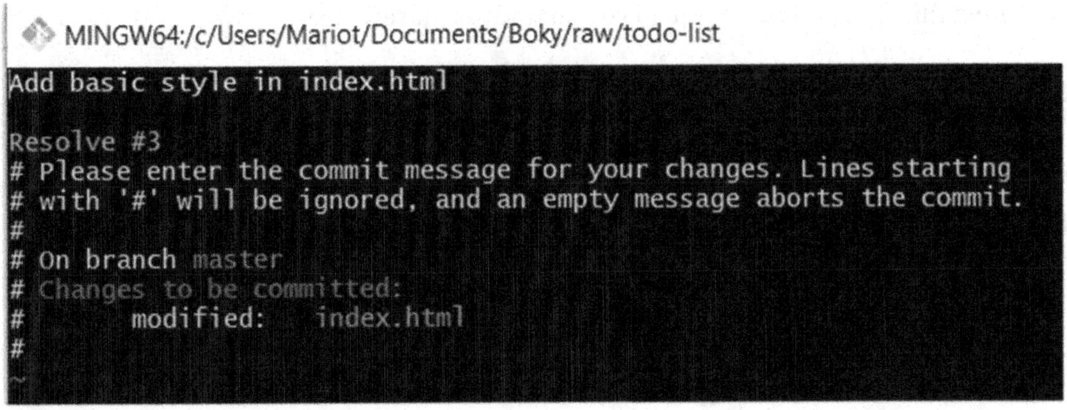

Figure 10-21. *Resolving an issue by commit message*

Like commit messages, the issue references should use the imperative tone, so it is preferred to use *resolve* instead of *resolved*. Now, it's time to push the commit and see for ourselves!

Navigate to the issue you worked on (you won't find it in the open issues, use the filter to see the closed issues) and open the details page. You should see a new comment on it, just like mine, as shown in Figure 10-22.

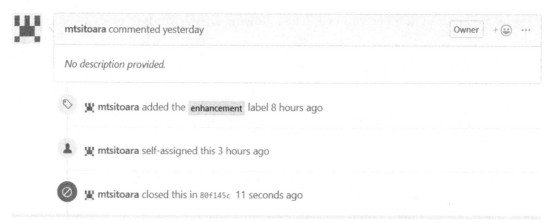

Figure 10-22. *Issue close by keywords*

If you tap the commit name, you again see the `git show` view of the commit.

The little feature of GitHub is useful, but be very careful when using it. Only close an issue when you are perfectly sure that it was resolved. Closing and reopening issues confuse people and generate a lot of notifications. And don't close a different issue by mistake! 83% of all workplace violence is due to issues closing mistakes. And just because I invented this statistic doesn't mean you should take it seriously!

Summary

Phew! This chapter was a bit lengthy, wasn't it? It delved into understanding issues, notably learning how to link them to commits. Always remember to log all your actions into issues before executing them. And ensure you triage them using labels and assignees.

That wraps up basic project management. By now, you should be familiar with planning your GitHub moves. Yet, project management isn't solely about pre-planning tasks; having a clear record of past events and achieved milestones is crucial. Therefore, the next chapter dives into "proper" project management. It also provides a concise summary of various GitHub workflows. Let's proceed!

CHAPTER 11

Diving into Project Management: Branches

In the last chapter, you discovered issues and used them to plan a project. You also learned how to link commits to issues so that you can track each change in a project. The workflow was simple: choose an issue, create a commit that can resolve it, and push it to GitHub. The issue was then marked as resolved and closed. However, this workflow is not well-suited for most real-world projects, as the potential for mistakes is too high.

What if you need more than one commit to resolve an issue? What if other team members have pushed commits that contain changes to the same files you're working on? How can you ensure that the pushed commits truly resolve the issue? These are some of the reasons why making direct changes to the project is not advisable, even if you're working alone.

Remember, closing an issue by using keywords in the commit message is convenient, but it requires caution. You may have overlooked issues in your work, or your changes might introduce new bugs into the project. That's why it's advisable to have someone else review your code before accepting the changes. This is the aspect covered in this chapter.

First, you are introduced to the most common GitHub workflow, which is how most teams work on GitHub. Then, you delve into the concept of branches.

But before beginning this chapter, here's a little thing that you should always remember: "You will make mistakes. A lot of the time. So, you must make sure to use as many safeguards as possible." Let's go!

© Mariot Tsitoara 2024
M. Tsitoara, *Beginning Git and GitHub*, https://doi.org/10.1007/979-8-8688-0215-7_11

GitHub Workflow

This section discusses the most common way that developers use GitHub. Remember that each team has its way of doing things, but each way of working is inspired by the basic workflow to present.

Remember the little fact about making mistakes? This omnipresent possibility of mistakes is why you need to follow this GitHub workflow so that even if mistakes happen, you isolate their repercussions in a controlled manner. The way of working from the previous chapter was to commit everything directly to the main project, which is very dangerous. The main project is usually the "production" line, the version the clients see and use. So, this version must be very clean and should always be exploitable. If errors are made in the main version, the clients will experience bugs, disrupting every team member.

One way to resolve this issue is to create a copy of the main project and work on this clone. Each change you make to this copy does not affect the main project, so none of your mistakes can impact clients. And when you (and other people) are perfectly sure that the changes you made resolve the issue, you can reproduce those changes in the main version.

These copies of the main project are called *branches*, and the concept of reproducing changes into another branch is called *merging*. You can make as many branches as you like and trade commits between them. When you first create a repository, Git creates a new branch for you, called `main`. Most developers put their main or production version in main and only re-create changes there when they are sure that it's okay to do so.

Just like tree branches, Git branches can have many ramifications, meaning that you can even create new branches from branches other than the main one, even if it's difficult to maintain such architecture. Most of the time, you create a branch when working on an issue and delete it after the issue is resolved.

To put all this into perspective, you will learn about the default or common GitHub workflow. As you know, everything should begin with an issue. You are already familiar with this. So, let's talk about each of the next steps of the workflow.

When you want to resolve an issue by making code changes, you should first copy the project's current working version and create a new branch.

Then, as usual, you make your changes and commit the state of the project. You can make any number of commits you need; it won't affect the main branch. You can also push your commits to GitHub so that your code can be seen.

Then, you link your branch to the main one so that others can compare the changes and review your code. This link is called a *pull request*; you request that your commits be applied to the main branch.

Other team members can then review and comment on your code on GitHub. You then push more commits addressing those comments until all problems are solved.

The pull request is accepted if every party (developers, managers, testers, or clients) agrees that your changes are okay and resolve the issue at hand. This means every commit you make on your branch is applied to the main branch. You can then delete the branch you created.

And that's it! You might wonder how it differs from directly pushing to the main branch. It's very different because mistakes and omissions are caught before applying the changes to the production version. This means that the number of production bugs is reduced to a minimum. It also makes it possible for various members of your team to review the changes before they are applied, which is the standard way of working in most tech companies. Bundling the changes into one pull request also solves the problem of multiple people pushing commits to solve different issues at the same time. It keeps the history log clean.

You might be tempted to open pull requests only when you feel that you are done with your work. Unless your work is very small and straightforward, don't wait long before opening a pull request. By opening a pull request early in your development, you can receive feedback before making too many changes. It is very useful for beginners especially because following the wrong path from the start takes a long time to correct, and you would wish that you were told the correct way earlier. Opening a pull request doesn't mean the work is done; it just means that you are considering applying commits from one branch to another.

Note   You can create branches from any branch and open pull requests. It's not only reserved for the main branch.

Figure 11-1 summarizes all the steps.

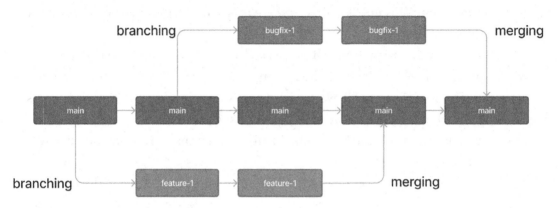

Figure 11-1. *Basic Git workflow*

As you can see, you can create branches from any branch in the project. Git created a branch called "main" at the initialization of the repository. You can then create more branches (for example, a bugfix branch or a feature branch) to introduce changes to the this branch.

Branches

Branches are the main feature behind code reviews. You must work on your own branch before publishing your work so that you won't be bothered by other people's changes. Simply put, a branch is your independent copy of the project at a certain time. Let's see how they work and create and delete some.

The logic behind branches is simple: make a copy of the current state of the project. In this copy, you can make your changes without affecting other people. You can use branches to have distinct channels of distribution or to try new things with the project.

When creating a repository, you get a branch by default: `main`. This branch is enough when working on very small projects, but most projects need more branches to get the best results. First, they need a production branch where clients can get the latest stable version of the software; this is the `main` branch. You will mostly work on the development branch, where most of the action happens. Finally, there are short-lived patching branches that you create to hold your commits before merging them into the development branch. These patching branches live and die with a pull request. You create one when you are solving an issue and delete them afterward.

To summarize a little bit, there are three sorts of branches.

- Production branch: where you release stable versions of your project

- Development branch: where you test your latest version

- Patching branch: where you work on your issues

Unless there is a *very* urgent major problem that needs solving immediately, you never commit directly to the production or the development branch. To update those branches, you use pull requests to review and test the changes. There are some companies where every developer commits directly to the development branch, but this is very counterintuitive because if a bug is discovered, they won't know which commit introduced it. Also, it forces the developer to push "do-it-all" commits, which is an anti-pattern. Do-it-all commits are commits that try to resolve many issues at the same time; for example, a commit that fixes a bug and introduces a new feature simultaneously. The laziness of developers often causes this practice when they don't want to create a new branch for another issue. This creates very bad pull requests and makes tracking the project's progress difficult. It also creates a big challenge for the testers as they don't know which version is stable. It's an all-around bad idea; don't do it even with small projects. Creating and deleting branches all the time may seem tiring, but it is the best workflow when working with Git.

The one thing to remember about Git branches is that they are simple references to commits; that's why creating and deleting them is so fast. Recall that Git stores its commits in chained links. Well, a branch is just a reference to one of those commits. A commit contains information about the author, the date, the snapshot, and, most importantly, the name of the previous commit. The name of the previous commit is called the *parent*, and every commit except the first one has at least one parent. Thus, each commit is linked to the previous one so that you can re-create the change history of the project.

For now, you only have the default "main" branch, which references your project's last commit. To create a new commit, Git checks where the reference is and uses the information in that commit to build the link between the new commit and the previously referenced one. So, each time you commit, the reference moves to the new commit, and the cycle continues. Thus, a branch is just a reference to a commit designed to be the parent of the next one.

But how does Git know which branch you are on? Well, it uses another reference called HEAD that references the current commit. If you are on a branch, HEAD references the last commit of that branch. But if you are checking out a previous version (like you did when you used git checkout <commit_name>), the HEAD references that commit, and you are in a state called *detached HEAD*.

Caution   You never want to be in a "detached HEAD" state. It is a very dangerous situation to find yourself in.

For most situations, you can think of HEAD as the reference to the current branch, and every commit you create uses the last commit in that branch as a parent.

When you merge a branch into another, a new commit is created. It has two parents: one from each branch. So, you can recognize a commit type from its number of parents.

- No parents: the very first commit

- One parent: normal commit in a branch

- Multiple parents: a commit created by the merge of branches

Creating a Branch

Now that you know a lot about branches, let's create one! It's very easy; you need to use the git branch command followed by the branch name. Remember that the branch name should only contain alphanumeric values and dashes or underscores; no spaces are allowed.

```
$ git branch <name>
```

For example, let's create a development branch for the project. Let's name it develop. Here's how to do it.

```
$ git branch develop
```

After executing the command, you notice that nothing has changed in your project. That's because creating a branch is simply about referencing the last commit of the current branch, and nothing else. To begin working with a branch, you must switch to it.

Switch to Another Branch

You created the development branch, and now it's time to switch to it. But here's the problem: I've forgotten the name I gave to the branch. Someone might suggest you turn back and look at the previous section to find the name. But I have a better idea: list all the current branches. To do so, execute the git branch command without any parameters.

```
$ git branch
```

This command gives you the list of branches you currently have and puts an asterisk next to the one you're currently on (the HEAD). Check out Figure 11-2 for an example of a branch list.

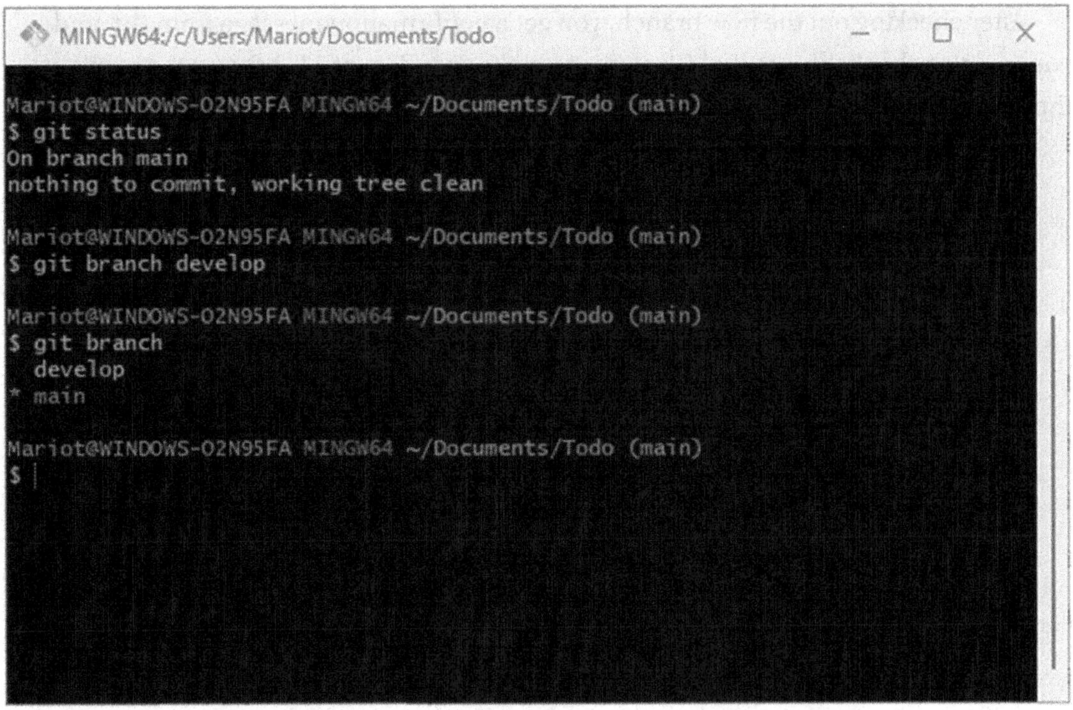

Figure 11-2. *List of branches in the project*

Notice that you are still on the main branch because you haven't created anything other than a branch. Now, let's switch to it.

You already know the command to switch between versions. Well, you use the same command to navigate between branches. Simply use `git checkout` with the name of the branch as a parameter.

```
$ git checkout <name>
```

So, if you want to switch to the `develop` branch, you must execute the following.

```
$ git checkout develop
```

Note   As when you navigated between versions, you can't switch branches if you have uncommitted changed files. Commit before you move. Or use a technique called *stashing*, which is covered in later chapters.

After checking out the new branch, you get a confirmation message from Git, and you can also check the result of Git status to make sure. Figure 11-3 shows the result of those commands.

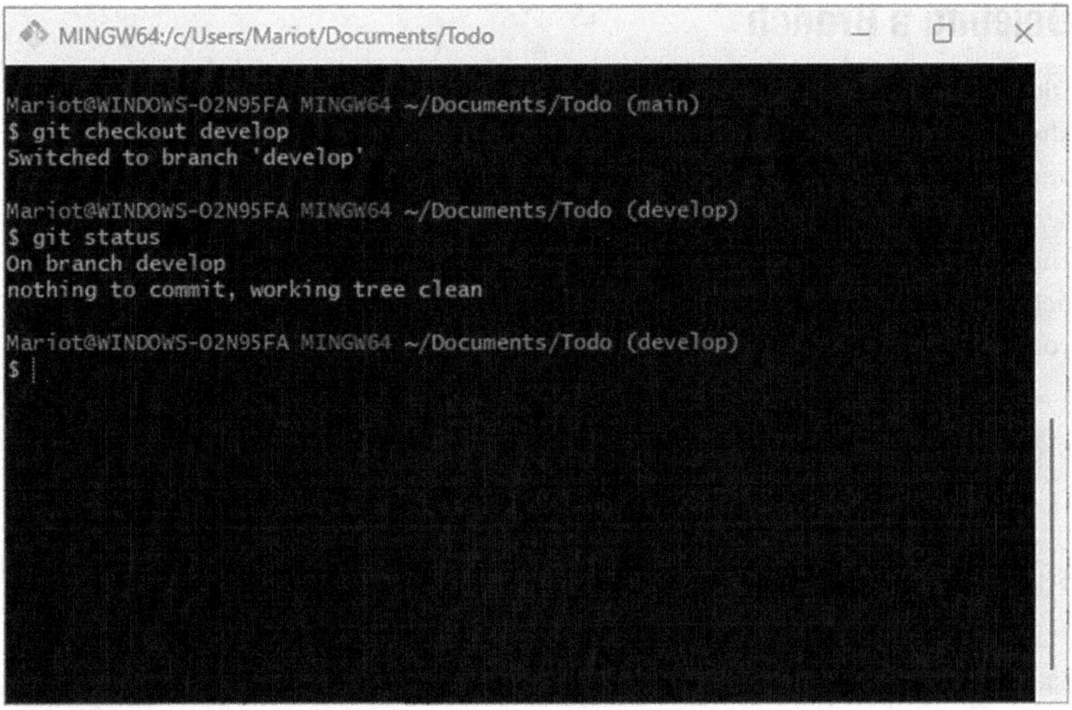

Figure 11-3. *Switching branches*

EXERCISE: CREATE A TESTING BRANCH

Let's do a simple exercise before moving on to the next task. It's very straightforward because all the answers are in this section. The exercise is to create a branch named `testing` where you test a project before merging all the commits to the main branch. You must do the following.

1. Go back to the main branch.

2. Create a new branch named `testing`.

3. Switch to the new branch.

Tip   To immediately switch to a new branch after creating it, use the `-b` option with the git checkout command. For example, is the same as `git branch testing` and then `git checkout testing`.

Deleting a Branch

Did you have fun creating the testing branch? Good. It's time to delete it because you already have a testing branch: develop. That's where you merge the patching branches, and all the testing is done there.

You can delete a pushed branch, which is present on the remote repository, by checking the "delete branch after PR merged" option when creating a pull request. This deletes the remote branch, but your local branches are unchanged. You have to delete your local branches manually.

To delete a branch, use the same command to create one but with the option -d.

```
$ git branch -d <name>
```

So, to delete the testing branch, use the following.

```
$ git branch -d testing
```

Like a real tree branch, you don't cut the Git branch you are currently standing on. Check out another branch before deleting the branch; for this reason, you can't have less than one branch in a project. If you try anyway, you get an error like the one shown in Figure 11-4.

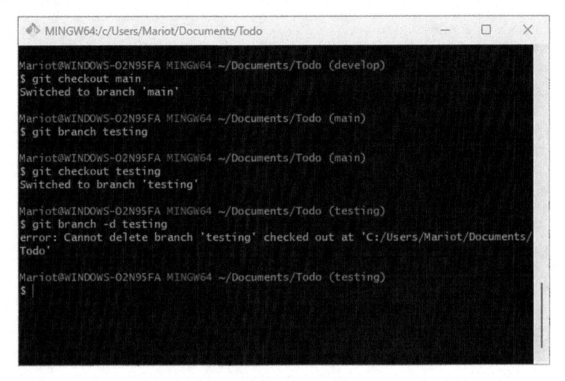

Figure 11-4. *Deleting current branch*

Thus, you must check out the main or develop branch before deleting the testing branch. If you did it correctly, you should get a result like mine shown in Figure 11-5.

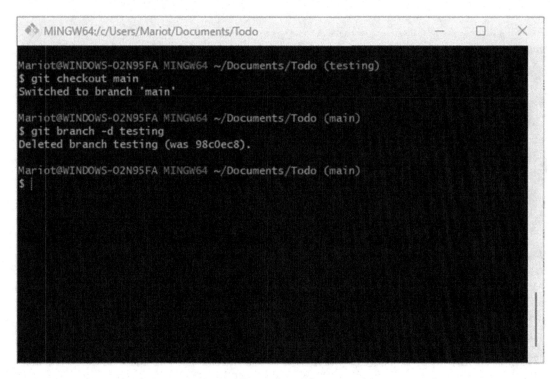

Figure 11-5. *Deleting of a branch (we hardly knew ye)*

Take note of the confirmation message; it gives you the SHA-1 name of the branch you just deleted. Since the branch you created and deleted contained no commits, it just referenced the last commit of the current branch. Let's check the history log to confirm this. Execute the git log command to get the list of the latest commits, just like in Figure 11-6.

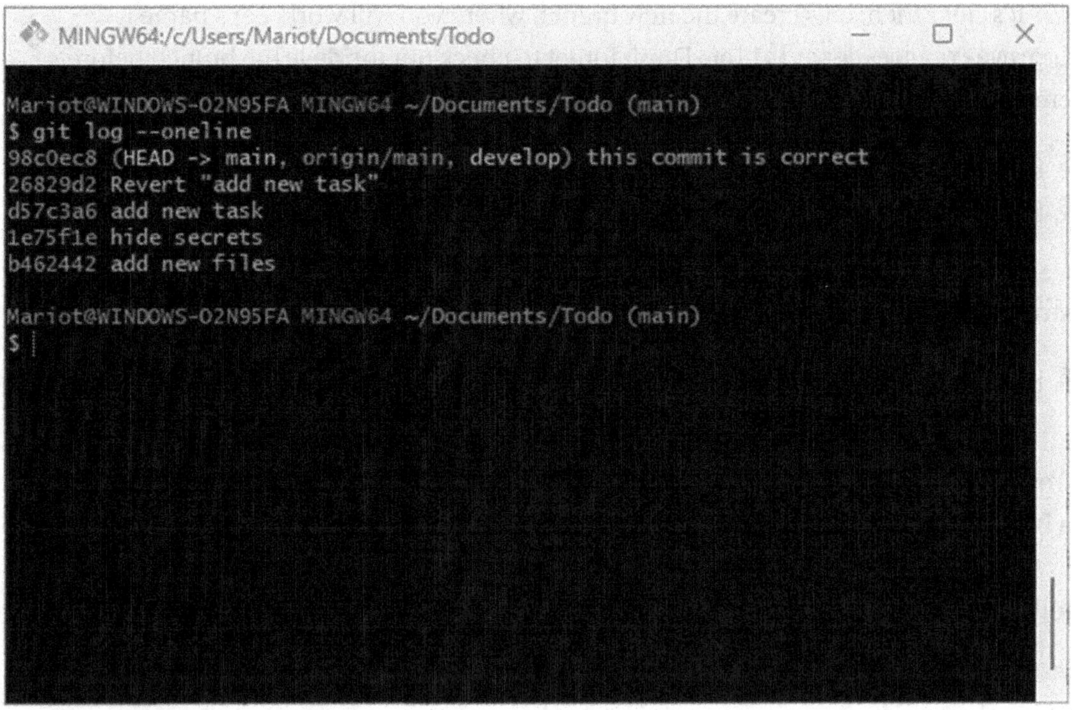

```
MINGW64:/c/Users/Mariot/Documents/Todo                          —    □    X

Mariot@WINDOWS-O2N95FA MINGW64 ~/Documents/Todo (main)
$ git log --oneline
98c0ec8 (HEAD -> main, origin/main, develop) this commit is correct
26829d2 Revert "add new task"
d57c3a6 add new task
1e75f1e hide secrets
b462442 add new files

Mariot@WINDOWS-O2N95FA MINGW64 ~/Documents/Todo (main)
$
```

Figure 11-6. *Commit name check*

The last commit name and the branch name are the same because you haven't made any commits in the branch. You also see on the history log where the branches are originating from. In this example, the develop branch originates from the 98c0ec8 commit, the branch's parent.

Merging Branches

Merging branches has been discussed in this chapter, but you haven't made a single merge. Let's change that.

Let's imagine that you want to improve the project's README file by adding a few pieces of information. This task is already listed in the GitHub issues, so there's no problem with that. The next step is to create a new branch from the development branch so you can merge them later. You must create a new branch from the develop branch instead of the main branch because you won't touch the main branch until everything is properly tested. If everything is clear and clean, you merge the development branch into the main branch.

It's clear then, let's create the new branch where you will work. Let's name it improve-readme-description. Don't forget to check out the develop branch before creating a new one. Thus, you execute the following.

```
$ git checkout develop
$ git branch improve-readme-description
```

Now that the branch has been created, switch to it so you can begin to work. To switch to the new branch, use the checkout command.

```
$ git checkout improve-readme-description
```

Perfect! Now you have a branch named improve-readme-description originating from the develop branch. You like branches so much that you created a branch from a branch!

Now let's get to work. Open the README.md file and change its content to the following.

```
# TODO list
A simple app to manage your daily tasks.
It uses HTML5 and CSS3.

## Features
* List of daily tasks
```

Now, stage the file and get ready to commit. I'll let you choose the commit message, but don't forget to put a reference to the issue you are trying to resolve! Thus, the following are the next steps.

```
$ git add README.md
$ git commit
```

There is nothing new here because every command is the same for any branch. The only slight change is that the branch name differs in the commit description. You can see it in my result shown in Figure 11-7.

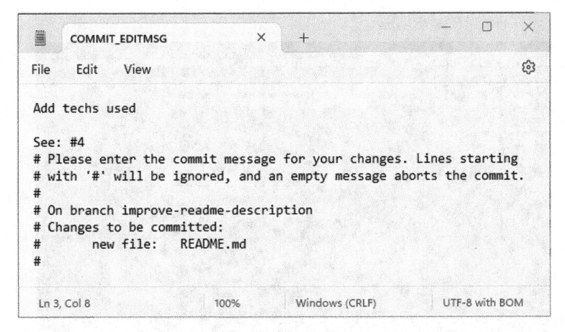

Figure 11-7. *Committing on another branch*

After you have made the commit, check the Git history to put everything you did in perspective. Execute the git log command to view the project's history.

```
$ git log
```

Tip   Use the --oneline option when using git log to get a prettier result

---

Your project history log should look like the one shown in Figure 11-8 after you have committed.

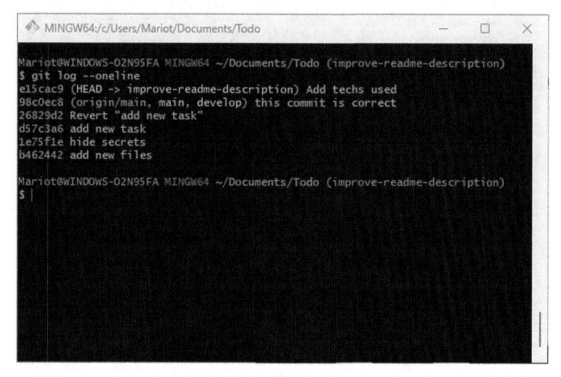

Figure 11-8. *History log after committing on a branch*

As you can see in the figure, HEAD now points to the last commit of the new branch. This means that every commit you create has that as a parent. Also, note that the main and develop branches didn't change because you only worked on the newly created branch.

If you are satisfied with the fix, let's merge the branch into the develop branch so you can test it. To merge the branch into develop, you first must check it out. So, navigate there by using the git checkout command.

```
$ git checkout develop
```

Now, let's try to merge this branch into the develop branch. *Merging* means reproducing all the commits from one branch into another. To do so, use the git merge command followed by the name of the branch to be merged.

```
$ git merge <name>
```

Since you want to merge improve-readme-description into develop, the following is the command to execute on the develop branch.

```
$ git merge improve-readme-description
```

This command integrates your commits from improve-readme-description into develop. You receive a similar result as a confirmation for the merge. Figure 11-9 shows an example.

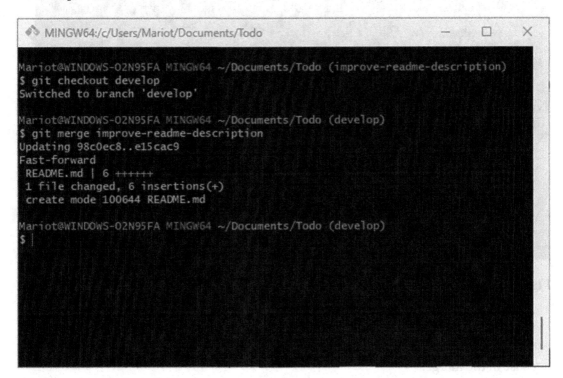

Figure 11-9. *Merge result*

Let's recheck the git log to better understand what happened. After executing git log --oneline, you see a result similar to mine, as shown in Figure 11-10.

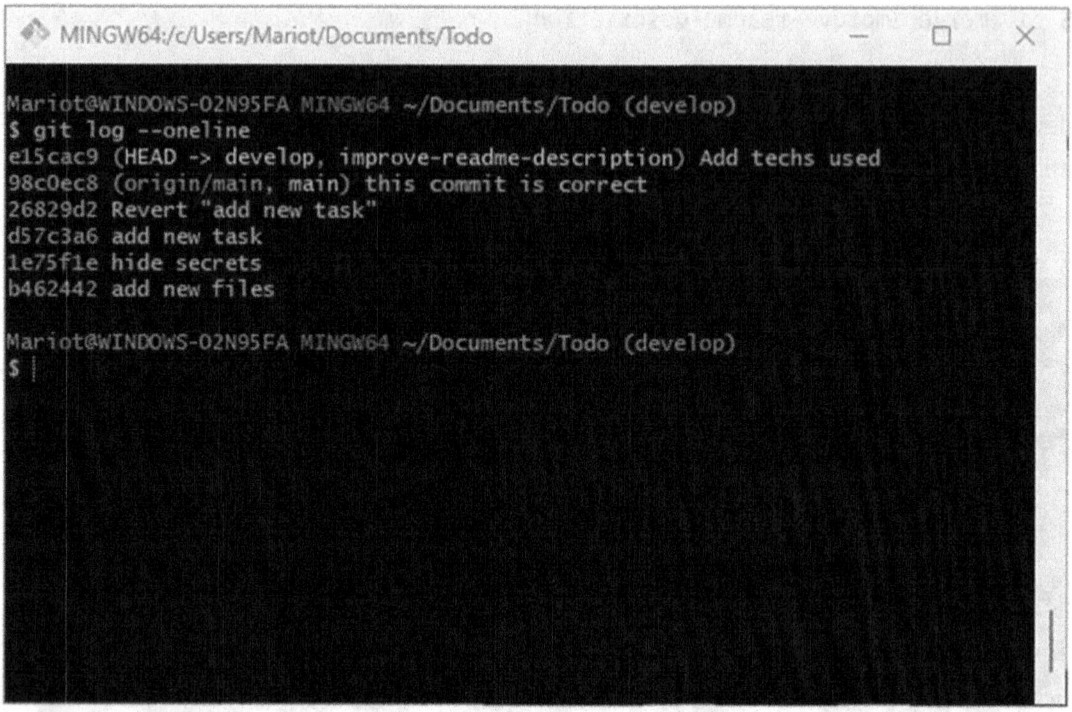

```
MINGW64:/c/Users/Mariot/Documents/Todo                        —     □     X

Mariot@WINDOWS-02N95FA MINGW64 ~/Documents/Todo (develop)
$ git log --oneline
e15cac9 (HEAD -> develop, improve-readme-description) Add techs used
98c0ec8 (origin/main, main) this commit is correct
26829d2 Revert "add new task"
d57c3a6 add new task
1e75f1e hide secrets
b462442 add new files

Mariot@WINDOWS-02N95FA MINGW64 ~/Documents/Todo (develop)
$
```

Figure 11-10. *History log after merge*

As you can see, HEAD now points to develop because it's the checked-out branch. Note that develop and improve-readme-description now point to the same commit because of the merge.

Congratulations on your first merge! It won't be so easy next time. (Hint: Merge conflicts appear when the same line of code has been modified in different commits.)

Pushing a Branch to Remote

Branches are not only made for working locally; you can also publish them to the world by pushing them to the remote repository. For example, let's push the development branch to GitHub so everyone can see the progress.

The command for pushing a branch to remote is (you guessed it!) git push, just like what you learned in a previous chapter. The command is as follows.

```
$ git push <remote_name> <branch_name>
```

The remote name hasn't changed; it's still origin. It's the branch name that is different this time. Instead of main, you push the develop branch. So, the command is as follows.

```
$ git push origin develop
```

Since you've already pushed to remote before, the result shown in Figure 11-11 is familiar to you.

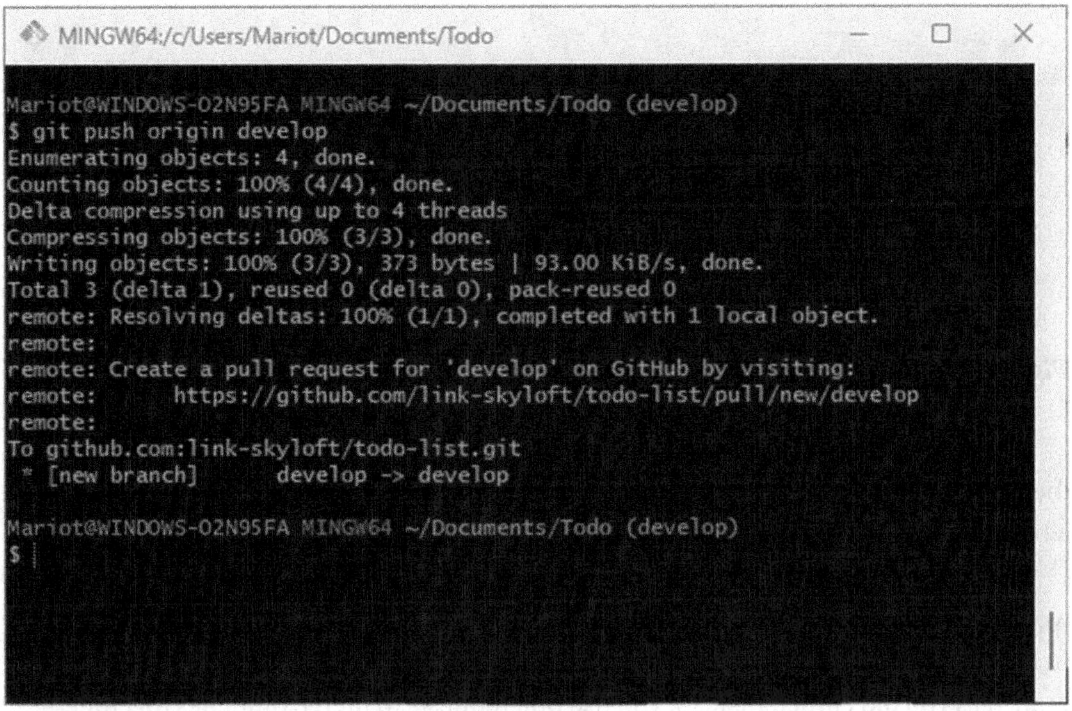

```
MINGW64:/c/Users/Mariot/Documents/Todo                          —     □     ×

Mariot@WINDOWS-O2N95FA MINGW64 ~/Documents/Todo (develop)
$ git push origin develop
Enumerating objects: 4, done.
Counting objects: 100% (4/4), done.
Delta compression using up to 4 threads
Compressing objects: 100% (3/3), done.
Writing objects: 100% (3/3), 373 bytes | 93.00 KiB/s, done.
Total 3 (delta 1), reused 0 (delta 0), pack-reused 0
remote: Resolving deltas: 100% (1/1), completed with 1 local object.
remote:
remote: Create a pull request for 'develop' on GitHub by visiting:
remote:      https://github.com/link-skyloft/todo-list/pull/new/develop
remote:
To github.com:link-skyloft/todo-list.git
 * [new branch]      develop -> develop

Mariot@WINDOWS-O2N95FA MINGW64 ~/Documents/Todo (develop)
$
```

Figure 11-11. *Pushing to a remote branch*

As you can see, there is a little difference in the result. It has a link to create a pull request to ask for permission to reproduce the commits on develop into main. Take note of the link because you will learn about pull requests in the next chapter.

If you return to GitHub to check your project page, you also have the call-to-action button for creating pull requests. Ignore this for now and instead navigate between the main branch and the develop branch. Figure 11-12 shows an example of a project page after a new branch has been pushed.

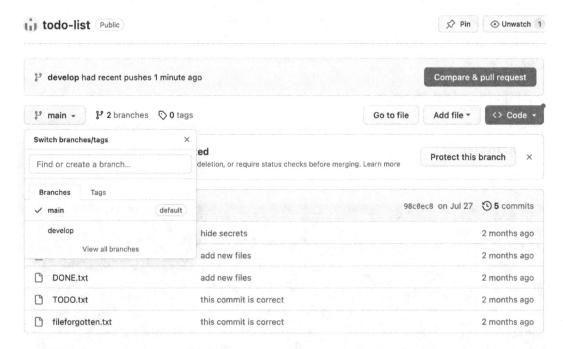

Figure 11-12. The new project page

It's all about branches for now. You now know how to create, merge, and delete them. And most importantly, you have a basic knowledge of the GitHub workflow: create a branch, work on that branch, and create a pull request.

Now, you may be wondering if you even used the workflow. No, you didn't use the workflow because you used the direct approach: directly messing with the branches. In a real-world project, you won't commit and push directly to the main or the develop branch as you did earlier. Instead, you use pull requests to merge branches together. That way, your work can be reviewed by your coworkers before you can merge them into the develop or main branch.

Summary

This chapter dealt with what makes Git a powerful tool for project management: branches. Branches are necessary for fast-paced development because you probably work on many issues at once. Keeping all those changes in the same place is a recipe for disaster. For example, you need to start in a clean environment to fix a bug or introduce a feature; trying to do both at the same time seriously increases the risk of introducing more bugs.

The main takeaway of this chapter is the importance of using a workflow when developing with Git. And those workflows all use branches to separate the different types of work necessary for clean issue resolution.

You've seen how to create, check out, and delete branches. Now, let's learn more about pull requests and code review so you can propose changes to the main branch!

## CHAPTER 12

Better Project Management: Pull Requests

In the last chapter, you learned about the typical GitHub workflow that most companies use or variations of it for their day-to-day work. You also learned about branches and how to use them. However, there is one crucial aspect you didn't cover: how to combine these two concepts effectively. The answer is simple: pull requests and code reviews.

The previous chapter highlighted many reasons why using a traditional approach to code management (where everybody commits to the same branch) is a bad idea. Even though you work alone on this project, you might not experience the inconveniences yet. But they do exist, and resolving them can be time-consuming. So, trust me, it's better to follow the workflow.

This chapter demonstrates how to implement the workflow presented in the previous chapter. You utilize the branches created to introduce changes to older branches. Additionally, you delve into code review and how to manage it effectively.

Why Use Pull Requests?

Many developers who don't follow a particular workflow argue that it wastes time because it consumes valuable development time. There is truth in this statement because adhering to the workflow may involve waiting for others to review your code. However, it's essential to remember that you don't have to sit idle while waiting for a review. You can continue working on other tasks, such as solving another issue. This is precisely why branches are so powerful in version control systems; they enable you to work on multiple issues concurrently. With the workflow, you can initiate work on an issue, seek ideas or guidance from your peers, and then switch to another issue while waiting for responses. Once you receive the necessary feedback, you can resume work on the first issue. You can also start working on an issue even if you don't have complete information about what needs to be done; you can pause midway to gather more information. Importantly, having someone else review your code is one of the most effective ways to reduce bugs. The time saved by not chasing bugs later is more significant than the time you gain by committing directly to the `main` branch.

The GitHub workflow is also the preferred method of work for open source contributors. It would be chaotic if anyone could push commits directly to a branch without any review. Instead, each contributor has a working clone of the project and can propose changes that other contributors review and discuss.

In conclusion, working with the GitHub workflow is the best approach, significantly reducing the likelihood of introducing bugs. As you saw in the last chapter, using branches is just the first step; you must also use pull requests to complete the workflow. Let's learn more about them!

Pull Requests Overview

Pull requests are a relatively easy-to-understand concept. Submitting a pull request is a way to ask for permission to apply all the commits in a branch to another branch. However, before diving into the subject, it's essential to understand what a *pull* is.

Pull

In Git terminology, a *pull* is essentially the opposite of a push (congratulations if you guessed that correctly!). When you *push*, you take your local branch and copy all its commits to a remote branch, creating the branch on the server if it doesn't exist. On the other hand, a pull is the reverse; it looks at a remote branch and copies the commits from that branch to your local repository. It's essentially an exchange of commits: *push* when moving from local to remote and *pull* when moving from remote to local.

The syntax is very similar, too.

```
$ git pull <remote_name> <branch_name>
```

So, for example, if you wanted to fetch the commits from the main branch on GitHub and bring them into your local repository, you would execute the following command while checking out the main branch.

```
$ git pull origin main
```

Always be on the branch corresponding to the one you are pulling before running any command. So, in this case, you must check out main before running git pull. After executing the command, you get a result like mine, as shown in Figure 12-1.

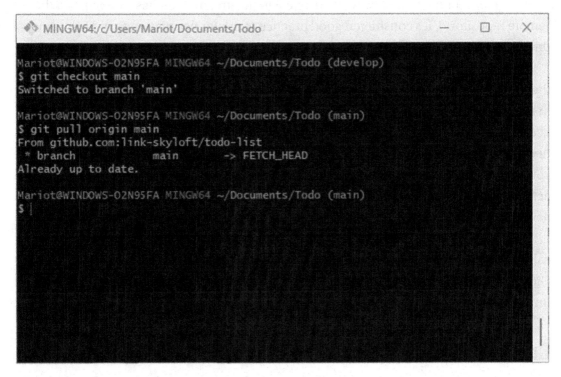

Figure 12-1. *Pulling main from origin*

Nothing happened since you have the same commits in your local repository and on GitHub. But once you start working with other people, you have to pull their branches to your local machine to review their changes, or review the changes on GitHub.

That's it! Pulling is just copying commits from a remote branch to a local one. And don't worry. You will have more opportunities to use git pull soon.

What Does a Pull Request Do?

Now that you know more about pulling, you should have a clearer idea of how a pull request works. It requests permission to execute a pull action on a remote repository. However, pulling a branch alone is not enough for the action to be complete; you must also merge the branches.

Remember when you merged a patch branch into the development branch? A pull request is just a way of formally asking for permission. You can do anything you want with your local branches, but when you deal with upstream branches (branches in the remote repository), it's considered good practice to ask for permission first. This ensures that every fix committed to the main branches is properly tested and reviewed.

So, to put it all together, a pull request is a request you make to get GitHub to perform these actions: pull your patching branch and merge it with another branch. For example, in this project, you currently have three local branches (`main`, `develop`, and `improve-readme-description`) and two remote branches (`main` and `develop`). If you made any new commits to `improve-readme-description` and wanted to merge it with `develop`, you would open a pull request. After it is accepted, GitHub performs the following actions: pulls the `improve-readme-description` branch and merges it with the `develop` branch.

You might wonder, "If the end goal of a pull request is to merge a branch, why not call it a *merge request*?" Well, many people (including other Git hosting services like GitLab) do call it a merge request. It means the same thing. This book uses the two terms interchangeably.

Create a Pull Request

Let's get down to business! Creating a new pull request is very easy. You only need two branches: one to work on and another to merge into. Let's do it!

First, let's create an issue to work on. So, go to GitHub and create an issue called "Improve the app style". Yes, there was a similar issue previously, but since you've already solved that issue, you will open a new one. Recycling issues is not a good idea because it makes it harder to follow your progress.

After you've created the issue, it's time to go back to your terminal because each pull request begins with a branch. Create a branch named `improve-app-style` from the latest development branch (`develop`). As you saw in the last chapter, the way to create a new branch from another is to check out the source branch and execute the branch creation command. So, you have to execute those commands one after another.

```
$ git checkout develop
$ git branch improve-app-style
$ git checkout improve-app-style
```

After executing those three commands, the new branch is checked out, as seen in Figure 12-2.

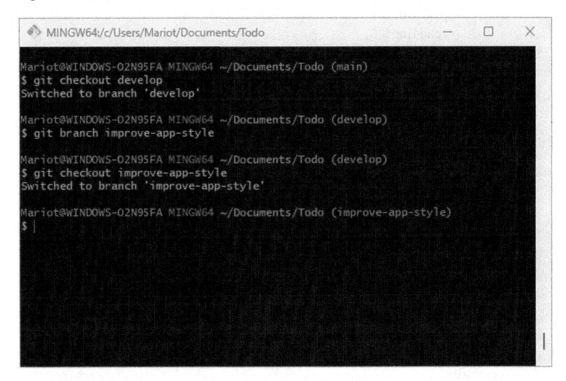

Figure 12-2. *Creation of a new branch*

Let's work on the issue within the newly created branch. Open index.html and replace its contents with the following.

```html
<!doctype html>
<html>
    <head>
        <meta charset="utf-8">
        <title>TODO list</title>
```

```
    <style>
        h1 {
            text-align:center;
        }
        h3 {
            text-transform: uppercase;
        }
        ul {
            margin: 0;
            padding: 0;
        }
        ul li {
            cursor: pointer;
            position: relative;
            padding: 12px 8px 12px 40px;
            background: #eee;
            font-size: 18px;
            transition: 0.2s;
        }
        ul li:nth-child(odd) {
            background: #f9f9f9;
        }
        ul li:hover {
            background: #ddd;
        }
    </style>
</head>
<body>
    <h1>TODO list</h1>

    <h3>Todo</h3>
    <ul>
        <li>Buy a hat for the bat</li>
        <li>Clear the fogs for the frogs</li>
        <li>Bring a box to the fox</li>
    </ul>
```

```
    <h3>Done</h3>
    <ul>
        <li>Put the mittens on the kittens</li>
    </ul>
  </body>
</html>
```

Then, stage the file and prepare to commit. Put something very simple as a commit message; there's no need to reference the issue. You'll do this later. As a commit message, you can state: "Add basic color changes on item rows". As usual, you get a confirmation message after the commit, like the one shown in Figure 12-3.

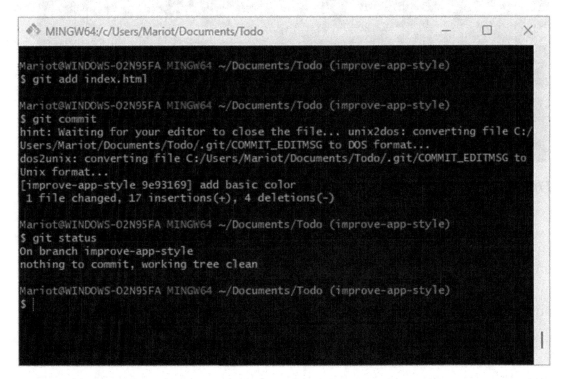

Figure 12-3. *Commit confirmation*

Now it's time to push it to GitHub. As you've seen, you have to use the git push command, followed by the remote name and the branch name. So, the command is as follows.

```
$ git push origin improve-app-style
```

After you've pushed your branch to GitHub, you get another familiar confirmation message. Figure 12-4 shows an example of this.

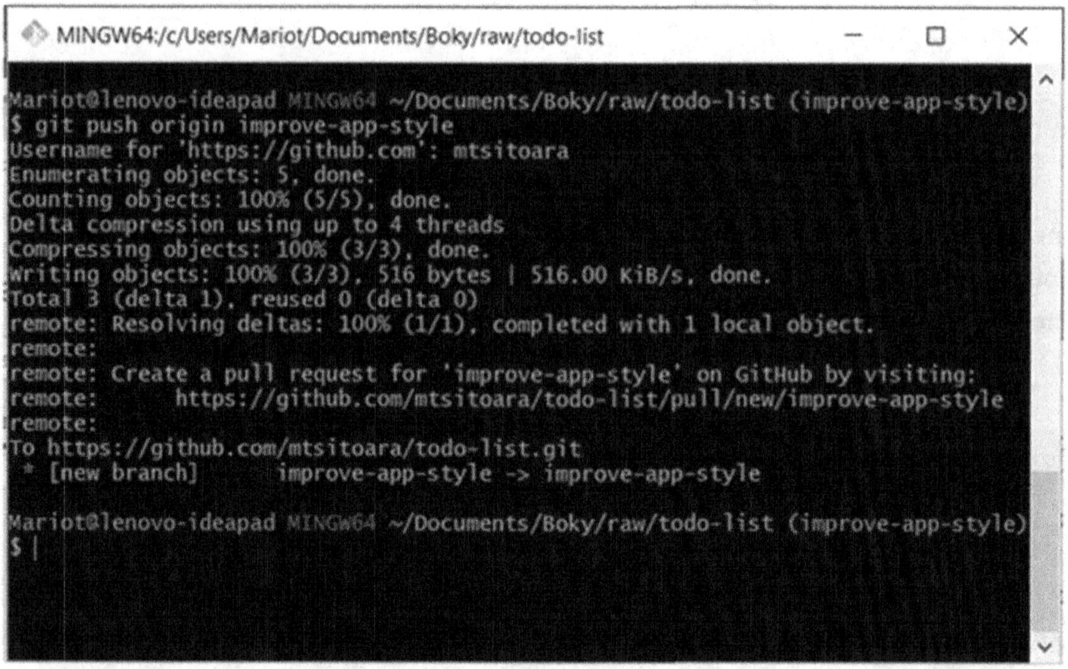

Figure 12-4. *Pushing the branch to GitHub*

As you can see in the confirmation message, Git provides a link for you to follow so you can create a pull request. However, let's create it using another method: directly on GitHub.

Go to your project page and look for something different in the layout. After a recent push to a new branch, your project page should look like the one shown in Figure 12-5.

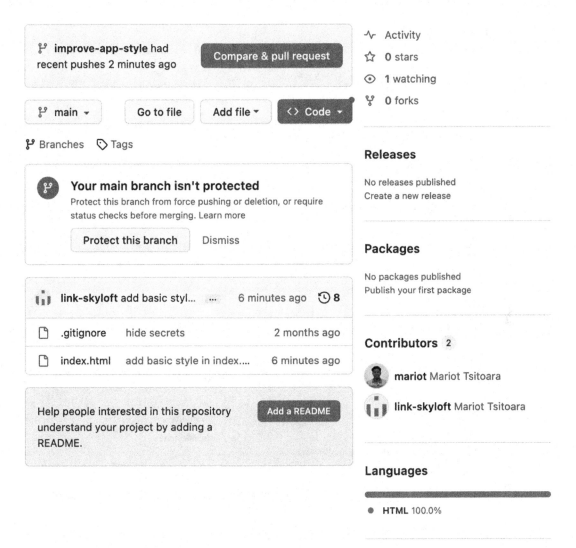

Figure 12-5. *Project page after a recent push*

As you can see, there is a new call to action on the page above the list of branches. It displays the name of the branch that you just created and a prominent button for creating a pull request. Click the button to proceed, and you should be taken to the creation form, as shown in Figure 12-6.

Comparing changes

Choose two branches to see what's changed or to start a new pull request. If you need to, you can also compare across forks.

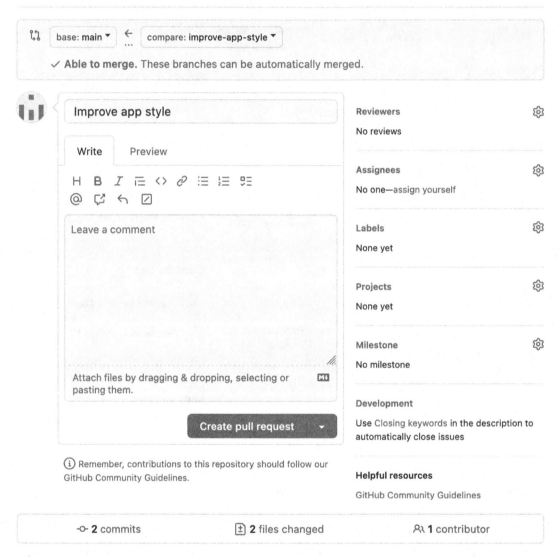

Figure 12-6. *Pull request creation form*

You can note that the pull request creation form is similar to the issue creation form. On the right, you can find the same information about assignees and labels; they work the same. At the bottom of the page, you can see the commits that the pull request applies; if you scroll down, you'll find the differences between the versions. Figure 12-7 shows an example of this.

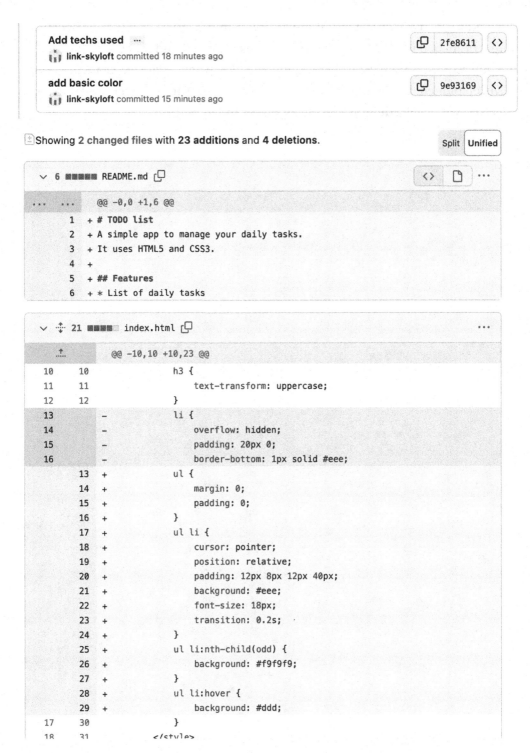

Figure 12-7. *Differences between versions*

But you might ask yourself why there are two commits to be applied. It's because of the target branch. If you examine Figure 12-6 closely, you'll find that the base branch for the pull request is set to main. This is not what you want because you are targeting the develop branch. Change the base branch to develop. After you change it, the page reloads, and you'll get a different result, as shown in Figure 12-8.

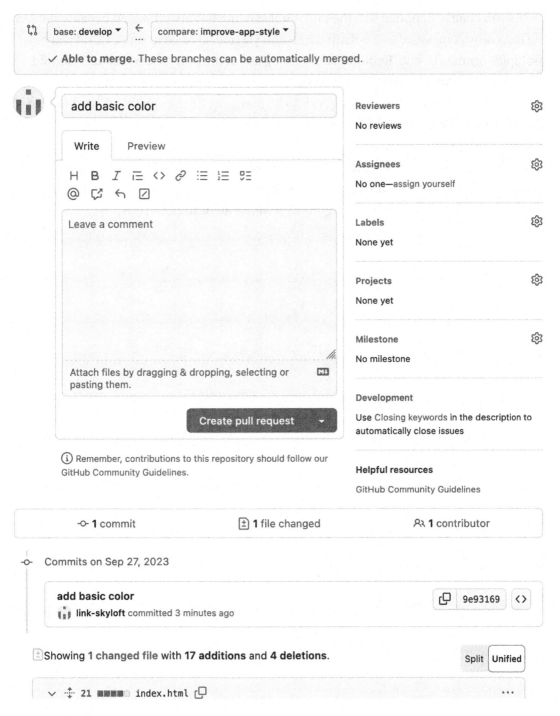

Figure 12-8. Pull request on develop

As you change it, notice that the pull request name has also changed because it takes the last commit message as a default name. But you can change it, especially if you have multiple commits in one. Remember one thing about the pull request name: it should be as clear and straight to the point as commit messages. The name should answer this question: What will this pull request do if I merge it? Be thoughtful when choosing a name and description so the reviewers know which problem you are trying to solve without reading your code.

You can expand your pull request explanation in the description textbox, and don't hesitate to provide more information about the changes. You should also include keywords for closing issues there. Figure 12-9 shows an example of this.

Comparing changes

Choose two branches to see what's changed or to start a new pull request. If you need to, you can also compare across forks.

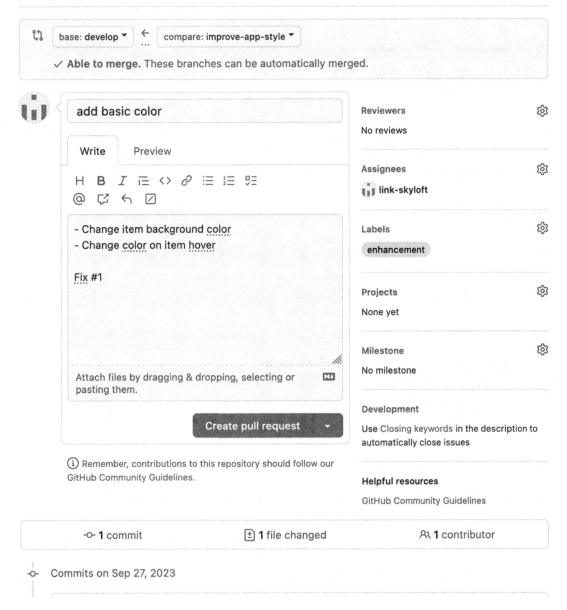

Figure 12-9. *A completed pull request*

Once you are ready, click "Create pull request" to submit it; you are taken to a page similar to the one shown in Figure 12-10.

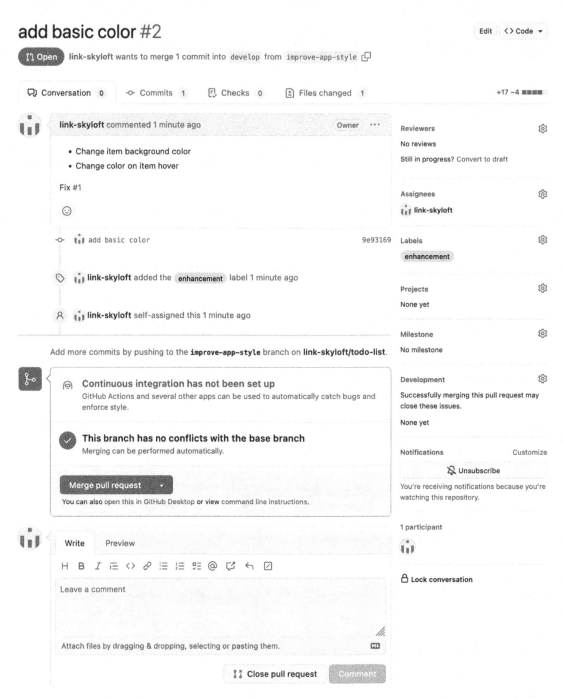

Figure 12-10. *Your new pull request*

Again, this view is very similar to its issues counterpart, with the pull request number following the issues number. The only difference is the "Merge pull request" button. Tapping it merges the branches. But don't do that yet! Let's play around with the pull request before merging it.

Once the pull request is submitted, it's time to review it! Remove your developer hat for a while and put on your tech lead hat; it's time to do a code review!

Code Reviews

Code reviews are one of the best features of GitHub. Long gone are the days when you had to schedule a one-on-one meeting with your tech lead so they could check your code. There is no need to send each other long chains of emails (with many annoyed people on the cc list) for each change request in the code. Now, everything is done in GitHub. Let's see!

Give a Code Review

Figure 12-9 provided a glimpse of the code review process. You saw all the changes made to the files compared to the current version, but you couldn't interact with them yet. This section teaches how to review your co-contributors' code.

Figure 12-10 shows that the pull request page has many sections, just like the Issues page. You must click "Files changed" to begin the code review. You then arrive on a page like the one shown in Figure 12-11.

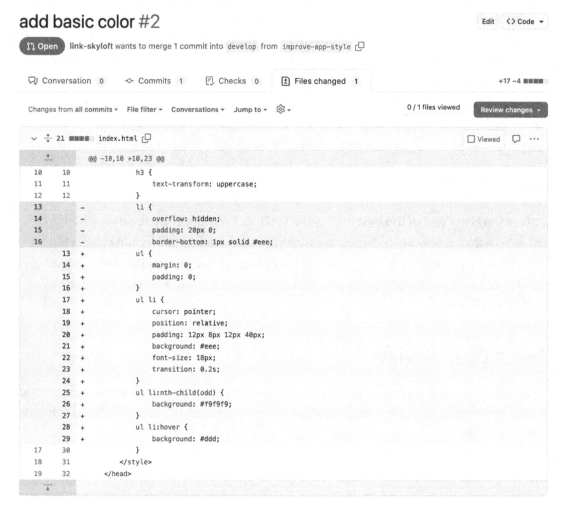

Figure 12-11. *The Code Review section*

This view should remind you of the git diff results because it's essentially the same thing. It shows you the differences between the versions in detail, which means that you see what has been added, removed, or replaced.

Leave a Review Comment

Now, let's pretend to review this code. During code reviews, you can comment on the overall changes or a specific piece of code. For example, let's put a comment on the ul li CSS definition on line 17. As you move your cursor around, the code review changes, and a little plus icon (+) follows it. It means that you can comment there. Let's do that. Place your cursor on line 17, and when the plus icon appears, click it. It opens a small comment section like in Figure 12-12.

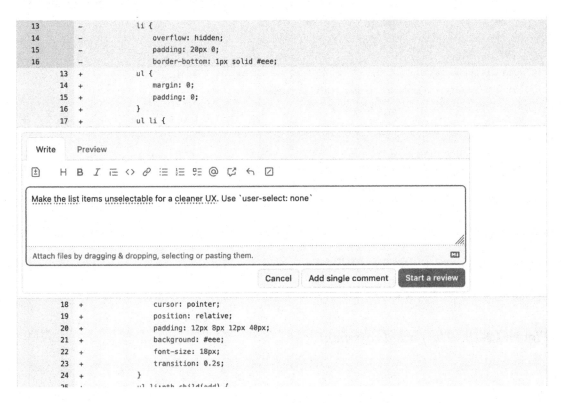

Figure 12-12. *A code review on a line*

As always, you can make all kinds of comments in this section with the help of Markdown syntax. For this example, add this comment: "Make the list items unselectable for a cleaner UX. Use `user-select: none`". You should check the preview before you submit the comment.

If you are satisfied with your comment, tap "Start a review" to go to the next step. The comment is displayed on the Review page, and there is also a Reply button on the comment, just like in the result shown in Figure 12-13.

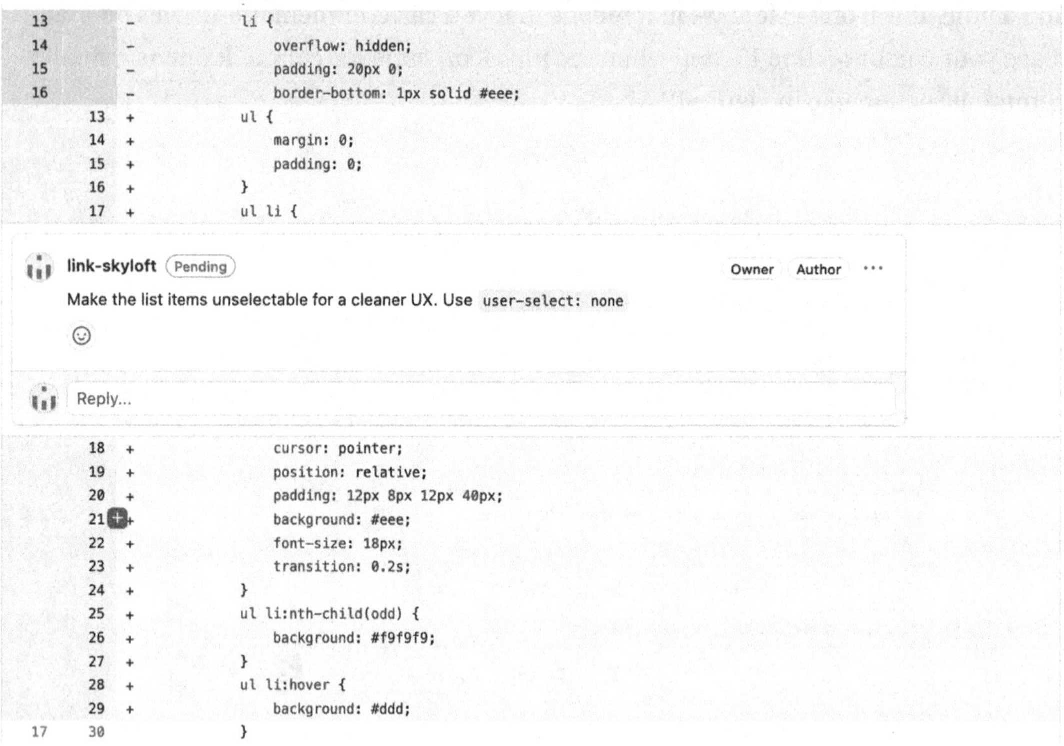

```
13      -           li {
14      -               overflow: hidden;
15      -               padding: 20px 0;
16      -               border-bottom: 1px solid #eee;
     13 +           ul {
     14 +               margin: 0;
     15 +               padding: 0;
     16 +           }
     17 +           ul li {
```

link-skyloft (Pending)   Owner   Author   ···

Make the list items unselectable for a cleaner UX. Use `user-select: none`

☺

Reply...

```
     18 +               cursor: pointer;
     19 +               position: relative;
     20 +               padding: 12px 8px 12px 40px;
     21 +               background: #eee;
     22 +               font-size: 18px;
     23 +               transition: 0.2s;
     24 +           }
     25 +           ul li:nth-child(odd) {
     26 +               background: #f9f9f9;
     27 +           }
     28 +           ul li:hover {
     29 +               background: #ddd;
17   30           }
```

Figure 12-13. *The posted comment*

Using this button, the developer can discuss the comment with the reviewer before reworking the pull request. You can comment more if you want because comments constitute a code review. If you are satisfied, tap the "Finish your review" button at the top of the page. You are again greeted with a small section, similar to the one shown in Figure 12-15.

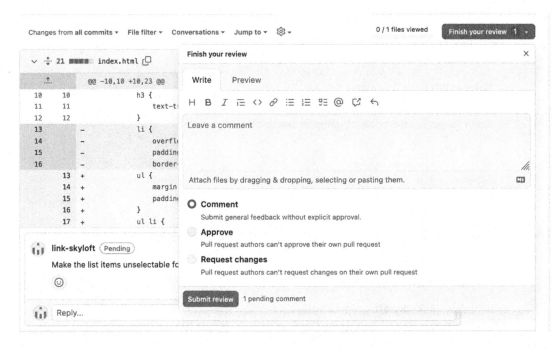

Figure 12-14. *Finishing the review*

Upon finishing the review, you get three choices: Comment, Approve, or Request changes. Since it's your own pull request, you cannot approve or request changes to it. Choose the default option, which is general feedback on the changes. Let's put: "Don't forget to take into account different browsers" as a comment and submit the review. You return to the pull request details page, as shown in Figure 12-15.

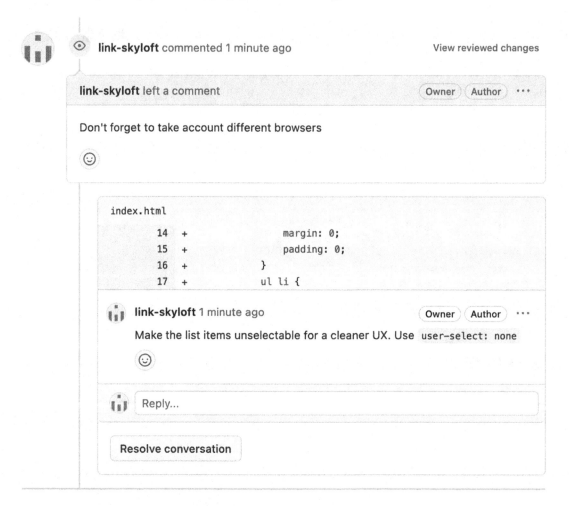

Figure 12-15. *Your completed code review*

The details page shows overall comments and those by the reviewer. Let's address these comments.

Update a Pull Request

The comment left by the reviewer suggested that you should make some changes to the code before the pull request can be accepted. So, let's do that! You must update it by pushing new commits to the patching branch.

Note   The patching branch is also called the *topic branch* because each branch should have its own topic to resolve.

Open index.html once again and change its contents to the following.

```html
<!doctype html>
<html>
    <head>
        <meta charset="utf-8">
        <title>TODO list</title>
        <style>
            h1 {
                text-align:center;
            }
            h3 {
                text-transform: uppercase;
            }
            ul {
                margin: 0;
                padding: 0;
            }
            ul li {
                cursor: pointer;
                position: relative;
                padding: 12px 8px 12px 40px;
                background: #eee;
                font-size: 18px;
                transition: 0.2s;
                -webkit-user-select: none;
```

```
                -moz-user-select: none;
                -ms-user-select: none;
                user-select: none;
            }
            ul li:nth-child(odd) {
                background: #f9f9f9;
            }
            ul li:hover {
                background: #ddd;
            }
        </style>
    </head>
    <body>
        <h1>TODO list</h1>

        <h3>Todo</h3>
        <ul>
            <li>Buy a hat for the bat</li>
            <li>Clear the fogs for the frogs</li>
            <li>Bring a box to the fox</li>
        </ul>

        <h3>Done</h3>
        <ul>
            <li>Put the mittens on the kittens</li>
        </ul>
    </body>
</html>
```

Stage the file again and commit the changes with the message: "Make the list items unselectable". Then, push the branch to GitHub again using the git push origin improve-app-style command.

After you've pushed the branch, return to the Pull Requests page. Notice a new comment on the details page, as shown in Figure 12-16.

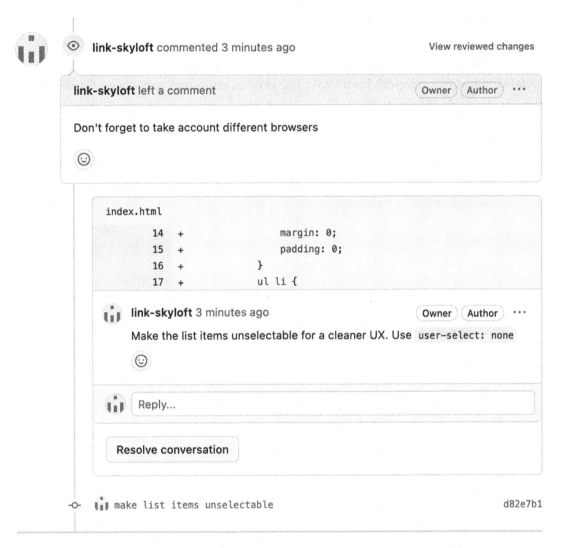

Add more commits by pushing to the **improve-app-style** branch on **link-skyloft/todo-list**.

Figure 12-16. *New changes detected by GitHub*

After each commit you push, GitHub updates the pull request to reflect the changes made to the branch. Click "View changes" to review the new changes. You arrive on the Code Review page again, but this time, you only see the new changes that haven't been reviewed yet. This makes it easier for the reviewer to track the progress of the pull request.

Since there aren't any additional comments, click "Finish review" and provide a general comment. In a work environment, you would have the option to approve the changes, but since you're working alone, leave a general comment like "Good job!" to acknowledge the developer's hard work. The general comment appears on the details page, as shown in Figure 12-17.

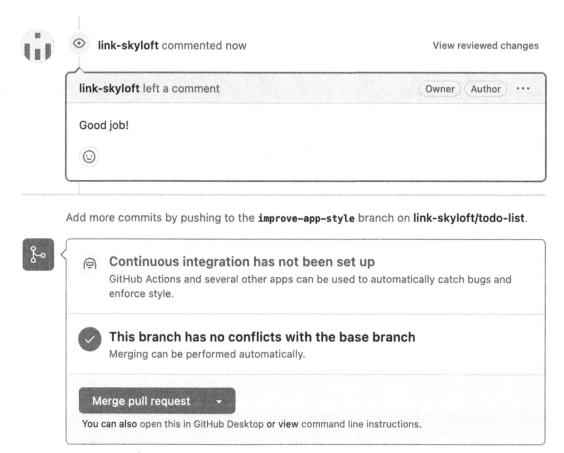

Figure 12-17. *A final comment has been made*

You can safely merge your branch into the base branch because your code has been properly reviewed. Click the big green "Merge pull request" button to accept and merge it. You are asked for confirmation before the branch is merged. After you confirm, the branches are merged, and the pull request is closed. You can even delete the source branch, as Figure 12-18 shows.

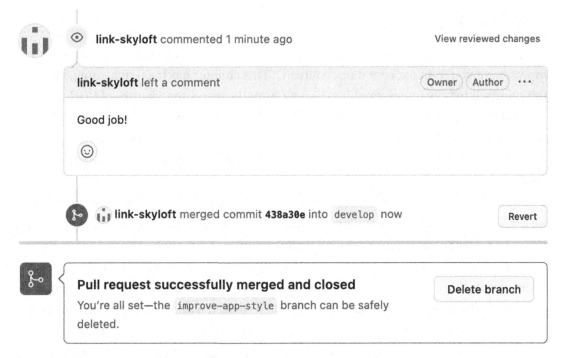

Figure 12-18. *Pull request accepted*

Whether or not you want to delete the branch is up to you. Sometimes, teams don't delete branches until a tester has confirmed that everything is working as expected.

You might wonder why your issue wasn't automatically closed. That's because the issue is associated with the develop branch, which is not the default branch. Only fixes merged into the default branch (main) automatically close issues. But since you're concerned about that issue, let's complete an exercise before moving on to the next chapter.

EXERCISE: MERGE DEVELOP INTO MAIN

Let's pretend a tester tested a new feature and said it was okay to release. So, you must merge the develop into the main branch. The exercise is to do the following.

1. Go back to the project page.

2. Open a pull request to merge develop.

3. Accept the pull request and merge.

Summary

Congratulations on getting your first pull requests accepted! (Although it would be more impressive if you didn't accept them yourself). This chapter has been quite long, but it's important to fully understand it to benefit from the awesome features of GitHub. Remember to open a pull request for your issues instead of committing directly to the `main` branch. Keep in mind that in most professional settings, committing to the `main` branch is discouraged and denied by default in GitHub. Each change should come from a pull request.

You should now be comfortable with using pull requests. If not, consider revisiting the first sections of this chapter. The key thing to remember is that a pull request is just a formal way of requesting permission to apply commits to a branch.

You might have some questions now, like "What if somebody else pushed some changes to the base branch before I completed my pull request?" or "What if someone else modified the same file as me?" or "What if I'm tasked with resolving another issue while I'm working on a pull request?" These are indeed important questions, so they are addressed in the next chapter. You'll learn about merge conflicts and how to resolve them. But first, you'll learn how to avoid them altogether! Let's go!

PART III

Teamwork with Git

## CHAPTER 13

Merge Conflicts

This chapter revisits how branch merging works and discuss some common problems you might encounter in your development journey. You explore the solutions to these problems, particularly when resolving merge conflicts. While merge conflicts can be frustrating, they are a natural part of collaborative development and can be managed effectively. Let's dive into these topics to better understand and address the challenges of working with branches and merging changes.

How Does a Merge Work?

It's important to understand the fundamental purpose of merging in Git. Merging combines the changes made in one branch with another. However, even with careful planning, conflicts can arise when multiple people work on the same file. Git allows for distributed development, meaning each contributor has their own copy of the project and can make changes independently. When these changes conflict, merging is necessary to reconcile the differences.

A key principle to remember is that you should only merge a branch when you are certain that the commits in that branch are final and the work is complete. Merging incomplete or unfinished work can lead to confusion and disrupt the clarity of your project's history. It's acceptable to open a pull request for review even if you don't intend to merge it immediately, but merging should be reserved for fully completed work. This ensures that your project's history remains coherent and understandable.

© Mariot Tsitoara 2024
M. Tsitoara, *Beginning Git and GitHub*, https://doi.org/10.1007/979-8-8688-0215-7_13

Pulling

Let's revisit the pulling command once again. Pulling means copying a remote branch to the local repository. For example, you have merged a branch into develop and main but have not made any changes to the local branches. This means that you are "behind" in the history timeline because there are commits in the remote repository that you don't have.

The word *behind* is a bit of a misnomer because, as established, every repository is independent, and there are no central repositories in Git. A main remote repository makes team collaboration easier. However, in practice, you can exchange commits as you like; the concept of being "behind" was introduced to simplify developers' workflows.

Let's attempt to pull the main branch into the local repository. Please ensure that you have completed the exercise from the last chapter (merging develop into main) before proceeding with the steps in this chapter. First, check out your local main branch and ensure it's clean.

```
$ git checkout main
$ git status
```

If you haven't made any unexpected changes in your working directory, you should see the same result depicted in Figure 13-1: a clean directory.

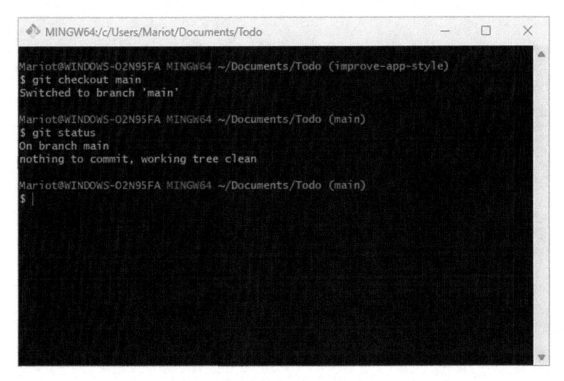

Figure 13-1. *A clean directory is needed before a pull*

Now, let's check the history log before making any changes.

```
$ git log --online
```

This displays the commit history of the main branch, which does not include the recent changes you made because those changes are currently only in the remote repository. The main branch's history log should resemble the one shown in Figure 13-2.

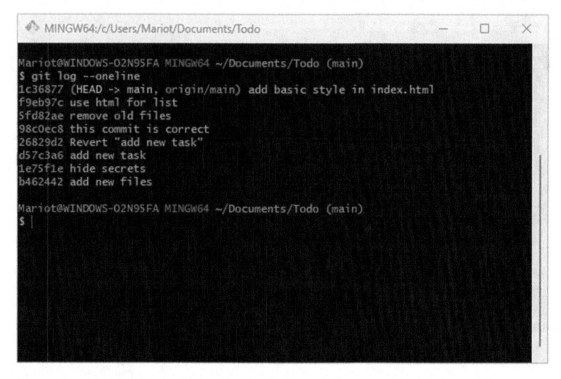

Figure 13-2. *The history log before the pull*

Figure 13-2 shows that the HEAD is pointing to the branch's last commit (most of the time, it is that way). According to this result, the local main branch and the remote main branch are on the same level, meaning they contain the same commits. However, you know that this isn't true because you've made changes on the remote main branch. Your local Git repository doesn't know this because you haven't yet fetched any commits from the server. Let's do that.

As you saw in the last chapter, the pull and push commands work the same way: you need to provide the remote repository name and the remote branch name as parameters. So, the command is as follows.

```
$ git pull origin main
```

After executing this code on a clean working directory, you get the result shown in Figure 13-3.

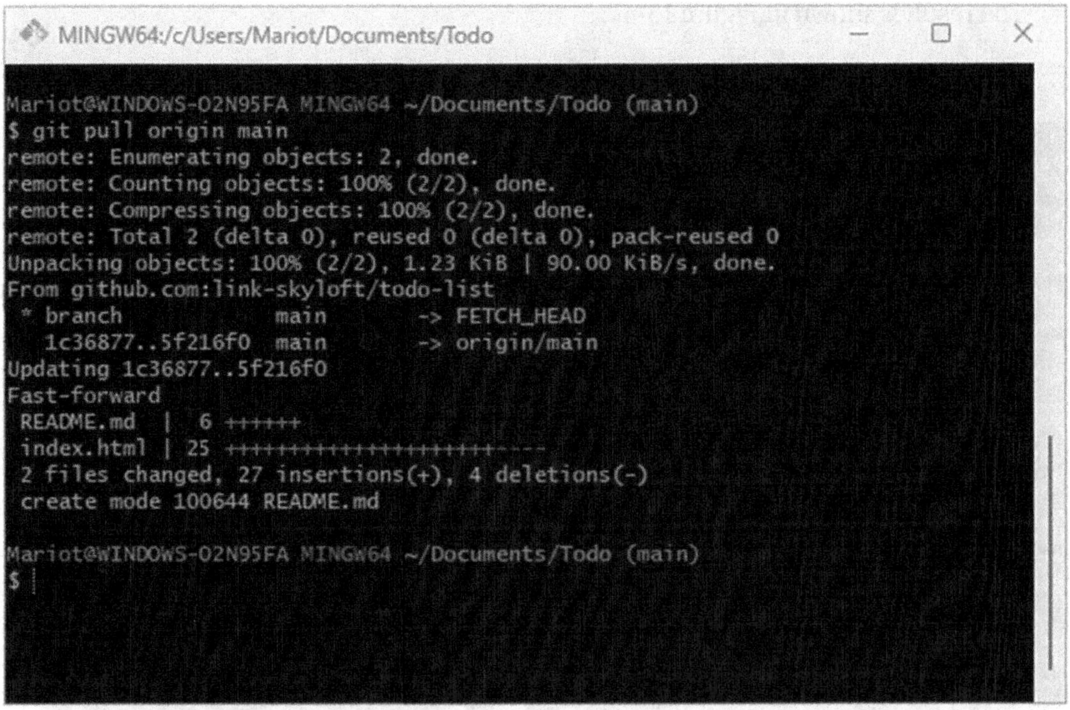

```
Mariot@WINDOWS-02N95FA MINGW64 ~/Documents/Todo (main)
$ git pull origin main
remote: Enumerating objects: 2, done.
remote: Counting objects: 100% (2/2), done.
remote: Compressing objects: 100% (2/2), done.
remote: Total 2 (delta 0), reused 0 (delta 0), pack-reused 0
Unpacking objects: 100% (2/2), 1.23 KiB | 90.00 KiB/s, done.
From github.com:link-skyloft/todo-list
 * branch            main        -> FETCH_HEAD
   1c36877..5f216f0  main        -> origin/main
Updating 1c36877..5f216f0
Fast-forward
 README.md  |  6 ++++++
 index.html | 25 +++++++++++++++++++++++----
 2 files changed, 27 insertions(+), 4 deletions(-)
 create mode 100644 README.md

Mariot@WINDOWS-02N95FA MINGW64 ~/Documents/Todo (main)
$
```

Figure 13-3. Pulling main from origin

Fast-Forward Merge

After you've pulled main from origin, you receive a summary of the operation. This summary includes the number of files changed and the type of merging performed. In this case, it is a fast-forward merge, which is the easiest type. A fast-forward merge occurs when the commits on the remote branch are on the same timeline as the local branch. Consequently, Git only needs to move HEAD to the last commit of the origin branch. Recall the discussion on commits being linked to one another through parent-child relationships. If Git recognizes this link between the commits on the first branch and the branch to be merged, it performs a fast-forward merge. Only a pointer move is necessary, making Git very efficient. You should always aim to use fast-forward merging because it's the easiest and, most importantly, the cleanest method for the history log.

Speaking of the history log, let's check it to see the changes you've fetched from the server. Once again, use the --oneline option to obtain a more readable result.

```
$ git log --oneline
```

The result is shown in Figure 13-4.

```
MINGW64:/c/Users/Mariot/Documents/Todo                          —    □    ×

Mariot@WINDOWS-O2N95FA MINGW64 ~/Documents/Todo (main)
$ git log --oneline
5f216f0 (HEAD -> main, origin/main) Merge pull request #3 from link-skyloft/deve
lop
438a30e Merge pull request #2 from link-skyloft/improve-app-style
d82e7b1 (origin/improve-app-style, improve-app-style) make list items unselectab
le
9e93169 add basic color
2fe8611 (origin/develop, develop) Add techs used
1c36877 add basic style in index.html
f9eb97c use html for list
5fd82ae remove old files
98c0ec8 this commit is correct
26829d2 Revert "add new task"
d57c3a6 add new task
1e75f1e hide secrets
b462442 add new files

Mariot@WINDOWS-O2N95FA MINGW64 ~/Documents/Todo (main)
$
```

Figure 13-4. *History log after pulling from origin*

You have additional commits now! Commits from the remote branch have been merged into your local branch. Consequently, your local main branch now points to the same commit as the origin branch.

Let's break this down. First, let's discuss the branch colors. Green branches represent your local branches, while red branches are remote branches. Remote branches have two names, as their names are combined with the remote repository name.

You can observe that improve-readme-description, develop, and origin/develop are at the same level. You know this is not correct because you made changes to develop on GitHub. Git won't know these changes until you pull the develop branch from origin.

You'll also notice there are commits in this history that you didn't make. Specifically, "Merge pull request #3 from link-skyloft/develop" and "Merge pull request #2 from link-skyloft/improve-app-style". These are called *merge commits*, which Git creates when you merge two or more commits. This project merges improve-app-style into develop and develop into main. Each of these merges generates a merge commit.

Like regular commits, you can view more information about them using the `git show` command. Let's examine the details of the first merge commit.

```
$ git show 438a30e
```

This results in a familiar view: the commit intel view. You should get the same result shown in Figure 13-5.

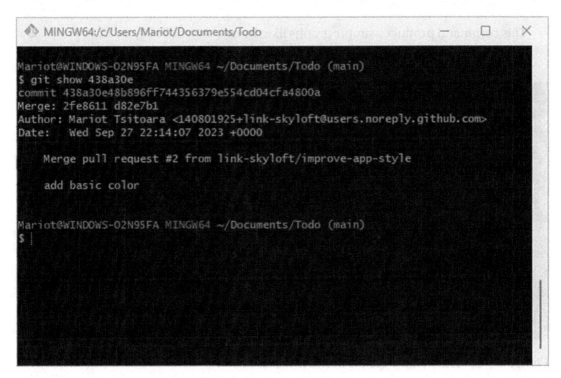

Figure 13-5. A detailed view of a merge commit

This view might not seem particularly interesting as it primarily displays the commit parents and the user who performed the merge. However, it's important to note that the committer and the merger can be different individuals. Additionally, it's advisable to include keywords for resolving issues in the merge commit message rather than in the commit messages themselves. Most of the time, a single commit won't be sufficient to address a problem, so including these keywords in the pull request message ensures that the issue is only closed when the branch is merged.

The history log displayed in Figure 13-4 is visually appealing but doesn't effectively illustrate the concept of branches and merges. To get a more appropriate representation, you can use the `--graph` parameter with `--oneline` when using the `git log` command. This combination provides a graph-style view of your commit history, making it easier to understand branching and merging.

```
$ git log --oneline --graph
```

This command produces simple graphs like the one shown in Figure 13-6.

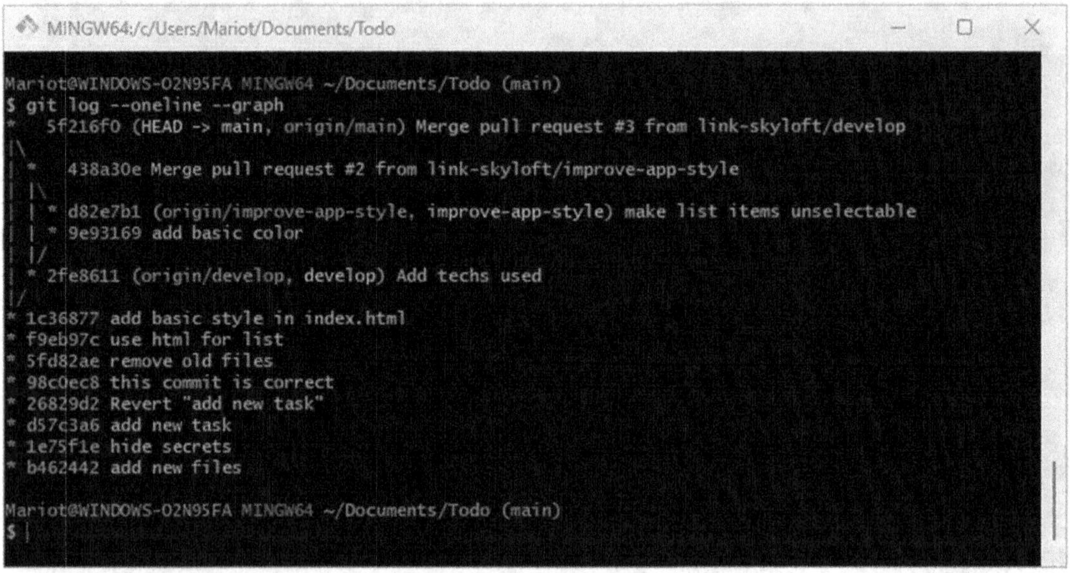

Figure 13-6. *The history graph of the project*

The log graph indeed provides a more detailed history of your project. Each asterisk represents a commit, as usual, but there's a new element shown on this graph: branches. You can see how the project's history has diverged and merged over time. For example, you diverged from the main branch to create the develop branch, which in turn diverged to form the improve-app-style branch. Commits were made to this branch before merging it back into develop. Finally, the develop branch was merged into the main branch.

When working on a project with many branches and frequent merges (as you should in a collaborative environment), the graph view is more helpful than the traditional view. It provides a clearer visual representation of your project's history, and the use of colors can make it even more intuitive.

If you want to maintain a cleaner history log, consider deleting the local `improve-app-style` branch, especially if it's no longer needed for your current work. However, ensure that you've already pushed any relevant changes to the remote repository or merged them into other branches before deleting the branch locally.

```
$ git branch -D improve-app-style
```

Deleting an already merged branch carries little risk, but many developers avoid it in case they need to revisit it later. Most of the time, this situation doesn't arise. A good rule of thumb is to delete branches only when you're certain you won't need to check them out again for testing or other purposes.

What is demonstrated here is the simplest form of merging: a fast-forward. However, you're in a completely separate context after you've diverged from a branch, as you did with `main` and `develop`. You won't automatically receive updates from the other branches; you need to request them explicitly. This also means that the other branches evolve independently of your branch. When you create a pull request on a branch, that branch may have already changed. For instance, multiple contributors can create new branches from `develop` and work on their respective issues. These issues may not be resolved simultaneously, so each pull request is accepted one after the other. This is where the challenge arises: your target branch can change independently while you're working on your issue. The reality you're working with might evolve when you finish your changes. Perhaps multiple people have modified the same files in their respective branches. These situations occur frequently in your career, and often, a pull request won't go as smoothly as ours did in this chapter. These challenges are known as *conflicts*, and learning how to resolve them is crucial to your Git journey. Let's delve into it!

Merge Conflicts

The best way to understand merge conflicts is to create one. So, let's deliberately introduce a conflict into the project! First, ensure that you're on your local `develop` branch. Since you haven't made any changes to this branch, it should still be clean.

```
$ git checkout develop
```

Next, let's check the history log to see the current state of the branch.

```
$ git log --oneline --graph
```

You get the same result because you haven't pulled from "origin" yet. The result is depicted in Figure 13-7.

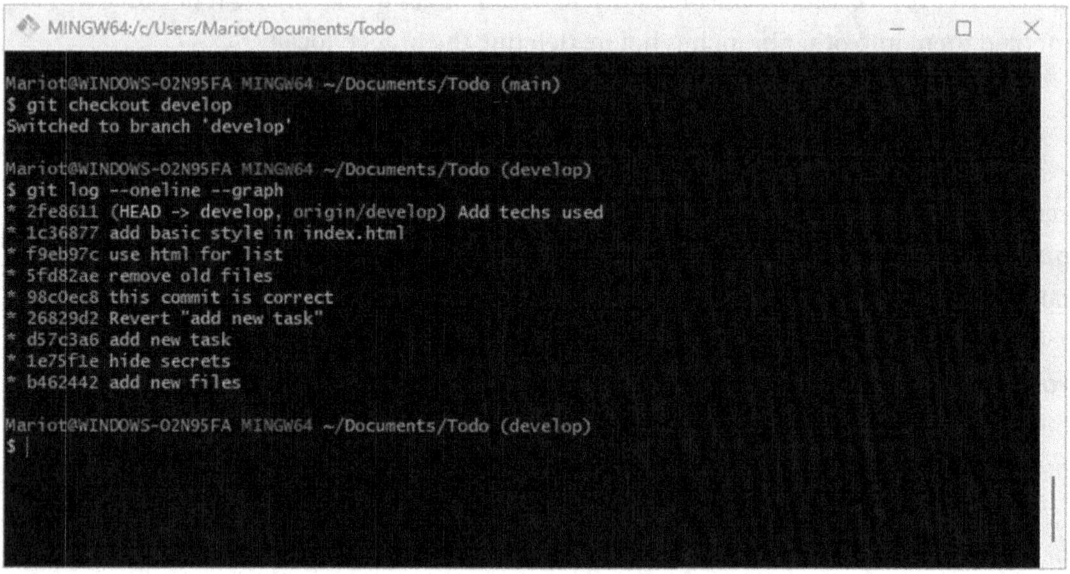

Figure 13-7. *develop history log before pull*

There is nothing spectacular here—just a good old log without any problems. Since you deleted the improve-readme-description branch, no branch is left in the develop history log.

The log says that develop and origin/develop are in the same state, but this isn't true because you made changes on GitHub. But instead of pulling from origin, let's make changes in the branch first—changes that cause conflicts with the changes from origin.

Open index.html and replace its contents with the following code.

```
<!doctype html>
<html>
    <head>
        <meta charset="utf-8">
        <title>TODO list</title>
        <style>
            h1 {
                text-align: left;
            }
```

```
    h3 {
        text-transform: capitalize;
    }
    li {
        overflow: hidden;
        padding: 22px 0;
        border-bottom: 2px solid #eee;
    }
    </style>
</head>
<body>
    <h1>TODO list</h1>

    <h3>Todo</h3>
    <ul>
        <li>Buy a hat for the bat</li>
        <li>Clear the fogs for the frogs</li>
        <li>Bring a box to the fox</li>
    </ul>

    <h3>Done</h3>
    <ul>
        <li>Put the mittens on the kittens</li>
    </ul>
</body>
</html>
```

Run git diff to review your changes. These were only small changes, so it shouldn't be a big deal, right?

```
$ git diff
```

The result is very familiar because you see it all the time on GitHub and with git show. Your result should be the same as mine, as shown in Figure 13-8.

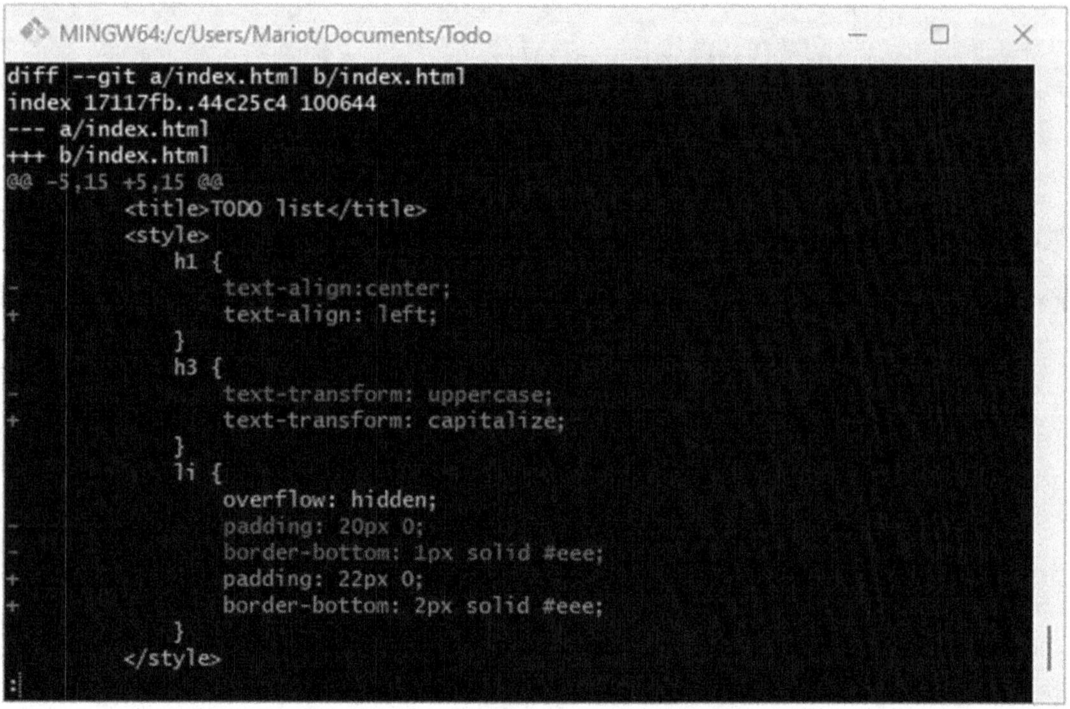

```
MINGW64:/c/Users/Mariot/Documents/Todo                                    —    □    ✕

diff --git a/index.html b/index.html
index 17117fb..44c25c4 100644
--- a/index.html
+++ b/index.html
@@ -5,15 +5,15 @@
            <title>TODO list</title>
            <style>
               h1 {
-                   text-align:center;
+                   text-align: left;
               }
               h3 {
-                   text-transform: uppercase;
+                   text-transform: capitalize;
               }
               li {
                   overflow: hidden;
-                  padding: 20px 0;
-                  border-bottom: 1px solid #eee;
+                  padding: 22px 0;
+                  border-bottom: 2px solid #eee;
               }
            </style>
:
```

Figure 13-8. *Difference between develop and the working directory*

Nothing new here. Let's add the changed file to the staging area and then commit the current project.

```
$ git add index.html
```

Tip   Is opening your text editor for each commit tiresome? Well, you can skip it if you are in a hurry. To commit the project while skipping the commit message editing phase, you can pass the commit message as a parameter.

```
$ git commit -m "<commit_message>"
```

Don't forget the -m!

```
$ git commit -m "Change CSS to introduce conflicts"
```

Caution   Using the shorthand form of the `git commit` command can save you a few seconds, but it also makes it easier to make mistakes because you won't have the chance to review your changes before committing. I highly suggest only using it when you have only one changed file. Plus, you can't use it to write a multiline commit message.

This won't produce any results that you haven't seen before. Figure 13-9 shows a standard result because there is no conflict yet.

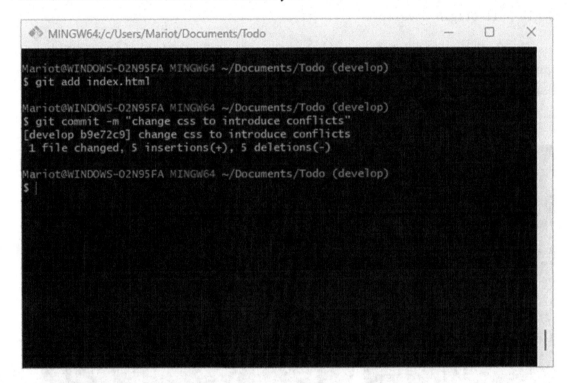

Figure 13-9. *The commit that introduces conflicts*

To produce the conflict, you need to retrieve the commits you pushed to develop when merging a branch into it.

Pulling Commits from origin

You've already seen the pull command in action, but in this scenario, you encounter a little problem: you've made changes to the same file in different commits. This leads to conflicts that must be resolved before you can complete the pull operation. Don't forget that pulling means copying remote commits into your local repository.

Let's start by directly pulling the develop branch from origin. Again, the command is very similar to the push command. You need to specify the remote repository and branch name.

```
$ git pull origin develop
```

The result is quite different from what you've seen earlier. Instead of a successful merge, you encounter a conflict, and the repository is now in a state where it's stuck between two conflicting versions. Figure 13-10 shows an example of this.

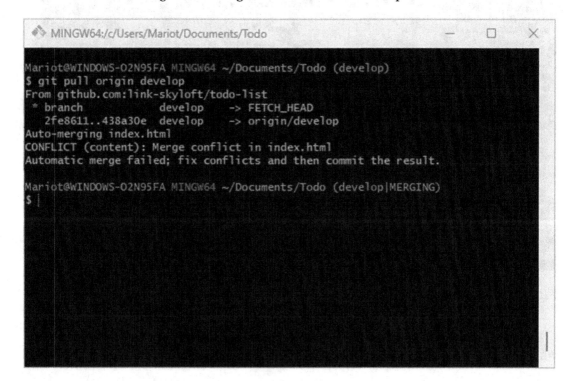

Figure 13-10. *Merge conflict during the pull command*

Let's break down the result step by step. First, the URL is being used for the pull, which is straightforward.

Next, you encounter the first action performed by Git, which is called *fetch*. Its role is to copy the selected branch from the remote repository to the local repository. This branch is then stored in a temporary storage area called FETCH_HEAD. Just like HEAD refers to the last commit you are working from, FETCH_HEAD references the tip of the branch that you just fetched from origin.

The following action is a basic merge, like you've seen before. You fetched the remote branch, and it's time to merge it with the current branch. The details of the action specify the branches being merged, which are develop and origin/develop. It even specifies the commits that would be used. Your commit names are different, but to verify the first commit, you can use the following command to check the commit log.

```
$ git log --oneline
```

You find the commit name on the second to last commit, as shown in Figure 13-11.

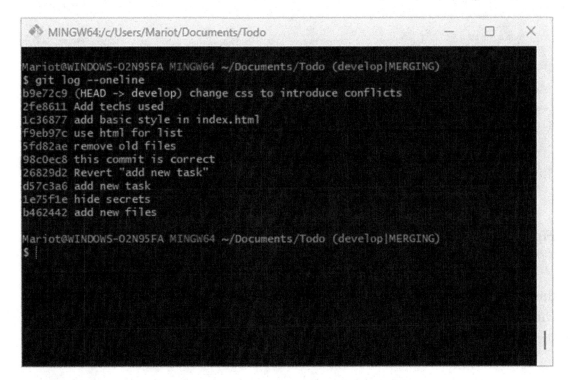

Figure 13-11. *The second to last commit is used for the merge*

Note that the merge won't use the last commit because that's the commit you are currently working on, the one that introduced the changes.

Figure 13-10 also references another commit for the merge, and you can find that commit on `origin/develop`. Select the `develop` branch to see the history log of the remote branch on your project page on GitHub. Alternatively, you can directly access it using your GitHub link, such as `https://github.com/link-skyloft/todo-list/commits/develop`. This provides you with a view of the latest commits, as shown in Figure 13-12.

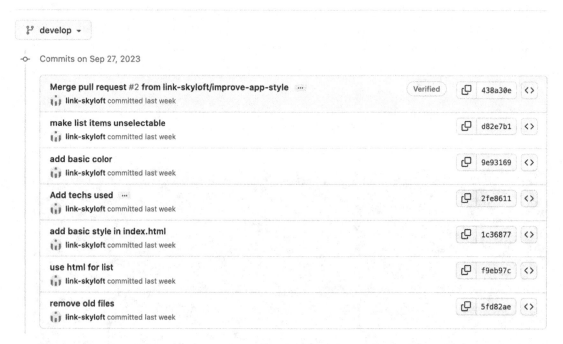

Figure 13-12. *The commits on origin/develop*

As you can see, the second commit referenced in Figure 13-10 is the latest commit of the remote branch, the one that was created by the previous merge on GitHub. You can click it and access the commit details to gather even more information. You can refer to Figure 13-13 for an example of this.

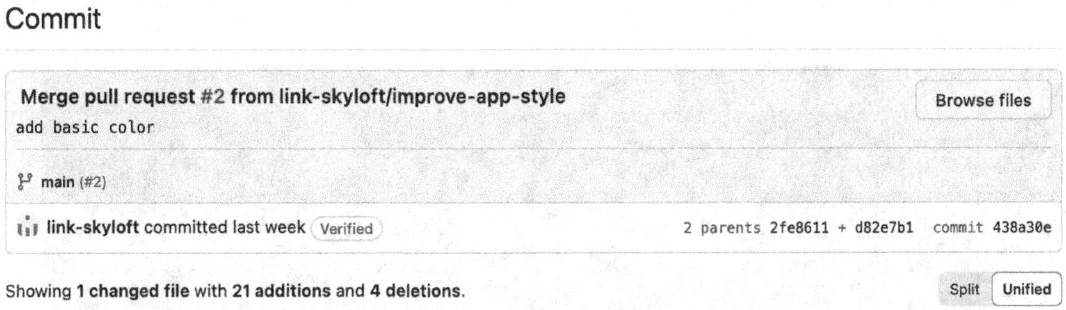

Commit

Merge pull request #2 from link-skyloft/improve-app-style	Browse files
add basic color	

ᛋ **main** (#2)

ᵢᵢᵢ **link-skyloft** committed last week (Verified)   2 parents `2fe8611` + `d82e7b1` `commit` `438a30e`

Showing **1 changed file** with **21 additions** and **4 deletions**.   Split Unified

Figure 13-13. *More info on the merge commit*

Figure 13-13 shows that this commit has two parents because it's a commit created by merging two branches. One of the parents is also referenced in Figure 13-10 because it was the last commit pushed before you merged the branches on GitHub.

Now, let's return to Figure 13-10. In the next part of the result, Git attempts to merge the branches automatically. This usually goes smoothly when different files or different parts of the files have been changed in the branches to be merged. However, in this case, conflicts were found, so the merge failed. It's now up to you to resolve these conflicts.

Git tried to merge the local `develop` branch with `FETCH_HEAD`. Because both branches contain changes to the same parts of the `index.html` file, you must decide which changes to keep. You'll see how to do that in the next section.

The last information to note from Figure 13-10 is the state of the local repository. If you look at the left part of the console, you'll see that the repository is in the `develop|MERGING` state instead of the standard `develop` branch. This indicates that there are unresolved conflicts in the project, and the merge (and, by extension, the pull) is not complete. You can use the `git status` command to get more information about the current state of the repository.

```
$ git status
```

This provide you with a new result that you haven't seen before, as shown in Figure 13-14.

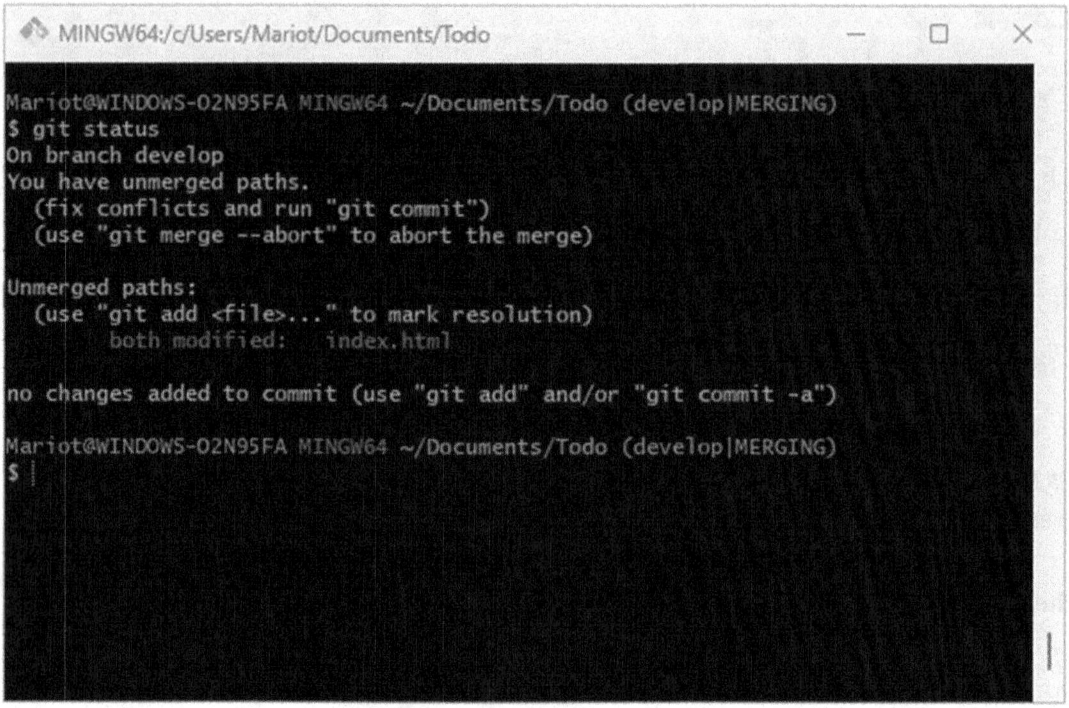

Figure 13-14. *Status of the merge*

This result is quite straightforward and provides helpful guidance for the next steps. First, it advises on what to do: resolve conflicts and commit the project. Additionally, it mentions a way to abort the current merge if you decide to give up on resolving the conflicts. In some cases, this can be a good option because you can work on the local branch to resolve the conflicts before attempting the merge again. For example, you could abort this merge, revert the commit that introduced the conflicts, and then pull again. This would result in an automatic merge without any conflicts. However, for the sake of learning, let's resolve the conflicts the hard way!

Next, there's a list of files affected by the merge. In this case, only index.html is involved and has been modified in both branches. Let's open this file to examine the conflicts. You'll see substantial changes in it, as shown in Figures 13-15 and 13-16.

Figure 13-15. *index.html in Visual Studio Code*

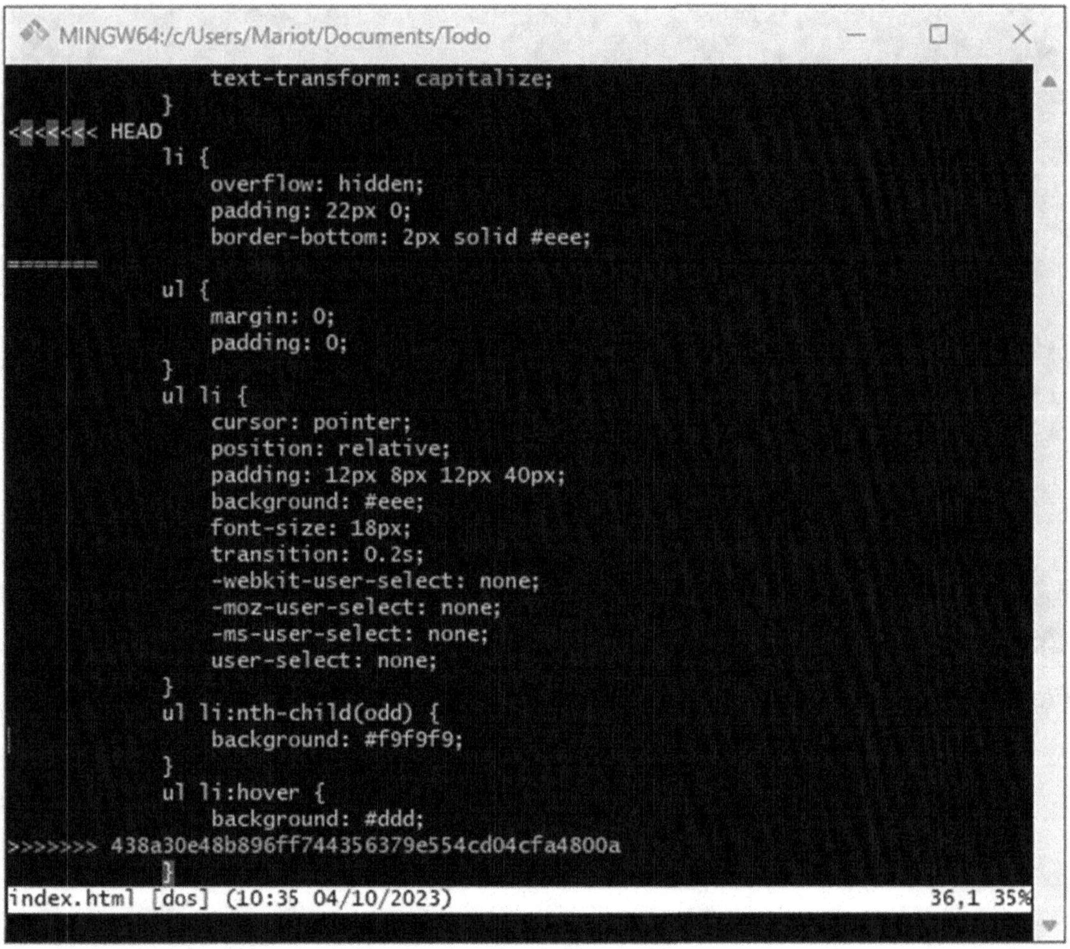
MINGW64:/c/Users/Mariot/Documents/Todo
text-transform: capitalize;
}
<<<<<<< HEAD
li {
overflow: hidden;
padding: 22px 0;
border-bottom: 2px solid #eee;
=======
ul {
margin: 0;
padding: 0;
}
ul li {
cursor: pointer;
position: relative;
padding: 12px 8px 12px 40px;
background: #eee;
font-size: 18px;
transition: 0.2s;
-webkit-user-select: none;
-moz-user-select: none;
-ms-user-select: none;
user-select: none;
}
ul li:nth-child(odd) {
background: #f9f9f9;
}
ul li:hover {
background: #ddd;
>>>>>>> 438a30e48b896ff744356379e554cd04cfa4800a
}
index.html [dos] (10:35 04/10/2023)
36,1 35%

Figure 13-16. *index.html in vim*

You'll notice the three prominent lines that divide your code within the file. These lines are consistent in every code conflict but might appear differently depending on your text editor. For instance, an integrated development environment (IDE) like Visual Studio Code may render the code with different colors and even provide buttons to interact with the code, as shown in Figure 13-15. On the other hand, a basic text editor might display these lines as regular lines of code, potentially disrupting your color scheme. In Figure 13-16, I used Vim without additional tools, resulting in a more straightforward rendering. However, there are many plugins available to enhance this experience.

Resolving Merge Conflicts

Let's start by explaining the meaning of those three lines. The "<<<<<<<" and ">>>>>>>" lines delineate the region where a conflict exists. It's important to note that a file can have multiple conflicting regions.

These regions are separated by the "=======" line, which displays the code from the two branches. The first part represents the code from your current branch, while the second part represents the code from the branch you're attempting to merge.

To resolve the merge conflict, you need to edit the file so that only one changeset remains. This doesn't necessarily mean you must choose between the two changesets; you need to combine them into one coherent code. In this case, retaining most of the second part is advisable since those changes have already been reviewed and accepted. However, there might be some elements from the first part that should be incorporated.

To achieve this, copy the code you need from the first part and paste it into the second part. The resulting code should look like the following.

```
<!doctype html>
<html>
    <head>
        <meta charset="utf-8">
        <title>TODO list</title>
        <style>
            h1 {
                text-align: left;
            }
            h3 {
                text-transform: capitalize;
            }
<<<<<<< HEAD
            li {
                overflow: hidden;
                padding: 22px 0;
                border-bottom: 2px solid #eee;

=======
```

```
        ul {
            margin: 0;
            padding: 0;
        }
        ul li {
            cursor: pointer;
            position: relative;
            padding: 12px 8px 12px 40px;
            background: #eee;
            font-size: 18px;
            transition: 0.2s;
            -webkit-user-select: none;
            -moz-user-select: none;
            -ms-user-select: none;
            user-select: none;
            overflow: hidden;
        }
        ul li:nth-child(odd) {
            background: #f9f9f9;
        }
        ul li:hover {
            background: #ddd;
>>>>>>> 33753ecaebae2ba1c3ffdc1e543d372385884c78
        }
    </style>
  </head>
  <body>
    <h1>TODO list</h1>

    <h3>Todo</h3>
    <ul>
        <li>Buy a hat for the bat</li>
        <li>Clear the fogs for the frogs</li>
        <li>Bring a box to the fox</li>
    </ul>
```

```
    <h3>Done</h3>
    <ul>
        <li>Put the mittens on the kittens</li>
    </ul>
  </body>
</html>
```

You've only copied one line from the first part since the second part was already almost complete. Now, it's time to clean the file of unnecessary parts. First, you can remove the first part of the code conflict (between "<<<<<<<" and "=======") because you don't need it anymore. Then, you can simply remove the remaining line (">>>>>>>") because it doesn't make sense to keep it. The file then looks like the following.

```
<!doctype html>
<html>
    <head>
        <meta charset="utf-8">
        <title>TODO list</title>
        <style>
            h1 {
                text-align: left;
            }
            h3 {
                text-transform: capitalize;
            }
            ul {
                margin: 0;
                padding: 0;
            }
            ul li {
                cursor: pointer;
                position: relative;
                padding: 12px 8px 12px 40px;
                background: #eee;
                font-size: 18px;
                transition: 0.2s;
```

```
                -webkit-user-select: none;
                -moz-user-select: none;
                -ms-user-select: none;
                user-select: none;
                overflow: hidden;
            }
            ul li:nth-child(odd) {
                background: #f9f9f9;
            }
            ul li:hover {
                background: #ddd;
            }
        </style>
    </head>
    <body>
        <h1>TODO list</h1>

        <h3>Todo</h3>
        <ul>
            <li>Buy a hat for the bat</li>
            <li>Clear the fogs for the frogs</li>
            <li>Bring a box to the fox</li>
        </ul>

        <h3>Done</h3>
        <ul>
            <li>Put the mittens on the kittens</li>
        </ul>
    </body>
</html>
```

The file is back to normal, with a merged version of the conflicting codes and no more of those three big lines. Now, you can continue the merge process. If you forgot the next step, you could run git status again (see Figure 13-14).

So, now that the file is ready, you must stage it.

```
$ git add index.html
```

After that, you must commit the project as usual.

```
$ git commit
```

You are greeted by the familiar commit message view, but with a little twist: the commit message is already written. Figure 13-17 shows an example of this.

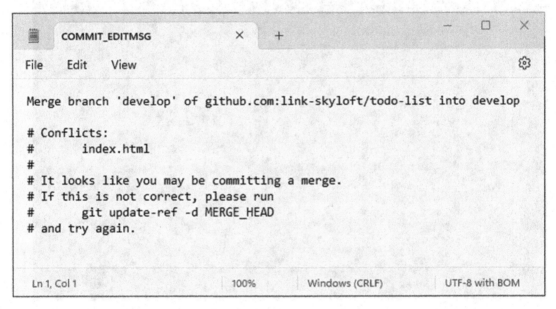

Figure 13-17. *The default commit message*

Of course, you can always modify the commit message, but I suggest leaving the default one unless you follow a personal or company guideline. You can save the commit message and move on.

If you look at the command result (see Figure 13-18), you see that you are back on the develop branch and no longer in the merging state.

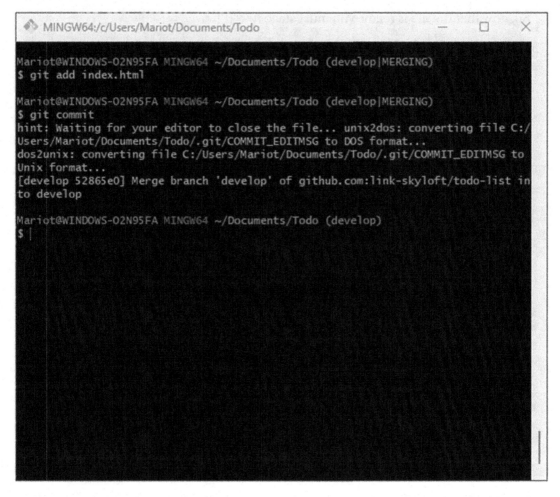

Figure 13-18. *Back to normal state*

You can also check if the merge has been completed by checking the history log. Make sure to add a graph option for a beautiful result.

```
$ git log --oneline --graph
```

This produces this stunning visual shown in Figure 13-19.

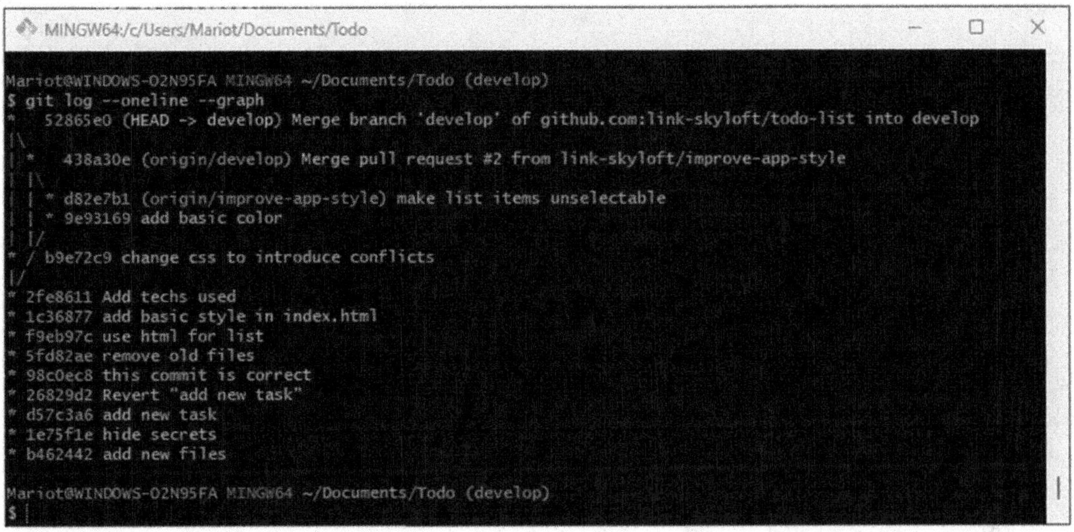

Figure 13-19. *The recent history of the project*

You can see on that graph that when the origin/develop branch was merged, all its history was imported. So, it seems like there is a branch from a branch. In big Git projects, it happens all the time.

Summary

Congratulations on completing this chapter! You've learned about pulling code from a remote server, handling merge conflicts when two branches modify the same code, and resolving those conflicts.

Remember that pulling involves two steps: fetching, which copies the remote branch into a temporary branch, and merging, which combines the temporary branch with the current one. When conflicts arise, you must manually decide which code to keep, stage the changes, and commit them.

Merge conflicts can be frustrating, but they are a common part of working with Git. In the next chapter, you'll learn how to reduce the occurrence of conflicts and manage branches more effectively. Keep up the good work!

CHAPTER 14

More About Conflicts

The last chapter was intense, wasn't it? It talked about what merge conflicts are and when they would happen. You also saw how to resolve them manually. Don't worry. This chapter is much easier to digest. It covers how to push your branch to remote after a merge conflict. Also, you will see some strategies to adopt to reduce the number of conflicts that might happen. Let's go!

Pushing After a Conflict Resolution

I've made some grammar and style improvements to the text. Here's the revised version.

As you saw in the earlier chapters, pushing means copying the local commits to a remote branch. This means that every commit you have locally is applied to the remote repository.

You learned in the last section that a pull action is just two actions executed one after the other: a fetch action that copies the remote branch into a temporary location and a merge action that merges the temporary branch with the local one. Since the pull and push actions are essentially the same but in different directions, they work similarly when pushing your local branch to origin.

So, a push action is divided into two parts: the copy of your local branch to the remote and the merging of the branches. The only difference between push and pull actions is who initiates the action: you or the server.

Under normal circumstances, the push goes smoothly because the merge is automatically performed using *fast-forward*, which is possible when the commits on your local branch can be directly linked to the commits on the remote branch. For example, simply adding commits one after another to the `main` branch (like you've done until now) and then pushing them results in a fast-forward merge, with no need to create a merge commit.

© Mariot Tsitoara 2024
M. Tsitoara, *Beginning Git and GitHub*, https://doi.org/10.1007/979-8-8688-0215-7_14

It also happens in this situation since you've only added new commits to the develop branch. You won't encounter any problems unless you or someone else tampered with the commit history in the past. Never attempt to do this.

With that said, let's push the develop branch using the usual command.

```
$ git push origin develop
```

As expected, you get the usual result shown in Figure 14-1.

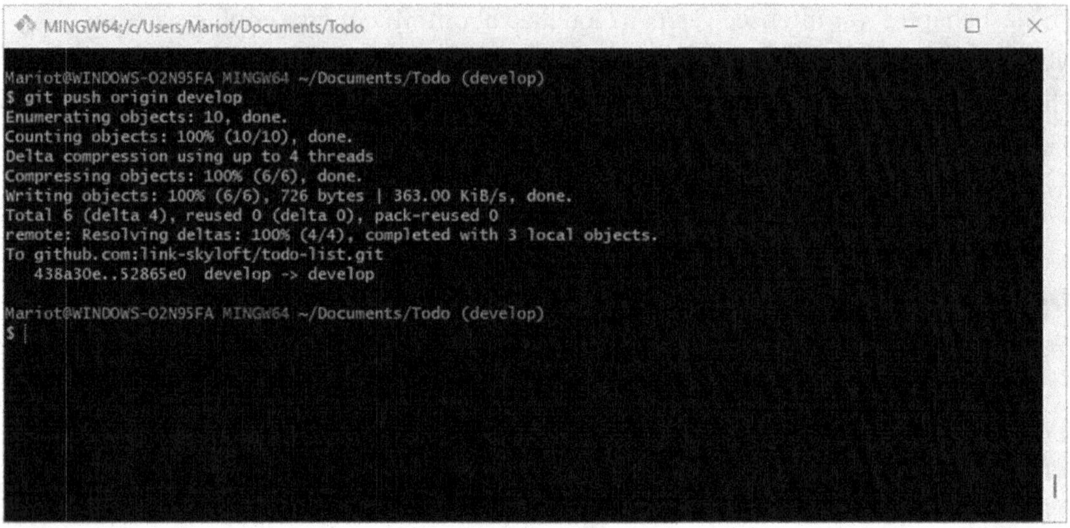

Figure 14-1. *Pushing the develop branch*

In conclusion, pushing a branch back to origin after pulling and merging the changes shouldn't lead to unexpected behavior unless someone has tampered with the commit history.

Review Changes Before Merging

Before attempting any merge, reviewing all the changes your branch introduces is crucial. This step should not be ignored, as it can save you countless hours of battling with Git.

Check the Branch Location

First, ensure that you are in the correct branch location. You must have the target branch checked out to merge two branches together. For instance, if you intend to merge develop into main, you should first check out main. The commands would be as follows (please don't execute the second command at this moment).

```
$ git checkout main
$ git merge develop
```

Review the Branch Differences

Reviewing differences is not limited to commits; you can also use it to check the variances between two branches. This is particularly helpful in delicate situations like merging. The command is relatively straightforward.

```
$ git diff branch1..branch2
```

Take note of the two dots between the two branch names. This command displays the differences between the two branches in a familiar diff view. Let's compare develop to main.

```
$ git diff main..develop
```

The result is quite like the diff output when comparing commits. Refer to Figure 14-2 as an example.

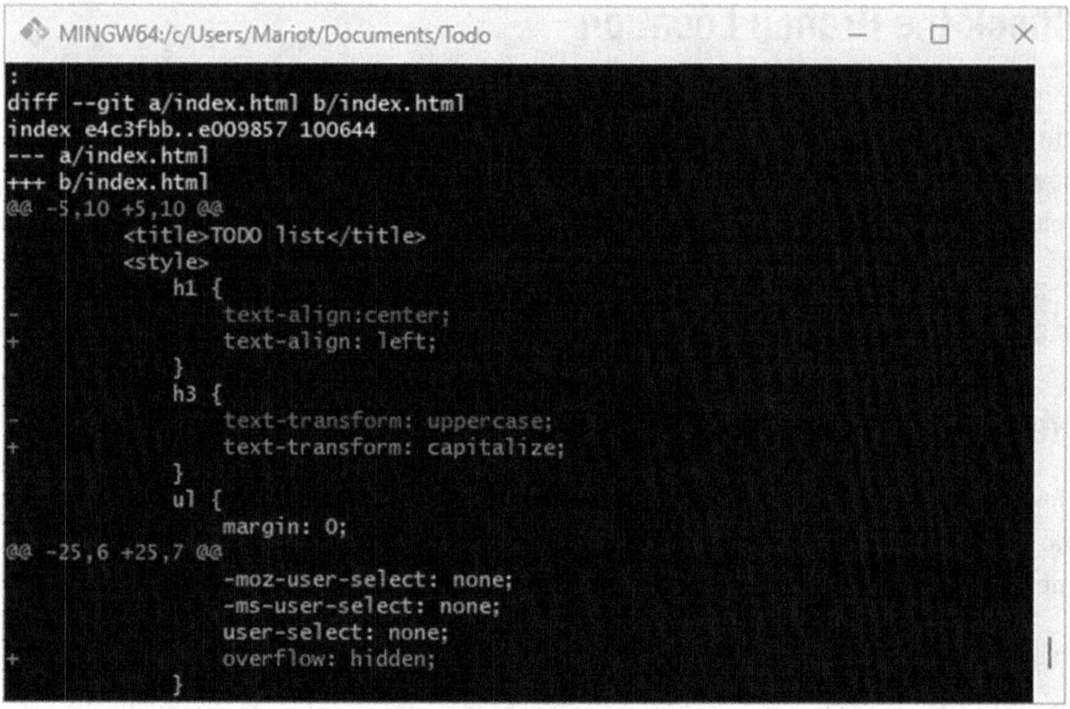

Figure 14-2. *Differences between branches*

If you've made numerous changes and don't want to scroll through them all in the terminal, you can also view them on GitHub. Simply push the branch and open a pull request!

Merging

You've learned various concepts about Git merges, but let's summarize them to better understand this feature. As discussed, merging involves combining two branches or, more accurately, integrating the changes from one branch into another.

Branches can be created from any other branch, and once a branch is created, it becomes independent from its parent branch. Changes made in one branch do not immediately affect the other; they remain separate until it's time to merge.

Consider a scenario where you create a child branch and make commits on that new branch. When it's time to merge, several situations can arise.

- No changes in parent branch: If the parent branch hasn't changed (no new commits have been made), and you attempt to merge, Git performs a `fast-forward` merge. Technically, this isn't a merge but a reference change in Git. Git moves the reference of the parent branch forward, effectively appending the commits from the child branch to the parent branch. This is the easiest type of `merge` but is less common, especially in collaborative settings.

- Parent branch has changes: If the parent branch has changed (received new commits), a fast-forward merge is not possible. Instead, a true merge, or a three-way merge, occurs. This type of merge was discussed in the last chapter. It creates a new commit that incorporates all the changes from the child branch and appends this commit to the parent branch. This new commit is called a *merge commit*, it has two parents: one from the parent branch and one from the child branch. A conflict can arise if different commits in both branches modify the same lines of code, requiring the developer to manually select which changes to keep.

In essence, merges are a sophisticated way of creating commits that contain all the changes from a child branch and adding them to the parent branch. Understanding this process is crucial for minimizing the frequency of merge conflicts.

Reducing Conflicts

In the previous chapter, you learned that resolving conflicts can be a challenging and time-consuming process, especially when conflicts are extensive. Therefore, it's advantageous to adopt strategies to minimize conflicts. This section explores these strategies.

Having a Good Workflow

Many problems in Git and GitHub can be mitigated by implementing a well-defined workflow. The most common Git workflow was covered in previous chapters, but let's revisit it for clarity.

First and foremost, it's essential not to commit directly to your main branches. In other words, any changes you intend to make to your primary or development branches should be carried out through merging. Each merge should be initiated via a pull request. This approach allows you to receive feedback as you work, provides testers with a clear means of tracking project alterations, and ensures that all changes are well-documented in your project's history. Even if you're working solo, using PRs to introduce changes to main branches is advisable.

Every pull request should be focused on resolving a single issue. Whether it's a bug fix, a feature enhancement, or documentation changes, keep each pull request dedicated to one specific task. Avoid the temptation to address multiple issues in a single pull request, which can lead to merge conflicts.

Another aspect that developers often overlook is line endings and file formatting. As discussed in an earlier chapter, different operating systems use different line endings. Your team must agree on a consistent line-ending style for each project. Most teams opt for Unix-style line endings, so Windows users should configure their Git clients accordingly. The specifics can vary regarding formatting, but all team members must adhere to the same formatting standards for indentations and line returns.

Caution   Things might get heated when discussing tabs vs. spaces. Prepare your arguments in advance!

Aborting a Merge

Keep in mind that many merge conflicts won't necessarily arise from clashes in code logic; some can stem from differences in formatting and whitespace. For instance, a trailing space or variations in the number of indentation spaces can lead to conflicts, even if the code remains unchanged.

When you encounter conflicts of this nature, it's often best to abort the merge, reconcile the formatting differences, and then attempt the merge again. You can abort a merge using the following command.

```
$ git merge --abort
```

This action won't delete any of your commits; it simply cancels the ongoing merge and leaves you in your current state.

Using a Visual Git Tool

Resolving conflicts can be challenging when working with a basic text editor, as it often disrupts the code's color scheme and formatting. An effective solution to this issue is to employ specialized Git tools. These tools can take the form of IDE extensions or dedicated Git software. The next chapter explores these options in more detail!

Summary

This chapter was a valuable refresher on merge in Git. It explored the different types of Git merges and the scenarios in which they come into play. Additionally, it delved into the mechanics of how a merge functions, which is essentially about integrating commits from one branch into another.

The key takeaways from this chapter are the various strategies you can employ to reduce the occurrence of merge conflicts. While you might not be able to eliminate them entirely, following these guidelines helps keep conflicts to a minimum.

Up to this point, you've made significant progress in the Git journey, all through the command-line interface. It's time to add some color to the Git projects by exploring Git GUIs in the next chapter!

## CHAPTER 15

Git GUI Tools

The earlier chapters covered many important Git features and concepts. You've delved into commits, branches, pull requests, and merging. Armed with these concepts, you're already equipped to accomplish a wide range of tasks in Git. However, one small caveat: you've primarily used the terminal or console window for these operations. In this chapter, you won't encounter new Git concepts or features. Instead, you'll learn how to apply what you already know with style. ☺

Let's begin by exploring the default tools bundled with Git and then delve into integrated development environments that seamlessly integrate Git functionality. Finally, you'll look at specialized tools designed to enhance your Git experience.

Default Tools

If you've followed the installation steps outlined in the earlier chapters, you should already have these tools installed on your computer. If not, you can easily obtain them from your preferred software store. These default tools are bundled with Git to offer users straightforward GUIs (Graphical User Interfaces) for navigating their repositories and preparing commits. They are accessible on almost any operating system, so you needn't worry about compatibility. I'm presenting them in this book for historical context because they are integrated directly into Git.

Committing: git-gui

The first tool to explore is called `git-gui`, which serves as a graphical interface for committing changes in Git. You'll use it for committing your projects and reviewing proposed modifications. For more information about git-gui, visit `https://git-scm.com/docs/git-gui`.

© Mariot Tsitoara 2024
M. Tsitoara, *Beginning Git and GitHub*, https://doi.org/10.1007/979-8-8688-0215-7_15

To open git-gui, you can follow the same methods you use to open Git Bash: through the command line, context menu, or the Start page. Choose the method that suits you best. On Windows and Debian-based operating systems, you can open a Git GUI by navigating to the directory of your repository and right-clicking an empty space. Doing so brings up a menu similar to the one shown in Figure 15-1.

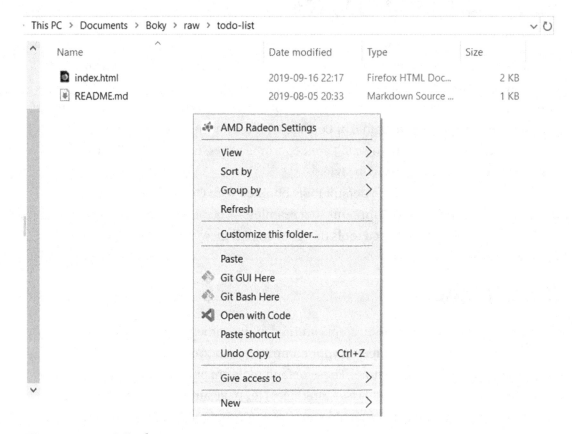

Figure 15-1. *Windows context menu*

The menu shows you can access Git GUI or Git Bash. Let's select Git GUI. This opens a small program window that provides details about the current status of your working directory. You can see what the window looks like in Figure 15-2.

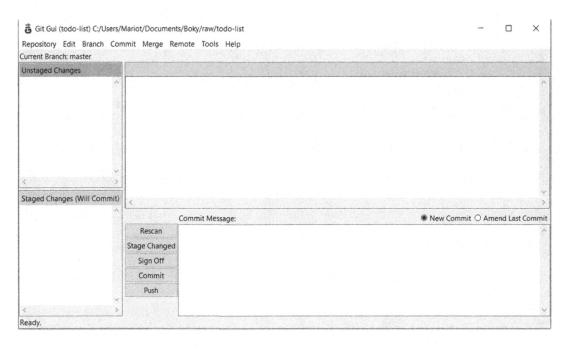

Figure 15-2. *Git GUI interface*

If you don't want to use the context menu or cannot, you can open Git GUI by launching a terminal or command prompt in the directory of your Git repository and running the following command.

```
$ git gui
```

The Git GUI interface is lightweight and consistent across different operating systems, making it easy to use. It is divided into four main sections.

- Top left: A list of edited files not staged for commit.

- Bottom left: A list of files that have been staged for commit.

- Top right: A diff view that displays the changes between the current state and the previous commit.

- Bottom right: A text area for entering the commit message.

Since you haven't made any changes to the project, everything is currently empty. To demonstrate how Git GUI works, let's make some additional commits. First, ensure that you are on the main branch, and then create a new branch from it. You can do this by going to the Branch menu and selecting "Checkout...". This opens the branch selection window, as shown in Figure 15-3.

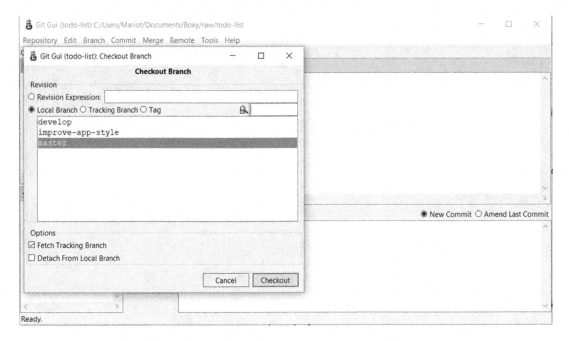

Figure 15-3. *Choosing a branch to check out*

You'll notice that information about its last commit appears when you hover your cursor over a branch. This can help identify the right branch, although it ideally shouldn't be necessary if you have clear and descriptive branch names.

To proceed, check out the `main` branch and create a new one. You can do this by selecting "Create..." from the Branch menu. This opens the branch creation window, as Figure 15-4 shows.

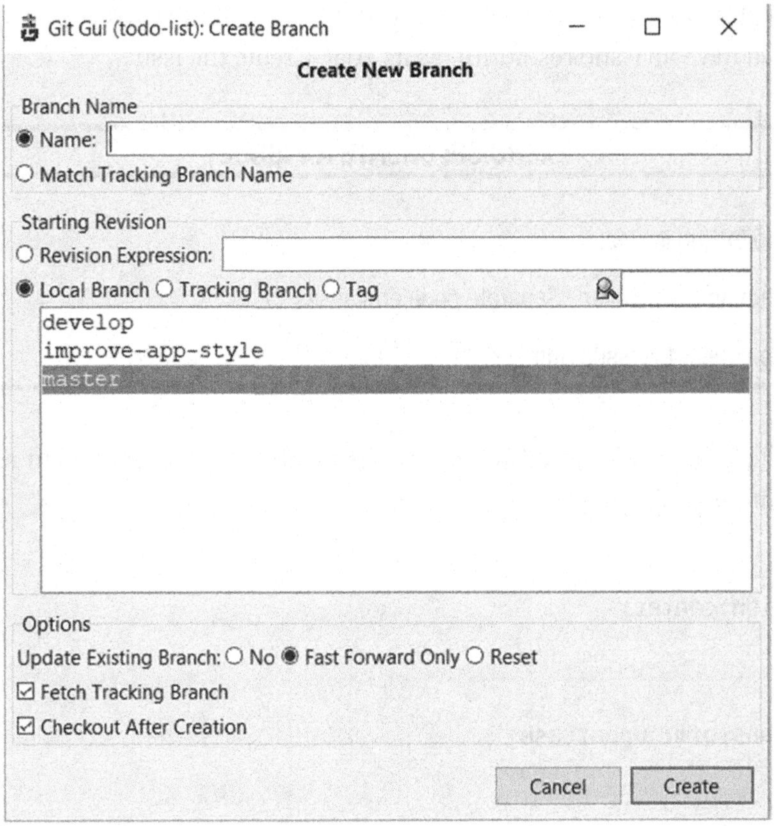

Figure 15-4. *Creating a new branch*

The first input area is crucial; it's where you provide the name of your new branch. Let's name the branch `separate-code-and-styles`.

The second input is a choice menu where you need to select the branch you want to create from. In this case, you want to create a new branch based on your local `main` branch. So, choose Local Branch and select `main`.

The third part consists of options, and it's generally a good idea to stick with the default settings. With the default options, Git fetches the latest commits from the remote tracking branch and checks out the new branch.

Now, click Create. You'll notice that the message box in the top left corner now lists `separate-code-and-styles` as the current branch. To provide some perspective, here are the equivalent command-line commands for what you just did.

```
$ git checkout main
$ git branch -b separate-code-and-styles
```

You can start working on the commit now that you're in the correct branch. Each commit should have an issue resolution as its goal. Create the issue.

EXERCISE: CREATE AN ISSUE

1. Go to GitHub issues.

2. Create an issue called "Separate code and styles".

3. Take note of the issue number.

Now you're ready to commit! Create a new file called `style.css` in your repository and paste it into the following code.

```css
h1 {
    text-align:center;
}
h3 {
    text-transform: uppercase;
}
ul {
    margin: 0;
    padding: 0;
}
ul li {
    cursor: pointer;
    position: relative;
    padding: 12px 8px 12px 40px;
    background: #eee;
    font-size: 18px;
    transition: 0.2s;
    -webkit-user-select: none;
    -moz-user-select: none;
    -ms-user-select: none;
    user-select: none;
}
```

```
ul li:nth-child(odd) {
    background: #f9f9f9;
}
ul li:hover {
    background: #ddd;
}
```

Then, open index.html and change its content to the following.

```
<!doctype html>
<html>
    <head>
        <meta charset="utf-8">
        <title>TODO list</title>
        <link rel="stylesheet" href="style.css" />
    </head>
    <body>
        <h1>TODO list</h1>

        <h3>Todo</h3>
        <ul>
            <li>Buy a hat for the bat</li>
            <li>Clear the fogs for the frogs</li>
            <li>Bring a box to the fox</li>
        </ul>

        <h3>Done</h3>
        <ul>
            <li>Put the mittens on the kittens</li>
        </ul>
    </body>
</html>
```

Save the two files, and now let's switch to Git GUI to see the result. Initially, you won't see any changes because Git GUI isn't aware of the recent modifications. To make Git GUI recognize the changes, click Rescan near the commit message box. This refreshes the view, and you'll see the result, which is depicted in Figure 15-5.

Figure 15-5. *Changes shown on Git GUI*

Now that the changes have been loaded, you can observe the list of modified files in the top left of Git GUI, which represents the unstaged files. You'll notice that these files have different icons, each indicating a different status.

- An empty file icon signifies a new file (never been committed).

- A file icon indicates a modified file (previously committed).

- A question mark (?) icon suggests a deleted file (also previously committed).

This view should remind you of the `git status` command. Clicking Rescan in Git GUI is equivalent to executing the following command in the terminal.

```
$ git status
```

In this case, you've modified `index.html` and created `style.css`. If you click the file names (not the icons), you'll see the diff view changes, as illustrated in Figure 15-6.

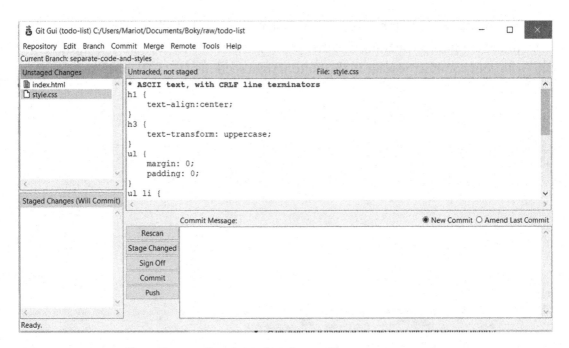

Figure 15-6. *Diff on the newly created style.css file*

It's certainly quicker than executing git diff! Also, it's easier on the eyes if you have a lot of changed files. So, clicking the file name is equivalent to executing the following commands.

```
$ git diff index.html
$ git diff style.css
```

Now is the time to stage the files in preparation for the commit. Staging and unstaging a file is easy: just click its icon. Alternatively, you can select the files you want to stage (by clicking their names) and select "Stage to Commit" in the Commit menu. Clicking the file icons is the same as executing the following commands.

```
$ git add index.html style.css
$ git reset HEAD index.html
$ git reset HEAD style.css
```

See? Way quicker than typing commands!

You can finally commit the project! But first, make sure that all the files you created or modified are staged, meaning that they are in the bottom-left section. Then, you can write your commit message in the bottom right section of Git GUI, just like in Figure 15-7.

Figure 15-7. *Writing of a commit message*

You're ready to commit now that the files are staged and the commit message is written. Click the Commit button near the commit message box. After doing so, Git GUI returns to its normal, empty state. You've committed using the graphical tool!

Clicking the Commit button has the same result as executing the following command.

```
$ git commit -m "Move style code to external file"
```

Since you're my best student (don't tell the others), I'll let you make another commit in the branch.

EXERCISE: MAKE ANOTHER COMMIT

---

1. Open README.md.

2. Add this line at the end of the file: License: MIT.

3. Create a new file called LICENSE.

4. Copy the license text from https://choosealicense.com/licenses/mit/ into the LICENSE file.

5. Stage both files.

6. Commit with the message, "Add MIT license".

Great job! Now you have two commits on your new branch, and it's time to push them to the remote repository. Clicking the Push button gives you the result shown in Figure 15-8.

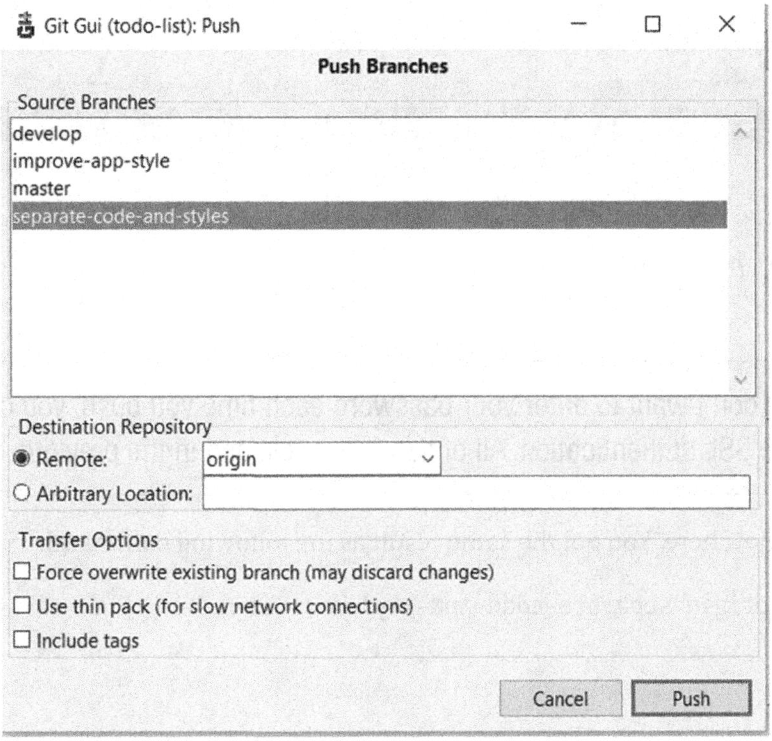

Figure 15-8. *Pushing a branch*

It's a straightforward interface. You just have to select the branch you want to push and the location where you want to push it.

The current branch is selected by default, so you don't have to change anything. The second section is the destination selection drop-down, and again, you don't have to change anything because you only have one remote repository. Ignore the options for now; you see them in a later chapter.

Press the Push button to push! If you use HTTPS authentication to connect with GitHub, you are asked for your GitHub username and password and then get the result shown in Figure 15-9.

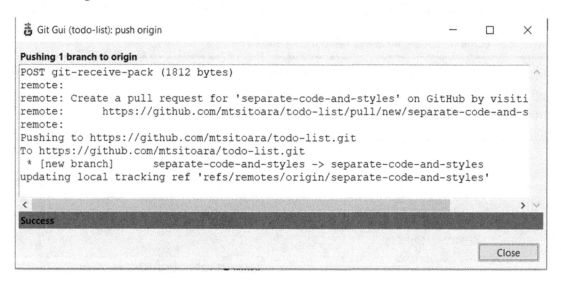

Figure 15-9. Push result

Tip   If you don't want to enter your password each time you push, you can cache them or use SSL authentication. All of this was explained in the previous chapters.

Nothing new here. You got the same result as the following command.

```
$ git push origin separate-code-and-styles
```

EXERCISE: CREATE A PULL REQUEST

1. Follow the link you got after pushing.

2. Create a pull request with this description: "Fix #10" (replace the number with the issue number you created earlier).

3. Merge the PR.

4. Rejoice.

And that's how you commit with Git GUI! Simple, right? And very quick, too. It's a great tool that can save you time when reviewing commits. Speaking of commits, let's look at the other default tool!

Browsing: gitk

The previous section explained creating and pushing commits. Now, you will visualize those commits in their natural habitat: the repository. gitk is a simple tool to visually represent your project's history. You can think of it as a more powerful version of the `git log` command. More information is available at `https://git-scm.com/docs/gitk`.

Since you already have the Git GUI open, let's use it to open gitk. Simply choose Visualize All Branch History from the Repository menu. You see the window shown in Figure 15-10.

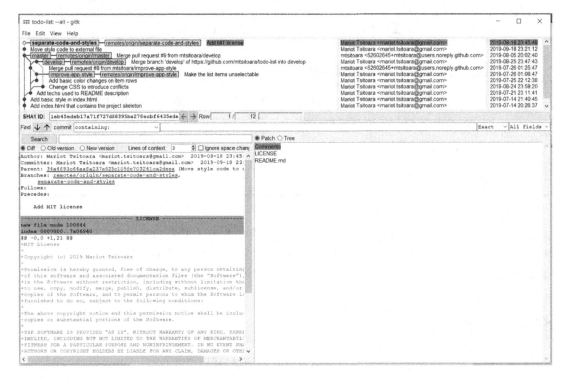

Figure 15-10. *The gitk interface*

At the top of the window is a list of all your project's commits from all branches. It is presented in a graphical view that you can reproduce in the console with the following command.

```
$ git log --oneline --graph
```

You can click the commits to get more information about them. Selecting a commit updates the views at the bottom of the window. The bottom-left is a diff view again, but with a twist: you can choose to view the old or the new version of the files. The bottom-right shows a list of all the files changed in the commit. You can click them to see the changes in the diff view. Clicking a commit is the equivalent of executing the following code.

```
$ git show <commit_name>
```

And that's it for gitk, the default browsing tool of Git! Since you can now commit and browse with the default graphical tools, it's time to introduce you to other tools.

IDE Tools

As you saw in the previous section, committing with a graphical tool is much faster than typing in the console. However, there's still a drawback: you must leave your integrated development environment (IDE) to use these tools. Wouldn't it be great if you could access these graphical tools directly from your code editor?

This is possible with many modern code editors. I'll introduce you to two popular IDEs that have Git integration built-in, allowing you to use Git seamlessly within your development environment. Additionally, if you prefer to use a different code editor or are already attached to your current one, chances are that it also has integrated Git tools or plugins, especially if it's a modern IDE. Each IDE offers a unique interface and user experience, so in this section, I'll provide an overview of the available features without going into specific details.

Visual Studio Code

Visual Studio Code, often abbreviated as VS Code, is a highly popular code editor. It's a lightweight IDE developed by Microsoft, and you can download it from `https://code.visualstudio.com`. Despite being relatively new, it has quickly gained popularity and boasts a wide range of integrated features, including robust Git integration. You can get a glimpse of the look and feel of VS Code in Figure 15-11.

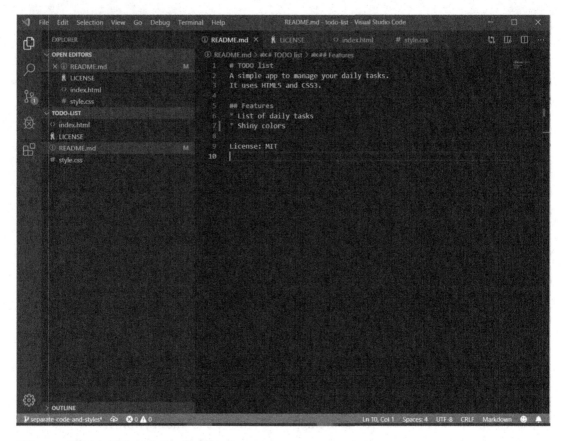

Figure 15-11. *Visual Studio Code*

It features a familiar interface like any other IDE but with a little bonus: you'll find traces of Git integration throughout the editor. First, the edited parts are highlighted when you modify a tracked file (in the example, README.md). There's no need to run git diff separately anymore.

You can see the current branch name in the bottom left of the window. If you click it, you can select the branch you want to switch to or create a new one. If you have unstaged changes, you'll see a little asterisk (*) next to your branch name and an M icon next to the file names with changes. If you've staged but not committed files, you'll see a plus sign (+).

Clicking the source control icon in the left-hand sidebar opens the Git tab, as illustrated in Figure 15-12.

Figure 15-12. *Source Control view*

This view looks and works very much like git-gui, so I'll let you discover it yourself!

Specialized Tools

The previous sections explored the default Git tools and Git integration in popular IDEs, and now, let's delve into some specialized tools designed specifically for Git.

GitHub Desktop

GitHub Desktop is a great choice if you appreciate the functionality of the default Git tools (like gitk and git-gui) but find their interfaces outdated. It offers a more modern and user-friendly interface while retaining all the essential features of those tools. You can download GitHub Desktop from `https://desktop.github.com/`. The interface of GitHub Desktop is depicted in Figure 15-13.

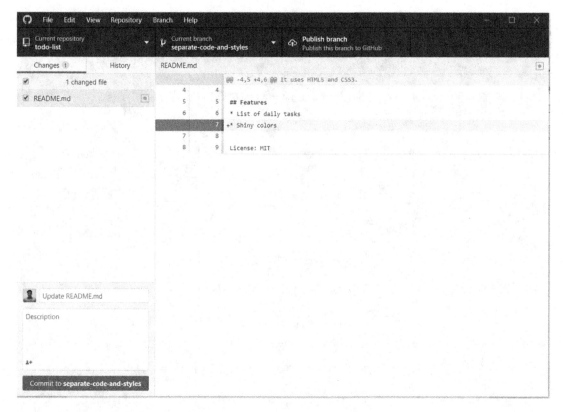

Figure 15-13. *GitHub desktop*

Summary

This chapter was fun, wasn't it? You learned how to use a graphical tool to make and browse commits. You also discovered many new tools available, whether integrated into an IDE or as specialized tools. And how can you forget about the good old default tool?!

You may wonder why the graphical tool wasn't used from the very beginning. It's because using a tool without understanding the concepts behind it is counterproductive and a waste of time. Trust me, learning to use the terminal was worth it! Speaking of terminals, let's get back to it for some more advanced Git commands!

CHAPTER 16

Advanced Git

In Chapter 15, you learned how to use basic Git features in a graphical context. Now, let's explore some additional Git commands that you won't use as frequently as the others but are powerful and necessary for improved productivity. These commands are easy to learn and invaluable if you ever make a mistake when using Git.

This chapter addresses common problems you will likely encounter after using Git for some time, and then you'll explore the easiest ways to resolve them. While this chapter may seem relatively straightforward, it dives into some powerful Git features.

Reverting

You've already learned how to revert a commit in previous chapters. However, often, you only want to revert a single file to a previous state. This situation typically arises when you've been working on a file for some time, only to realize that your entire approach was incorrect. Instead of manually undoing changes with hundreds of Ctrl+Z or Cmd+Z keystrokes, it's more efficient to revert the file.

You probably already know how to do this because Git provides instructions after you check the git status. First, let's open the README.md file and add some text to it.

```
# TODO list
A simple app to manage your daily tasks.
It uses HTML5 and CSS3.

## Features
* List of daily tasks
* Pretty colors

License: MIT
```

© Mariot Tsitoara 2024
M. Tsitoara, *Beginning Git and GitHub*, https://doi.org/10.1007/979-8-8688-0215-7_16

Now, let's see the status.

```
$ git status
```

As usual, you see the status of your repository (shown in Figure 16-1).

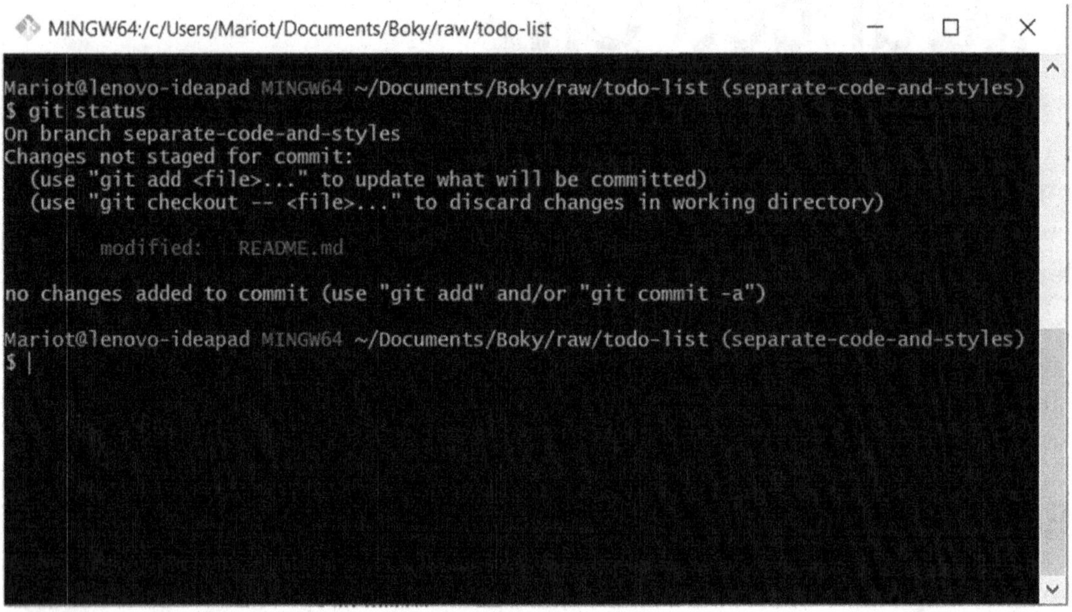

Figure 16-1. *Git status after a changed file*

There is nothing new here, but please direct your attention to the instructions above the modified file. As you can see, reverting a file to a previous state involves checking it out. The following is the command for this.

```
$ git checkout -- <file>
```

This command discards any changes you've made to a particular file. Be cautious when using it to avoid erasing valuable code. It might be better to use a GUI tool to quickly review the current changes before discarding them. Let's try to discard the changes to README.md using the following command.

```
$ git checkout -- README.md
```

You won't receive any response from this command, but if you check git status again, you'll see that README.md has been reverted to its previous state.

Stashing

You'll often want to navigate between branches but can't because your working directory is dirty. In this context, *dirty* means you have uncommitted changes in files, whether modified or staged. The only way to change branches is to first commit these changes. However, you often won't be ready to commit because the issue you're working on isn't resolved yet.

One solution to this dilemma is to make a temporary commit, switch branches, work on the new branch, and then go back and amend the temporary commit. However, this method has several drawbacks:

First, the working directory is clean after you commit, so you won't know which files were being changed anymore.

Second, it's a somewhat dirty and inelegant approach. This isn't why the amend command was created.

The ideal solution is to use a technique called *stashing*, which involves taking any modified tracked file in your working directory and putting it away for later. This allows you to have a clean directory and move around your repository without committing changes. These changes are stored in a small database called the *stash*. You can think of the stash as a temporary repository for your unfinished commits. It's designed as a last-in, first-out (LIFO) database, meaning the most recent changes you stashed are presented to you first. The best way to understand it is to try it out. So, let's make changes to the README.md file again.

```
# TODO list
A simple app to manage your daily tasks.
It uses HTML5 and CSS3.

## Features
* List of daily tasks
* Pretty colors

License: MIT
```

If you check the status, you'll see that README.md has been modified but is unstaged, resulting in the same result as before (see Figure 16-1).

Let's suppose that while you're working on this issue, an urgent one requires your attention. You can't switch to the main branch now because your working directory is dirty, and you can't commit your current changes because you haven't quite finished yet. The solution is to stash your current changes somewhere so you can have a clean directory to work with. To do this, you'll use the stash command, which is straightforward.

```
$ git stash push
```

Note   Using the command git stash is the same as using git stash push. Using the full command is recommended because it's more intuitive and easier to understand.

This command stages your modified files and creates a temporary commit within the stash, leaving your working directory clean. Try it, and you get the result shown in Figure 16-2.

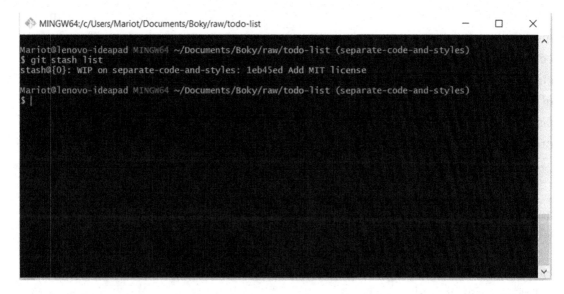

Figure 16-2. Stashing current changes

As you can see, your stashed changes were given a name and a description, just like a regular commit. This is normal because the stash is a temporary repository with only one branch. If you check the repository status, you will find a clean working directory as intended, as shown in Figure 16-3. Now, you can navigate to other branches without any issues.

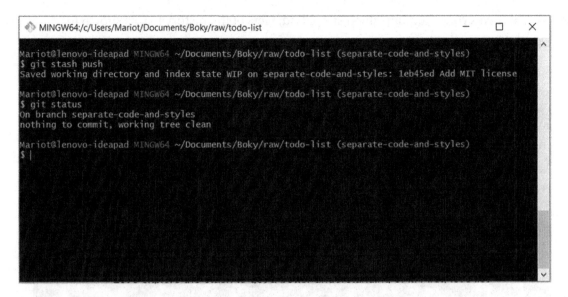

Figure 16-3. *A stash push produces a clean working directory*

Pushing changes into the stash can provide more flexibility and freedom to move between branches without losing your current work. This can be especially useful in fast-paced development environments where you frequently need to switch between different tasks and branches.

Caution   Even though this isn't a book about productivity, here's a little tip: if you find yourself jumping back and forth between issues, you may have a problem with your priorities, and resolving two issues at the same time can cost you precious time.

Since the stash is just a mini repository, you can execute most Git features, like checking the history log or getting a detailed view of the changes. Let's explore the stash to get a better understanding of it. First, show the history log using the git stash list command.

```
$ git stash list
```

This gives you a familiar, albeit simplified, view of the history log, as shown in Figure 16-4.

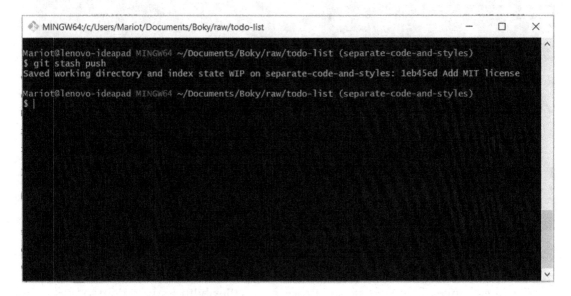

Figure 16-4. *List of stashed changes*

Again, this database works on a LIFO basis, so if you made other changes to the working directory and stashed them, they appear on top of the current stash.

Figure 16-4 shows that each stash has a number. It's easier to interact with them; unlike commits, where you must call them by their names. Let's look at the detailed view of the stashed change using the stash show command.

```
$ git stash show
```

This simple command shows you the files changed at the tip of the stash, meaning the last changes pushed into it. Figure 16-5 shows an example of this.

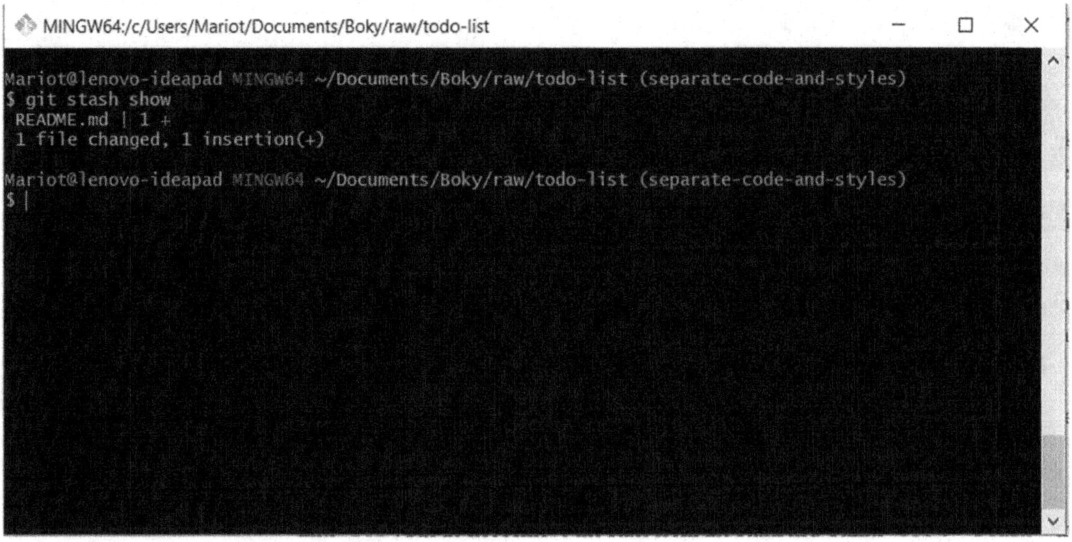

```
MINGW64:/c/Users/Mariot/Documents/Boky/raw/todo-list                              —    □    ×

Mariot@lenovo-ideapad MINGW64 ~/Documents/Boky/raw/todo-list (separate-code-and-styles)
$ git stash show
 README.md | 1 +
 1 file changed, 1 insertion(+)

Mariot@lenovo-ideapad MINGW64 ~/Documents/Boky/raw/todo-list (separate-code-and-styles)
$ |
```

Figure 16-5. *Detailed view of the tip of the stash*

The stash show command shows you the description of the changes in the stash, but not much else. To see the changes, you must apply the stash. Applying the stash is very simple: execute the following command.

```
$ git stash pop
```

This command applies the latest changes in the stash to the current branch. And as the name implies, popping the changes removes them from the stash. So, if you only had one set of changes in your stash, it would be empty after you popped the tip. If you execute the previous command, the result is the same as if you re-created the changes and then checked the status (see Figure 16-6).

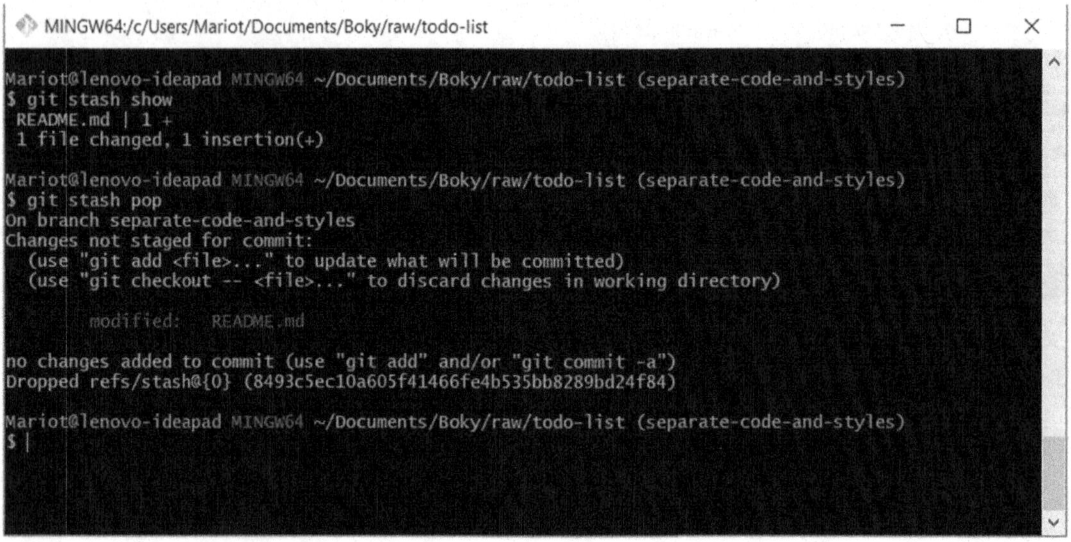

```
MINGW64:/c/Users/Mariot/Documents/Boky/raw/todo-list                    —    □    ×

Mariot@lenovo-ideapad MINGW64 ~/Documents/Boky/raw/todo-list (separate-code-and-styles)
$ git stash show
 README.md | 1 +
 1 file changed, 1 insertion(+)

Mariot@lenovo-ideapad MINGW64 ~/Documents/Boky/raw/todo-list (separate-code-and-styles)
$ git stash pop
On branch separate-code-and-styles
Changes not staged for commit:
  (use "git add <file>..." to update what will be committed)
  (use "git checkout -- <file>..." to discard changes in working directory)

        modified:   README.md

no changes added to commit (use "git add" and/or "git commit -a")
Dropped refs/stash@{0} (8493c5ec10a605f41466fe4b535bb8289bd24f84)

Mariot@lenovo-ideapad MINGW64 ~/Documents/Boky/raw/todo-list (separate-code-and-styles)
$ |
```

Figure 16-6. *Popping the last set of changes*

Back at the beginning! But you could have changed branches, made commits, or pushed to origin without losing precious changes. Stashing is particularly useful when setting aside your current changes to make quick changes elsewhere. As a rule of thumb, you might be handling your workflow incorrectly if you need to use more than one set of stashed changes.

Resetting

I hope you won't need to use this feature often because it's very destructive! Sometimes, you may want to discard everything you've done and start with a clean slate, even if you've already committed your project. Let's create a commit and discard it to better understand it. Make some modifications to README.md, stage it, and then commit the project, as shown in Figure 16-7.

Figure 16-7. *Add a bad commit to the project*

To put this into perspective, let's check the current history log after this commit using the git log command.

```
$ git log --oneline
```

This command shows you the latest commits on this branch, just like in Figure 16-8.

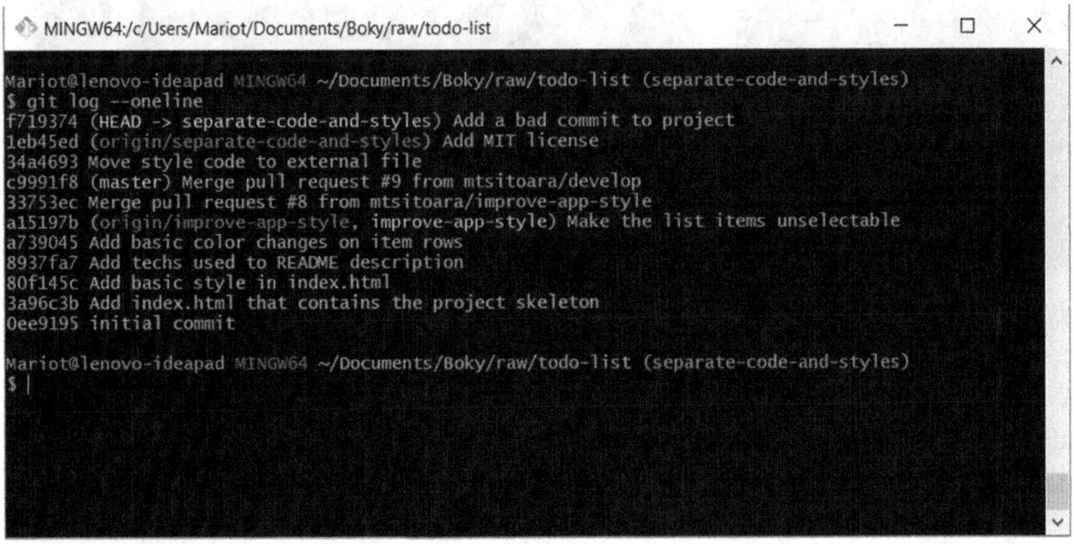

Figure 16-8. *History log of the current branch*

As you can see, the latest commit sits at the top of the log. Notice that the HEAD reference is pointed to it, which means that the next commit (or branch) has that commit as the parent. Note that the remote branch `origin/separate-code-and-styles` hasn't changed because you haven't pushed the project yet.

But let's imagine that you are utterly dissatisfied with that last commit and want to start over. Your only choice is to reset the branch back to a previous state. To reset the project, you use the git reset command followed by the state of the project to reset to. You must use the option `--hard` to accomplish this because it's a very dangerous command. For example, returning to the same state as the remote branch requires the following command.

```
$ git reset --hard origin/separate-code-and-styles
```

This command erases *everything* so the project can return to its previous state. Figure 16-9 shows the results.

Figure 16-9. Status of the project after a reset

Your commits made after the target state, current changes, and the staged files are all deleted because the `--hard` option overwrites everything in its path. It's the most dangerous command in Git, and you should think hard before using it.

Resetting should only be done as a last resort. Revert the commit, if possible, or work on a new branch. When used carelessly, a reset can destroy your data.

Summary

This chapter dealt with some advanced concepts of Git that are useful when confronted with certain situations. Use reset to revert a file to a previous state without much effort, and of course, you can revert those changes using the GUI, too. Stashing is also useful when you need a quick change of context. And finally, the hard reset is an all-powerful feature that is very destructive; don't use it unless you have no other choice.

This concludes the lesson about advanced Git commands. Let's return to GitHub to discover more features to help with project management.

PART IV

More with GitHub

CHAPTER 17

More with GitHub

You've seen almost every Git feature that you use daily in the previous chapters. Now, let's turn your eyes to GitHub, which only served as a code hosting site until now. But GitHub is so much more than that. You can use it to host project documentation and software releases. You also mainly use it as a project management tool and a way to connect with your collaborators. Let's learn about those features.

Wikis

Your project can be the best in its category, but you would get nowhere if other people don't know how to use it or how it works. That's why documentation is important, especially in software development. GitHub provides a nice way to document your project: wikis.

GitHub wikis work much like the world's most popular wiki: Wikipedia. Their goal is to provide in-depth information about your project: what it does, how it works, how someone can contribute, and so on.

Let's create a wiki page so you can better understand it. Go to your project's main page and click Wiki. You arrive at the page shown in Figure 17-1.

© Mariot Tsitoara 2024
M. Tsitoara, *Beginning Git and GitHub*, https://doi.org/10.1007/979-8-8688-0215-7_17

Welcome to the todo-list wiki!

Wikis provide a place in your repository to lay out the roadmap of your project, show the current status, and document software better, together.

Create the first page

Figure 17-1. *Wiki home page*

On the Wiki home page, click the button to create your first page. You'll arrive at the page creation page, shown in Figure 17-2.

Create new page

Home

| Write | Preview |

h1 h2 h3 🔗 🖼 B *i* <> ☰ ☰ " ᴴᴿ ⑦   Edit mode: Markdown ⬍

```
Welcome to the todo-list wiki!
```

Edit message

Initial Home page

Save Page

Figure 17-2. *Creation of a page*

As you can see, it's a very simple view that is divided into three sections: the title, the content, and the edit message. Think of the title as a web page title, so it must adhere to the same standards: clear and inviting. The content should be written in Markdown, just like README.md. You can write the wikis in other formats, but Markdown is the recommended choice because so many editors already use it, and it's much easier to read. The edit message is just like commit messages: a simple description of your proposed changes.

Change the content of your wiki. The following is an example.

```
# What is this

This is a simple app to track your daily goals

# Why another TODO app

Because that is never enough TODO apps in the world

# How does it work

Open `index.html` and update the goals as you wish

# How can I contribute to the project

You can contribute by forking the project and proposing pull requests.
Check [Issues](https://github.com/mtsitoara/issues) to see the current
areas that need help
```

Save the changes. You are redirected to the wiki home page, as shown in Figure 17-3.

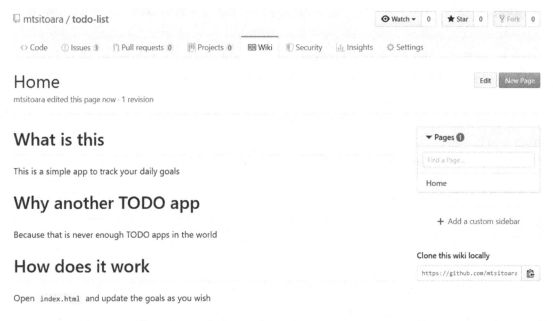

Figure 17-3. *Wiki home page showing the newly created wiki*

As you can see, the wiki you just created is automatically visible on your project page, and each page you create appears on the sidebar on the right. You can create as many wiki pages as you like, but make sure they are understandable and useful. Don't forget to add images and relevant links!

GitHub Pages

In simple terms, GitHub Pages is a website hosting service provided by GitHub. You can use it to showcase a project, host your portfolio, or even create an online version of your resume.

GitHub Pages can be used for your personal account, where you might showcase your portfolio or resume, or for your projects to create showcases for them. If you choose to use it for your account, you can create a single page. However, if it's for showcasing your projects, you can create a page for each. For a more detailed explanation, you can visit `https://pages.github.com/`.

Let's say you want to create a page to showcase your to-do list project. First, you'll need to go to your project page and click Settings, which takes you to the page displayed in Figure 17-4.

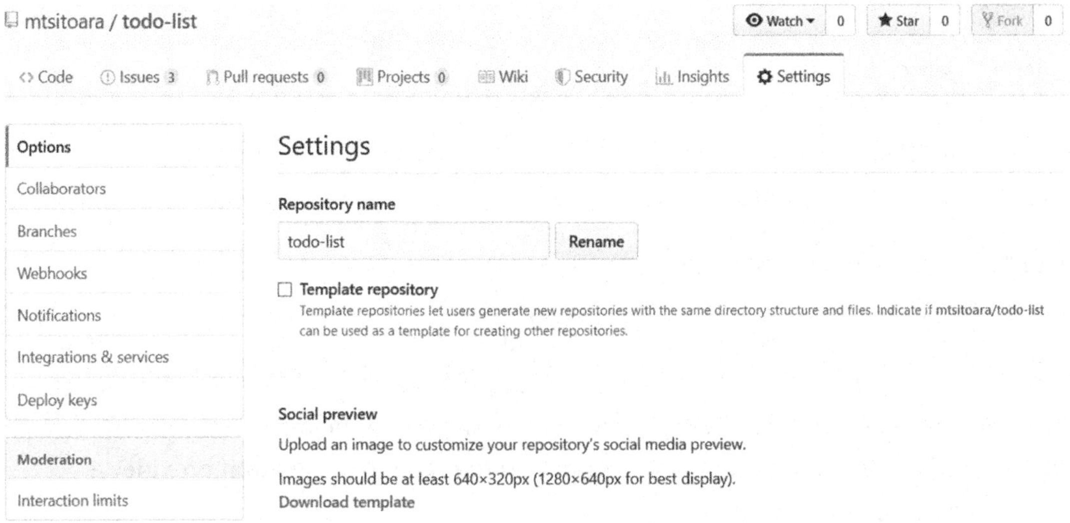

Figure 17-4. *Settings page*

Scroll down to the GitHub Pages settings, as shown in Figure 17-5.

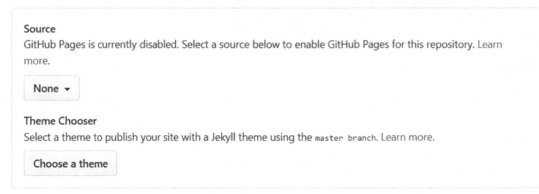

Figure 17-5. *GitHub Pages settings*

The first option is a drop-down list that contains the location of your page source. You must host your page on the main branch, but you have two choices for the source files. One is to place them directly on the main branch, and the other is to use a docs directory within the main branch. I recommend the second option as it provides a clearer structure for any visitors.

First, you need to create the docs directory. Then, using GitHub or Git tools, create a file called "index.html" within the directory. In this file, write the following basic HTML code.

```
<!doctype html>
<html>
    <head>
        <meta charset="utf-8">
        <title>Docs</title>
    </head>
    <body>
        <h1>Docs</h1>
        <p>Example of documentation</p>
    </body>
</html>
```

This serves as your documentation. Your main branch should now resemble what is shown in Figure 17-6.

Figure 17-6. Docs folder and index.html

You can then return to the settings page and choose the documentation source. Select the docs folder as the source, and the page refresh, displaying a link as shown in Figure 17-7.

GitHub Pages

GitHub Pages is designed to host your personal, organization, or project pages from a GitHub repository.

Your site is ready to be published at https://mtsitoara.github.io/todo-list/.

Source
Your GitHub Pages site is currently being built from the /docs folder in the master branch. Learn more.

master branch /docs folder ▾

Theme Chooser
Select a theme to publish your site with a Jekyll theme. Learn more.

Choose a theme

Figure 17-7. Page published

Following the provided link takes you to a splendid view of your GitHub project page! The possibilities are boundless, as you can design your page just like any other static website page. If you're looking for enhanced styling options, consider checking out `https://jekyllrb.com/`, which can assist you in generating GitHub Pages quickly!

Releases

Your project won't remain in development indefinitely; it must be released sooner or later. And what better platform to release your app than GitHub? It's straightforward.

To start, return to your project page and click Releases. You are directed to the main page, as depicted in Figure 17-8.

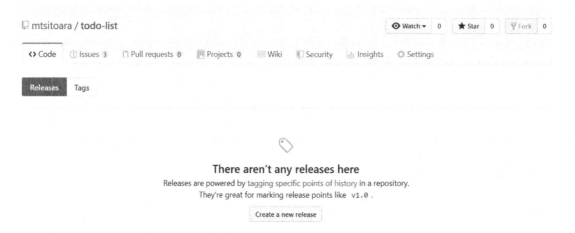

Figure 17-8. *Releases page*

Let's create your very first release! Click the "Create a new release" button to be directed to the release creation view shown in Figure 17-9.

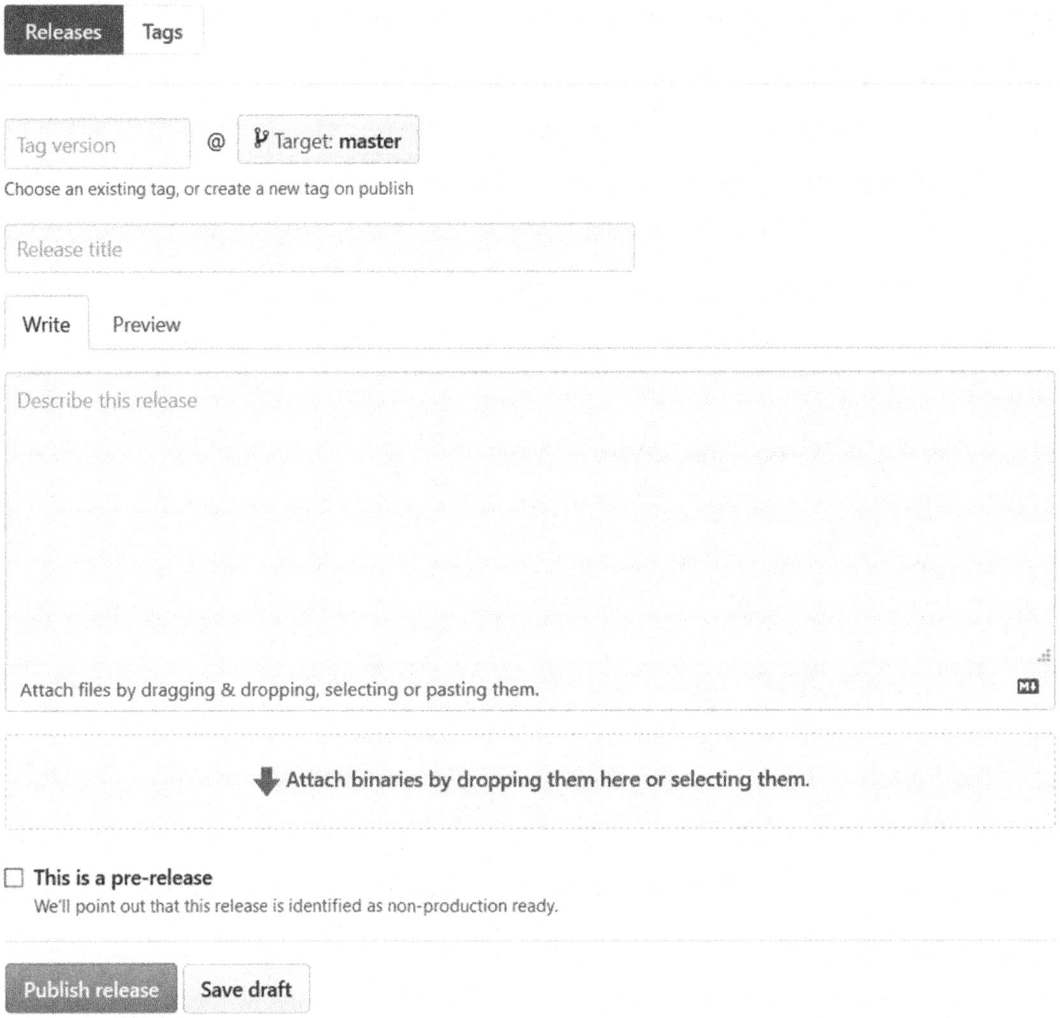

Figure 17-9. *Release creation form*

It's a straightforward form to fill out, with clear and easy-to-understand sections. The main task is to upload the release binaries by dragging and dropping them onto the form shown in Figure 17-9. Since this app is in HTML, let's attach compressed versions of the main branch. It would be an executable binary for installable apps, but here they are zip and 7z files. Don't forget to change the target of the release if necessary. The default option is the main branch, but you can specify another branch or a specific commit. The form then looks like the one shown in Figure 17-10.

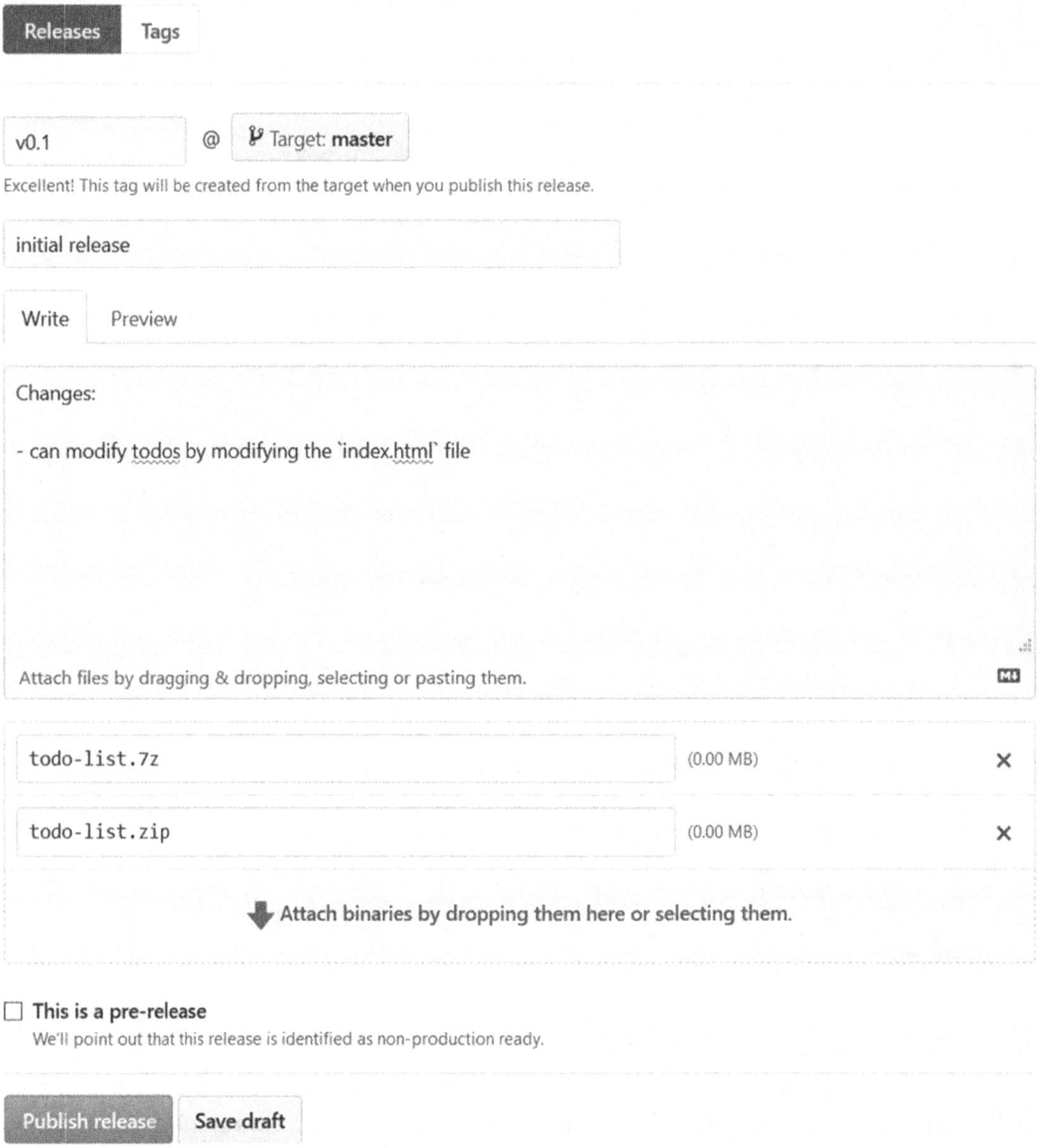

Releases   Tags

v0.1   @   ⑂ Target: **master**

Excellent! This tag will be created from the target when you publish this release.

initial release

Write   Preview

Changes:

- can modify todos by modifying the `index.html` file

Attach files by dragging & dropping, selecting or pasting them.

todo-list.7z   (0.00 MB)   ✕

todo-list.zip   (0.00 MB)   ✕

⬇ Attach binaries by dropping them here or selecting them.

☐ **This is a pre-release**
We'll point out that this release is identified as non-production ready.

Publish release   Save draft

Figure 17-10. *Filled release form with binaries*

Click "Publish release" to finalize it. You are then redirected back to the Releases list, where your new release is listed. You can refer to Figure 17-11 for an example.

Figure 17-11. *List of all the releases*

As you can see, GitHub also bundles the source code with your release! When creating a release, thoroughly test everything to ensure it functions correctly.

Project Boards

Project boards are a very useful feature of GitHub because they provide a way to track and organize your project. For example, you can create cards for any new ideas you have so you can discuss them with your team later. However, the main use of project boards is to track the advancement of your project. They go beyond issues because issues only describe a feature or a bug to be worked on, while project boards can show you if someone is actively working on it or if it's just a plan to be executed.

The best way to understand project boards is to experiment with them directly. So, go back to your project page and select Projects. You see the empty project board shown in Figure 17-12.

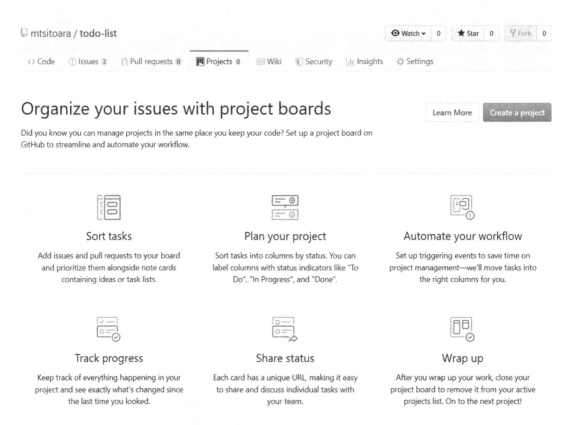

Figure 17-12. *Projects main page*

The project main page is still empty because you haven't created any projects yet. It also provides examples of situations where you might want to use project boards. Click "Create a project" to continue. You see the page shown in Figure 17-13.

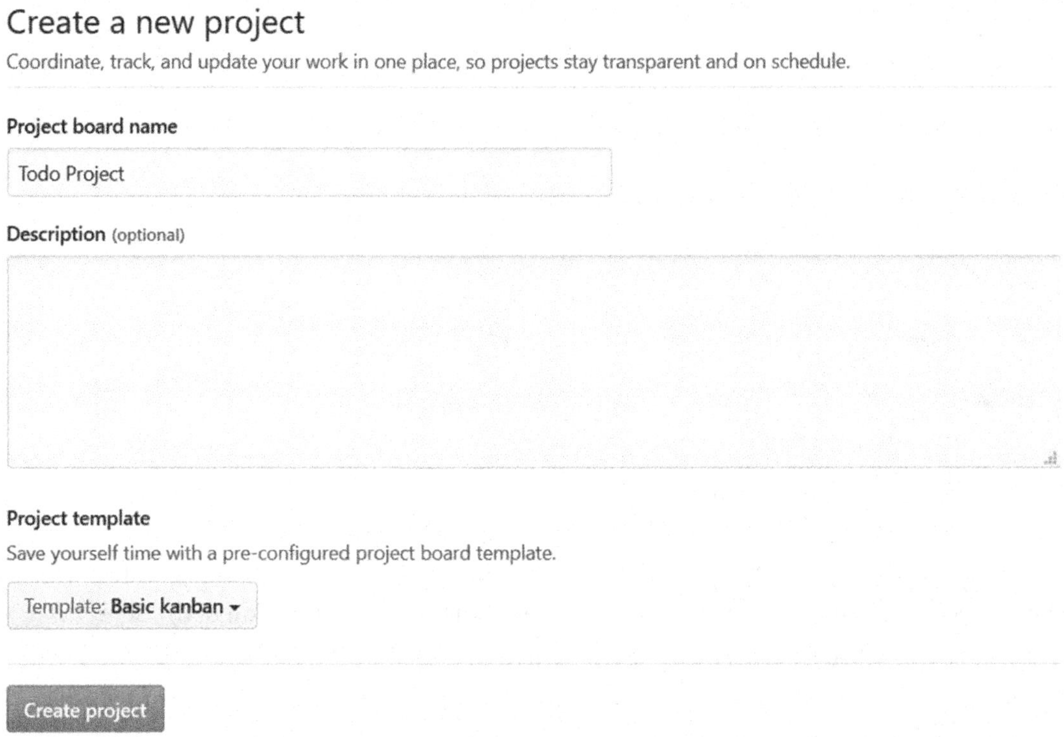

Create a new project

Coordinate, track, and update your work in one place, so projects stay transparent and on schedule.

Project board name

Todo Project

Description (optional)

Project template

Save yourself time with a pre-configured project board template.

Template: **Basic kanban** ▾

Create project

Figure 17-13. *Creation of a project*

Again, it's a very simple form, but pay attention to the Template section; it's quite important. As a beginner, you should use the basic kanban template because it is prefilled. You can create the boards yourself, but let's stick to the basics for now. Create the project. You will see the semi-empty board shown in Figure 17-14.

Figure 17-14. *New project created*

As you can see, there are three boards created: "To do," "In progress," and "Done," just like your app! You can see a list of the open issues on the right side of the screen. Drag and drop those issues into their respective boards. In the "To do" board, you have a little example of what you can do with your boards; it's not only for issues but also for pull requests or simple notes. After you've placed your issues in the desired boards, you get a result like Figure 17-15.

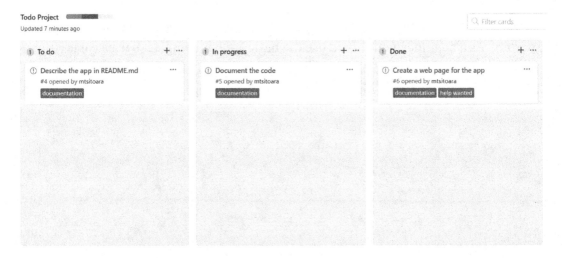

Figure 17-15. *Project boards*

As you move the issues around the board, the colored bar near the project name changes. It's a good way to track your progress!

Project boards are more than just project progress trackers! You can create project boards for many situations: release tracking, meeting notes, developer idea notes, user feedback, and so on. You can find the project board for this book in Figure 17-16, which is also available at `https://github.com/mariot/boky/projects/1`.

Figure 17-16. *A project board for this book*

I advise you to use project boards for future projects because having a clear view of your progress is a sure way to success. If you're feeling adventurous, check out the automated kanban, which automatically moves the cards for you. For example, every new issue is placed under "To do" and every closed issue is moved to "Done."

Summary

This chapter took you away from Git and focused on GitHub. You've seen that GitHub is more than just a storage place for your code; it's a complete tool for managing and releasing your projects. After this chapter, you should be able to create a basic website for your project, have some documentation for it, and make your first release.

The most important feature covered was project boards. Use them to better understand what you've accomplished and where you're headed. They may seem simple, but they are incredibly useful for project management.

You've now mastered the basics of Git and GitHub. However, there are still challenges ahead in a real-world working environment. The next chapter explores the common problems you'll encounter when collaborating with others and how to resolve them. Stay tuned!

## CHAPTER 18

Common Git Problems

You've come a long way since your first Git command! You've learned a lot about basic and advanced Git features and when to use them. However, since you are only human, you will encounter a lot of problems during your Git journey. Most of these problems result from inadvertent mistakes, so simply being aware of their existence is a significant step toward avoiding them. But if you still run into them, here are the best solutions!

Repository

The repository is the backbone of your Git experience; everything begins and ends there. It's very difficult to mess it up, but in the slight chance that something goes wrong, here are some tips.

Starting Over

This is the most radical "solution" in the chapter, and I hope you never have to use it. This solution is essentially a way to delete everything and start over. It should only be considered an option when you have a remote repository and want to delete your local one for some reason. Reasons to do this might include the following.

- Changing your work computer

- Encountering unreadable sectors in the hard drive

- Facing unrecoverable errors in the `.git` directory

To start over, you must clone the remote repository using the `git clone` command.

```
$ git clone <repository_location>
```

The repository location is the HTTPS or SSH link to your remote repository, which you can find on your GitHub project page.

© Mariot Tsitoara 2024
M. Tsitoara, *Beginning Git and GitHub*, https://doi.org/10.1007/979-8-8688-0215-7_18

Cloning has the same effect as initializing a repository but with a significant bonus: all history and commits are copied to your new local repository. You won't need to specify the origin link anymore.

Change Origin

Under normal circumstances, you would want to keep the remote repository's URL the same throughout your development. However, there are certain circumstances where it's necessary to change it.

- When switching between HTTPS and SSH links

- When transferring the repository to another host

- When adding a dedicated repository for release or testing

First, let's gather some more information about the current remotes. To do this, use the git remote command with the -v option.

```
$ git remote -v
```

It lists your current remotes, as shown in Figure 18-1.

Figure 18-1. List of current remotes

To modify the remote URL, use the `git remote set-url` subcommand in the following format.

```
$ git remote set-url <remote_name> <remote_url>
```

For example, you can execute the following command if you want to switch from using an HTTPS link to an SSH link for your GitHub access.

```
$ git remote set-url origin git@github.com:mtsitoara/todo-list.git
```

Doing this allows you to push to and pull from GitHub without providing your username and password. The authentication is handled using a private key stored on your local computer and a corresponding public key needed to upload to GitHub. If you're interested in using SSH for authentication, you can find more information in the GitHub Help documentation based on your operating system at https:// docs.github.com/en/get-started/getting-started-with-git/about-remote- repositories#choosing-a-url-for-your-remote-repository.

You can use a credential helper if you prefer to continue using HTTPS but want to cache your password to avoid typing it every time. More information about this can be found in the GitHub Help documentation, also based on your operating system at https://docs.github.com/en/get-started/getting-started-with-git/caching- your-github-credentials-in-git.

Caution   If you change your remote name, don't forget to use the new name for every push and pull action.

Working Directory

You spend most of your time in the working directory, and here again, there are few things you can break.

git diff Is Empty

This comes up a lot, but it's not dangerous. Sometimes, you've made a lot of changes and want to check the differences. But when you run git diff, the result is empty. Don't panic! git diff only shows modified files, so if your file is staged, you won't see it there. To see changes done to staged files, you must run the following.

```
$ git diff --staged
```

Tip   Using a GUI tool greatly helps when reviewing changes.

Undo Changes to a File

This comes up a lot when you use Git. Sometimes, you want to revert a file back to its previous state without having to check out an entire commit and then copy-paste the code. You've already seen the command earlier.

```
$ git checkout <commit_name> -- <file_name>
```

This command checks out the file as it was in the commit and, thus, changes your working directory. Be careful not to lose any uncommitted changes!

Commits

Most problems arise when you try to commit your current project. But don't worry, there is always a simple solution for these problems. The most important thing to consider is: are the commands you are using destructive? Commands like reset or checkout change your working directory, so please make sure that you know what you are doing before executing them.

An Error in a Commit

This is a basic error in Git. After you commit your hard work, you'll sometimes notice that a little grammatical error found its way into your commit message or that you forgot to stage a file. The solution to these problems is to amend the commit, meaning that you cancel the immediate commit and make a new one. The command is simple.

```
$ git commit --amend
```

The commit name changes because you are changing its content. That's why you should not amend a commit you've already pushed to a remote branch, especially if somebody else works on that branch. This is rewriting history, and you should never do it.

That said, if you've pushed your commit and are alone on the branch, you can amend a commit and try to push it again. But since the commit name changed, Git won't allow you to change history without a fight. You have to erase all the history on the remote branch and replace it with yours, meaning that you overwrite everything on the remote branch. That's why you should never amend a commit if you aren't alone on a branch. To push a branch with amended commits, you must force it.

```
$ git push <remote_name> <branch_name> -f
```

The "-f" option forces Git to overwrite everything on the remote branch and replace it with your current branch history.

Caution   Rewriting history on a branch where somebody else is working is just plain rude and selfish. Don't do it.

Undo Commits

If you committed on a branch but then realized it's the wrong one, you can undo it, but only when you haven't pushed to a remote branch.

The command is simple but dangerous: it's the reset command. But in contrast to a hard reset where everything is cleared, a *soft* reset is necessary to undo the commit but keep the changes.

```
$ git reset HEAD~ --soft
```

The commit disappears, leaving you with options to stash the changes and apply them to another branch.

Again, this is rewriting history and should not be used if you've already pushed to a remote branch.

Branches

You need to work with branches a lot to have an optimized workflow. When working on a new feature or bugfix, your first instinct should be creating a branch. But the more you get comfortable with branches, the more likely you are to forget a little detail that can lead to problems. Here are the most common problems that you encounter with Git.

Detached HEAD

HEAD refers to the currently checked-out commit, which means it points to the parent commit of any future commit you create. Usually, HEAD points to the last commit of the current branch, and all future branches and commits have it as their parent.

When you check out branches, HEAD moves back and forth between the last commits of the branches. But when you check out a specific commit, you enter a state called detached HEAD, which means that you are in a state where nothing you create is attached to anything. Trying to commit during this state is useless because any changes are lost.

Git informs you when you are in that state (as shown in Figure 18-2), so you will never be in that state unknowingly.

```
MINGW64:/c/Users/Mariot/Documents/Boky/raw/todo-list                    —    □    ×

Mariot@lenovo-ideapad MINGW64 ~/Documents/Boky/raw/todo-list (master)
$ git checkout c9991f8f066bb9ccOcfOffd771f7d9fe33dee4c9
Note: checking out 'c9991f8f066bb9ccOcfOffd771f7d9fe33dee4c9'.

You are in 'detached HEAD' state. You can look around, make experimental
changes and commit them, and you can discard any commits you make in this
state without impacting any branches by performing another checkout.

If you want to create a new branch to retain commits you create, you may
do so (now or later) by using -b with the checkout command again. Example:

  git checkout -b <new-branch-name>

HEAD is now at c9991f8 Merge pull request #9 from mtsitoara/develop

Mariot@lenovo-ideapad MINGW64 ~/Documents/Boky/raw/todo-list ((c9991f8...))
$
```

Figure 18-2. *Checking out a commit*

Checking out a commit is thus only needed to test something on your software. You can, however, create a branch from that specific commit if you want to keep the commits you intend to make. The command is the same as creating a branch from another branch.

```
$ git checkout -b <branch_name>
```

Working in the Wrong Branch

Working in the wrong branch happens a lot. The situation is usually like this: you receive a task and are so eager to complete it that you begin to code immediately. You are already an hour into the task when you notice that you were working in the main branch all along! Don't worry. It's very simple to resolve this.

If you modify some files on the wrong branch, you can create a new branch (and check it out) to take the current changes there. It's the same command again.

```
$ git checkout -b <branch_name>
```

It creates a new branch with your current changes and checks it out. You can then stage your modified files and commit the project.

However, this won't work if you've already pushed the branch to a remote repository; history is history, so don't change it. The only way to fix that is to revert to the commit you push and live with that shame all your life.

Catch up with the Parent Branch

When you create a branch from another (usually main), their histories are not linked anymore, so what happens in one branch doesn't have any incidence on the other. This means that while you are working on your branch, other people can commit on the base branch, and those commits won't be available to your branch.

If you are still working on your branch but are interested in having those new commits on the base branch, you must first have a clean plate, which means that you need to commit your project (or stash your current changes).

Then, you must check out the parent branch, pull the new commits, and then go back to your branch.

```
$ git checkout main
$ git pull origin main
$ git checkout <branch_name>
```

Safely on your local branch, you can then catch up to the parent branch. The concept is simple: Git takes out your current commits and creates a new branch from the tip of the parent branch; your commits can then be applied to your new branch. It would be like you create a branch from the latest commit of the main branch. The command is called rebase.

```
$ git rebase main
```

The commits on main might introduce conflicts in your branch, so be prepared to get your hands dirty. Resolving those merge conflicts is the same as what've you've done previously: open each conflicted file and choose which code you want to keep; then, you can stage them and commit.

You can find an example of rebase conflict in Figure 18-3, on which both commits on main and test_branch modified README.md.

```
MINGW64:/c/Users/Mariot/Documents/Boky/raw/todo-list                    —    □    ×

Mariot@lenovo-ideapad MINGW64 ~/Documents/Boky/raw/todo-list (test_branch)
$ git rebase master
First, rewinding head to replay your work on top of it...
Applying: another commit
Using index info to reconstruct a base tree...
M       README.md
Falling back to patching base and 3-way merge...
Auto-merging README.md
CONFLICT (content): Merge conflict in README.md
error: Failed to merge in the changes.
hint: Use 'git am --show-current-patch' to see the failed patch
Patch failed at 0001 another commit
Resolve all conflicts manually, mark them as resolved with
"git add/rm <conflicted_files>", then run "git rebase --continue".
You can instead skip this commit: run "git rebase --skip".
To abort and get back to the state before "git rebase", run "git rebase --abort".

Mariot@lenovo-ideapad MINGW64 ~/Documents/Boky/raw/todo-list (test_branch|REBASE 1/1)
$ |
```

Figure 18-3. *Merge conflict during rebase*

As you can see, it's almost exactly like any merge conflict, and the resolution is the same.

```
$ git add <conflicted_files>
$ git rebase --continue
```

If you are not feeling brave enough for conflicts, you can abort the rebase and return to the initial state.

```
$ git rebase --abort
```

If you work on a branch for a long time, it's a good idea to rebase occasionally so you aren't left too far behind the parent branch. Of course, you can face merge conflicts, but those are more likely to appear the bigger your changes are. And if you delay rebases for fear of conflicts, you only set yourself up for failures because those conflicts appear again when you attempt to merge the branches anyway. It's better to occasionally deal with small conflicts with a rebase than having to merge many conflicted files simultaneously.

Branches Have Diverged

This can happen if you're using an inefficient Git workflow. It's advisable to work on your own branch when resolving an issue because multiple people committing to the same branch can lead to problems.

The term *diverged* describes a situation where you can't push to your remote branch anymore due to changes in the commit history. This occurs when you've committed changes to your local branch, but others have pushed their commits to the remote branch before you. When you attempt to push, Git prevents you from doing so because the latest commit on the remote branch doesn't exist in your local history. You'll encounter an error message like the one shown in Figure 18-4.

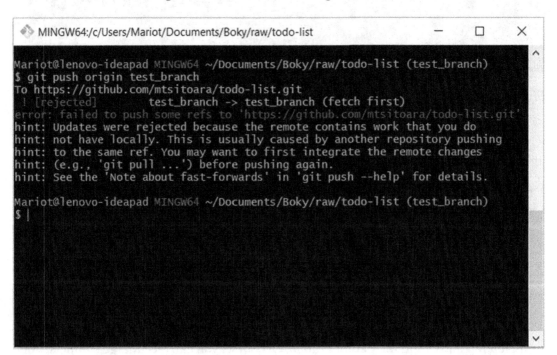

Figure 18-4. *Rejected changes*

The most practical solution is to pull the commits from the remote branch and merge your changes. This way, you incorporate their changes into your history (after resolving any potential merge conflicts) and then push your changes.

```
$ git pull origin <branch_name>
$ git push origin <branch_name>
```

This approach may result in a messy history log, but it ensures that all commits are preserved. You can see an example of this in Figure 18-5.

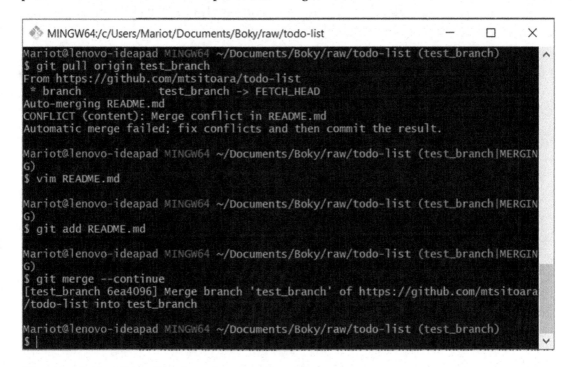

Figure 18-5. *Merge local and remote branch*

Another solution is more drastic: overwriting everything on the remote branch and replacing its history with yours. To do this, you can push with the force option.

```
$ git push origin <branch_name> -f
```

However, this approach results in lost commits and potential conflicts, and it's strongly discouraged. It's best to avoid this situation altogether by following a well-structured Git and GitHub workflow.

Summary

This chapter guides you toward the right solutions when faced with common Git problems. While you may encounter more complex issues as you gain experience, this chapter provides a solid starting point. The key takeaway is always to double-check your context before taking any actions, especially when committing.

However, these problems should ideally not arise if you adhere to the standard Git and GitHub workflow. So, let's revisit this workflow in the next chapter. It's worth revisiting now that you're familiar with the most commonly used Git and GitHub features.

## CHAPTER 19

Git and GitHub Workflow

A substantial amount of information was covered in the previous chapters, particularly the technical aspects of Git. You now have a solid understanding of how to effectively version control your projects and how to address common issues that may arise. You've also learned the fundamentals of project management using GitHub.

It's time to bring it all together and create a comprehensive game plan for your projects. In this chapter, you'll be introduced to a meticulously designed workflow that you can follow to ensure the success of your projects. Think of it as a "best practices" section or a practical "how-to" guide for your project management needs.

How to Use This Workflow

The workflow outlined in this chapter has been crafted with both beginners and experienced users in mind. It's widely utilized in open source projects, so many developers are already familiar with it. However, it's essential to understand that this workflow isn't set in stone. If those changes are reasonable, you can adjust to align with your specific project requirements.

For beginners, I recommend following this workflow diligently. It helps you grasp the workings and rituals of Git and GitHub. As you gain more experience, you can tailor the workflow to increase efficiency. But never compromise security for the sake of saving time. Skipping essential steps might seem like a time-saver initially, but it can lead to more bugs and merge conflicts, ultimately counterproductive.

After several years of using Git and GitHub, you'll become a main and can develop your workflow. Your changes should aim to enhance your team's efficiency and productivity.

© Mariot Tsitoara 2024
M. Tsitoara, *Beginning Git and GitHub*, https://doi.org/10.1007/979-8-8688-0215-7_19

GitHub Workflow

One of the most fundamental mistakes you can make when working with GitHub is viewing it solely as a code hosting service. In other words, use it solely to share code among collaborators or release your product to users. GitHub is an incredibly powerful tool, and it would be a tremendous missed opportunity not to leverage its full potential.

Consider GitHub as your primary project management tool. Every action you plan to take within your project should be meticulously tracked within GitHub. This ensures that you can always refer to and comprehend the project's history. You cannot simply make changes without adequately documenting the reasons behind those changes. Therefore, here are the golden rules of GitHub.

Every Project Starts with a Project

When starting a new project, it's advisable to create a GitHub project shortly after setting up the repository. This step should be taken as early as possible because utilizing project boards is the most effective means of monitoring your project's progress. At the very least, you should establish a kanban board to keep track of your project's to-do tasks. You can also utilize other boards to manage user feedback or compile a list of your spontaneous ideas. The key lesson here is to always document everything that crosses your mind, because you'll likely forget many details otherwise.

Every Action Starts with an Issue

Using issues is an effective method to keep track of the tasks that need to be addressed in your project. When you encounter a bug in your program, your initial response should not be to start fixing it in your integrated development environment (IDE) immediately but rather to create an issue to document and track it. The same principle applies to feature ideas; even if you're unsure whether you'll implement them in the future, create an issue to record your intent. You can close it later if you decide not to proceed with the implementation.

This practice emphasizes that every action you take in your local Git should ultimately contribute to resolving an issue. So, when working on something in your IDE, it's essential to ask yourself: Which issue does this address? You should create an issue, regardless of how small the task may seem.

No Direct Push to main

This primary ritual can be challenging to adhere to but significantly simplifies project management for everyone involved. The concept is straightforward: no one should push commits directly to the main branch. The sole method for introducing changes to the main branch is by merging other branches into it.

The direct consequence of this practice is that every change you make should be isolated on its own branch before it's eligible for merging into the main branch. Therefore, any new feature or bugfix should originate from a branch and then be merged into the main branch when it's considered "ready," which in this context means thoroughly reviewed and tested.

Any Merge into the Main Branch Needs a Pull Request

Since you can't push changes directly to the main branch, the only option is to merge branches into it. However, you shouldn't blindly merge any branches into main either. Instead, you must create pull requests to propose the changes. This way, another team member can thoroughly review your code to ensure everything is in order.

In the pull request description, you should include references to the issue numbers that the pull request resolves. This practice ensures that the associated issues are automatically closed when the pull request is accepted.

Use the Wiki to Document Your Code

This might seem like an additional burden, but it's the best way to document your code thoroughly. The README file, while helpful, isn't always sufficient for comprehensive code documentation, which is where the wiki comes in. It might appear to be a daunting task, but the most effective approach is to write documentation concurrently with your code development. This way, you only need to document small changes periodically. If you postpone documentation until later stages, you risk becoming overwhelmed and forgetting critical information.

Git Workflow

Let's now discuss Git. By this point, you're likely familiar with all of Git's most commonly used features. However, using them at the appropriate times is the best way to prevent errors and conflicts.

Always Know Where You Are

This is a fundamental aspect that's also easy to overlook. You should always be aware of the branch you're working on before making any changes or executing any commands. If you're using a modern IDE, your current branch is often displayed at the bottom of your screen. If not, you can always rely on the trusty git status command!

Pull Remote Changes Before Any Action

Before creating a branch from the remote main branch, it's a good practice to pull the latest changes from it. This helps you stay up-to-date with your colleagues and reduces the likelihood of merge conflicts. Additionally, while working on your local branch, consider rebasing occasionally to incorporate the latest updates. This reduces the chance of future merge conflicts and keeps your git log graph looking cleaner and more organized! ☺

Take Care of Your Commit Message

Referring to the chapter on commits is a valuable way to review how to write effective commit messages. This may seem like a minor detail, but it's crucial for maintaining a clear and organized history log. Writing good commit messages will not only save you a few minutes initially. But, it can also prevent countless hours of searching for the commit that introduced bugs when the inevitable bugfix time arrives. Trust me, it's worth the effort!

Don't Rewrite History

Just don't. This is one of the worst things you can do when using Git within a team. If you change a commit and force-push it to a remote branch, everything done to that branch is overwritten by your changes. That means if somebody else worked on that branch, they would have to discard everything they've done and reset their local branch. If you really must do it, make sure that you are the only one working on that branch.

Summary

Indeed, this chapter is short but packed with essential advice for a successful project. The main thing to remember is that GitHub is much more than just a code hosting service. You should use it to track your project's evolution. By following this workflow, you set yourself up for success and avoid most problems with Git and GitHub.

You now have all the tools you need to succeed with Git and GitHub! It all depends on your imagination and courage. Use these tools properly to steer your project down the right path. Good luck!

## CHAPTER 20

Making Git Yours with Aliases

Git is a powerful version control system that offers a multitude of commands and options. This flexibility is great but can lead to longer and more complex command sequences. This is where Git aliases come in. Git aliases allow you to create shortcuts or custom commands for frequently used Git actions, making your Git workflow more efficient and personalized.

What Are Git Aliases?

Git aliases are custom shortcuts for Git commands. They allow you to create your own Git commands or abbreviations for commonly used sequences of Git operations. With Git aliases, you can save time and keystrokes by creating shorter and more intuitive commands.

Using Git Aliases

Setting up Git aliases is straightforward and can be done by either using a git config file or by editing the git config file directly.

Using the Git Config File

You can define Git aliases in your global or local Git configuration file. Open your terminal to set up a global alias and use the following command.

```
git config --global alias.<alias-name> '<git-command>'
```

© Mariot Tsitoara 2024
M. Tsitoara, *Beginning Git and GitHub*, https://doi.org/10.1007/979-8-8688-0215-7_20

For example, you would use the following to create a global alias co for checkout.

```
git config --global alias.co 'checkout'
```

To set up a local alias for a specific Git repository, navigate to the repository's root directory and use the same command without the --global flag.

Editing the Git Config File Directly

You can manually edit your Git configuration file. The global configuration file is typically located at ~/.gitconfig. You can add aliases directly under this file's [alias] section.

```
[alias]
    co = checkout
```

Examples of Useful Git Aliases

The following are some commonly used Git aliases to get you started.

Common Command Shortcuts

- co for checkout

- ci for commit

- st for status

- br for branch

- df for diff

```
[alias]
    co = checkout
    ci = commit
    st = status
    br = branch
    df = diff
```

Listing Aliases

- **List aliases**

  - aliases to list all configured aliases

  ```
  [alias]
      aliases = config --get-regexp alias
  ```

- **View the Git log**

  - lg for a nicely formatted log

  - lga to include author information

  ```
  [alias]
      lg = log --graph --oneline --abbrev-commit --all
      lga = log --graph --oneline --abbrev-commit --all --author
  ```

- **Interactive rebase**

  - ri for an interactive rebase

  - rif for an interactive rebase with autosquash

  ```
  [alias]
      ri = rebase -i
      rif = rebase -i --autosquash
  ```

- **Push and pull**

  - pl for pull

  - pu for push

  - puf for a forced push

  ```
  [alias]
      pl = pull
      pu = push
      puf = push --force
  ```

- **Create and switch branches**

  - cb for creating and checking out a new branch

  - cof for checking out a branch by name (forces it)

  ```
  [alias]
      cb = "!f() { git checkout -b $1; }; f"
      cof = checkout -f
  ```

- **List commits with colors and annotations**

  - ls to list commits in short form, with colors and branch/tag annotations

  ```
  [alias]
      ls = log --pretty=format:"%C(yellow)%h%Cred%d\\
      %Creset%s%Cblue\\ [%cn]" --decorate
  ```

  This alias provides a visually appealing and informative log of commits.

- **List oneline commits with relative dates**

  - ld to list oneline commits showing relative dates

  ```
  [alias]
      ld = log --pretty=format:"%C(yellow)%h\\ %ad%Cred%d\\
      %Creset%s%Cblue\\ [%cn]" --decorate --date=relative
  ```

  This alias displays commits with human-friendly relative dates.

- **List oneline commits with dates**

  - lds to list oneline commits showing dates

  ```
  [alias]
      lds = log --pretty=format:"%C(yellow)%h\\ %ad%Cred%d\\
      %Creset%s%Cblue\\ [%cn]" --decorate --date=short
  ```

  This alias includes precise commit dates.

- **Show modified files in last commit**

  - dl to display modified files in the last commit

  ```
  [alias]
      dl = "!git ll -1"
  ```

  This alias provides a concise list of files changed in the most recent commit.

- **Show a diff of the last commit**

  - dlc to show a diff of the last commit

  ```
  [alias]
      dlc = diff --cached HEAD^
  ```

  This alias displays the changes made in the last commit.

- **Find a file path in the codebase**

  - f to find a file path in the codebase

  ```
  [alias]
      f = "!git ls-files | grep -i"
  ```

  This alias allows you to search for file paths within your codebase.

- **Search/grep your entire codebase for a string**

  - gr to search/grep your entire codebase for a string

  ```
  [alias]
      gr = grep -Ii
  ```

  This alias simplifies searching for text across your project.

- **List all files with TODO or FIXME comments**

  - todo-list to list all files containing TODO or FIXME comments

  ```
  [alias]
      todo-list = "! git grep --extended-regexp -I --line-number
      --count 'TODO|FIXME'"
  ```

  This alias helps you identify files with outstanding tasks or issues.

- **View details of the last commit**

  - last to view details about the most recent commit

  ```
  [alias]
      last = log -1 HEAD --stat
  ```

  This alias provides information about the latest commit, including the changed files.

These are just a few examples, and you can create aliases that suit your specific workflow and preferences. Customizing your Git workflow with aliases can significantly improve your productivity and make Git more intuitive and enjoyable.

Summary

Git aliases are a powerful tool for customizing your Git workflow. Creating shortcuts for commonly used Git commands and sequences can save time and make Git more user-friendly. Don't hesitate to experiment with aliases and tailor them to your needs. With the right aliases, you can make Git yours and enhance your version control experience.

Index

A

Assignees, 137–138, 146, 178

B

BitKeeper SCM, 10, 11
Branches, 12, 25, 43, 45, 120, 169, 171, 172,
       194, 237, 255–257, 261, 262,
       292, 293
  check out, 238
  commit, 147
  convention, 71
  creation, 152, 153, 239
  deletion, 156–159
  differences, 229, 230
  Git, 151
  Git workflow, 150
  location, 229
  logic, 150
  master, 272, 275
  merging, 159–164
  pushing, 246
  pushing to remote, 164–166
  separate-code-and-styles, 239
  stashing, 89
  switching, 153–155
  types, 151
Browsing, 247–248
Businesses, 101, 106, 172

C

Centralized VCS (CVCS), 8–9, 18
cmd, 40
Code reviews
  choices, 190
  co-contributors' code, 185
  review comment, 186–190
  section, 186
Collaboration, 11, 92, 199, 200, 231, 281
  and code release, 96
  online, 93
  team, 93
Commit log, 62, 63, 213
Commits, 48–52, 63, 66, 94, 95, 122, 147,
       148, 150, 151, 155, 159, 165, 204,
       232, 233, 237, 255, 260–262
  amending, 83, 84
  branch, 196, 199
  detached HEAD, 288, 289
  error, 287
  git-gui, 235
  GitHub workflow, 170
  and history, 93
  linking issues, 138
    closing, 144–147
    referencing, 140–143
    working, 139
  messages, 85, 86, 298
  modification, 77–84

© Mariot Tsitoara 2024
M. Tsitoara, *Beginning Git and GitHub*, https://doi.org/10.1007/979-8-8688-0215-7

Printed in the United States
by Baker & Taylor Publisher Services